zoom
MADE EASY

Establishing Lasting Connections

By James Bernstein

Bernstein, James
Zoom Made Easy
Book 17 in the Computers Made Easy series

For more information on reproducing sections of this book or sales of this book,
go to www.onlinecomputertips.com

Contents

Introduction

Thanks to modern technology and the fact that all of our devices are Internet enabled means that keeping connected with friends, family and coworkers is even easier than ever. We can use our computers, tablets and smartphones to do things such as make video calls, hold meetings and have presentations in addition to sending emails and text messages.

Fortunately, there are many ways to go about performing these tasks yet unfortunately you will need to choose the platform you are going to use to do this because you will need to decide on which method (or software) you will be using. It's important to choose a platform that is easy to use and also something the people you will be communicating with can also use without having too much of a learning curve in case they are not too tech savvy.

Just like with most software, there are a few vendors who dominate the market for their respective types of applications such as Microsoft does for operating systems (Windows) and word processors (Microsoft Word). You have most likely heard of other software such as Skype that allows video calls and GoToMeeting which is commonly used in the business sector for hosting online meetings that can be accessed from anywhere you have an Internet connection.

Recently, Zoom Video Communications has been gaining ground with their Zoom online meeting and webinar software as one of the most commonly used online tools being used today. The Zoom software is fairly easy to use and can be configured to suit just about anyone's needs. It's easy enough for the typical home user to use to host video calls with friends and family members and also robust enough for the business user who needs to hold meetings and host webinars for their clients.

For those of us who like things that are free, Zoom has a free version that has a lot of features included as well as other pay for versions with more advanced features. This way you can try it out and see if it does the job for you and if you later decide you would like to take advantage of more of the advanced features then you can get yourself a subscription to enable these features.

Regardless of what version you use, you should be able to get the hang of how Zoom works fairly quickly and be able to start hosting meetings and webinars in no time.

The goal of this book is to get you up and running with Zoom and show you how to host meetings and webinars as well as go over all of the basic features of Zoom and also some of the more advanced options. I will also go over the configuration settings so you will know how to customize Zoom to make it work just the way you want it to work. So on that note, let's get the communication channels open!

Chapter 1 – What is Zoom?

Like I mentioned in the introduction, Zoom is an online collaboration software platform that allows you to host meetings and webinars with other people. You can do things such as make video calls where you can see the other people you are talking to and share your screen so others can see what you are working on. A meeting can be between you and one other person or you can have hundreds of people on at one time. As you can see in figure 1.1 you can have many people in a single Zoom meeting and be able to interact and see them all at the same time.

Figure 1.1

If you don't want anyone participating in your meeting and would rather just have them watch your presentation then you can host a webinar instead of a meeting. This way you can have everyone attending focusing on you and what you are discussing (or selling). I will be discussing both meetings and webinars later in the book.

Many people use Zoom as a way to talk to family members in other parts of the country or even other countries since it's an easy to use way to make video calls over the Internet. This way you can have the entire family on one call and be able to see everyone on your screen as they are talking assuming they have some type of camera connected to their computer or are using their tablet or smartphone with its built in camera.

Before I get into the details of how to use Zoom I thought it would be best to give you a better idea of what you can do with Zoom.

Zoom Features
In order to decide whether or not Zoom will work for you, it's important to know what Zoom can and can't do. In this section, I will be going over the key features of the software so you will have a better understanding of what you can do with it.

The features that you will be able to use will vary on whether you are using the free version of Zoom or if you are using one of the subscription based services. As of this writing there is the free version and three subscription (paid) versions that you can use, each with their own set of features. I will be going over these different versions later in this chapter. I will also be going into more details on many of these features in later chapters as well.

As you might have figured out by now, you can use Zoom to host meetings and webinars which is a fancy word for a web seminar. While you are running a meeting or webinar you will be able to use some or all of these features to enhance their functionality. Here is a listing of some of the more commonly used features.

- **Individual and group chat messages** – This allows you to send messages to other users participating in your meeting or webinar.

- **Screen sharing** – Allows you so share all of your screen or just a certain program with other participants so they can see what you are working on.

- **Screen annotation** – Lets you mark up your screen to make notes or highlight certain aspects of your presentation.

- **Whiteboard** – This can be used just like a whiteboard you would have on the wall in a conference room where you can draw diagrams and write notes that can be shared with everyone in your meeting.

- **Keyboard and mouse control** – If you would like to give another participant control of the mouse and keyboard on your computer you can use this option.

- **Custom invitations and scheduling** – When you create a meeting or webinar you can send out invitations to others and also have it added to various calendars such as Outlook and Google.

- **Meeting recording** – If you need to review your meeting after it's complete you can have Zoom record it later and save it on your computer or in the cloud.

- **Breakout rooms** – This feature allows you to divide up your participants into separate rooms so they can collaborate on their own or with specific people.

- **Video effects** – If you want to add a little fun to your meeting you can use video effects such as background scenery to your meeting.

- **Templates** – When making webinars you can create templates that can be reused so you don't have to go through the setup process from scratch each time.

- **Mobile device support** – Zoom can run on a variety of smartphones and tablets so you can have your meetings from just about anywhere.

Zoom Plans

Anyone can use Zoom for free but as with most free software, there will be limitations as to what you can do with it compared to the version or versions you pay for. Zoom is the same way and has several plans to choose from based on what features you might need to use. For most home users, the Basic or free plan will be just fine but if you are planning to use Zoom for your business then you might want to consider one of the other more advanced plans.

As of this writing, there are four Zoom plans to choose from and I will now go over the features of each one.

Chapter 1 – What is Zoom?

Basic – Free

With the Basic plan, you can do things such as host meetings and webinars with video conferencing and chat features. Here are some of the more relevant features you get with the Basic plan.

- Host up to 100 participants
- Unlimited 1 to 1 meetings
- 40 mins limit on group meetings
- Unlimited number of meetings
- Ticket Support
- Video Conferencing Features
- Simultaneous Screen Share
- Virtual Background
- Waiting Room
- Desktop and application sharing
- Personal room or meeting ID
- Instant or scheduled meetings
- Chrome & Outlook plug-ins
- Scheduling w/ Chrome Extensions
- Local recording of meetings
- Private and group chat
- Breakout Rooms
- Mac, Windows, Linux, iOS and Android support
- Group messaging and presence
- Screen share any iPad/iPhone app
- Co-annotation on a shared screen
- Keyboard/mouse control
- Whiteboarding
- Multi-share
- Secure Socket Layer (SSL) encryption
- AES 256 bits encryption

Pro Plan - $15/month

The Pro plan includes all of the features of the Basic plan plus the following. There are also additional upgrades you can purchase if you require them.

- Includes 100 participants
- Meeting duration limit of 24 hrs. (30)
- User management
- Admin feature controls
- Reporting
- Custom Personal Meeting ID
- Assign scheduler
- 1GB of MP4 or M4A cloud recording
- REST API
- Skype for Business (Lync) interoperability
- Extra Cloud Recording Storage (starting at $40/mo.)
- H.323/SIP Room Connector (starting at $49/mo.)
- Join by Zoom Rooms (starting at $49/mo.)
- Join by Toll-free dialing or Call Me (starting at $100/mo.)
- Add Video Webinars (starting at $40/mo.)

Business Plan - $20/month

The Business plan includes all of the features of the Basic plan plus the following.

- Includes 300 participants
- Dedicated phone support
- Admin dashboard
- Vanity URL
- Option for on-premise deployment
- Managed domains
- Single sign-on
- Company branding
- Custom emails
- LTI integration
- Cloud Recording Transcripts
- Join by Toll-free dialing or Call Me (starting at $100/mo.)

Enterprise Plan - $20/month
The Enterprise and Enterprise Plus plans include all of the features of the Basic plan plus the following.

- Enterprise includes 500 participants
- Enterprise Plus includes 1,000 participants
- Unlimited Cloud Storage
- Dedicated Customer Success Manager
- Executive Business Reviews
- Bundle discounts on Webinars and Zoom Rooms

As you can see there are many features that come with Zoom so I would recommend starting with the Basic plan and then figure out if you need any of the more advanced features that come with the other versions and take it from there rather than signing up for a pay for plan and realizing you don't need it.

Chapter 2 - Signing up for Zoom

In order to start using Zoom, you will first need to sign up for an account using your email address because you will be signing into Zoom with the email address that you signed up with. During the signup process you will also need to create a password to secure your account. I will go over that part in a bit.

You might have noticed that most things in the technology industry change, and Zoom is no different when it comes to keeping us on our toes by changing the way their software looks and operates and the same goes for the signup process. So if things look a little different when you go to sign up for your account, just remember its Zoom, not you! Either way, you should still be able to successfully sign up by following along with my instructions.

Creating an Account

The process to create a Zoom account is fairly simple and if you have created accounts for other things such as online banking or shopping sites then you shouldn't have any problem signing up for a Zoom account. To begin you first need to go to the Zoom website by either doing a search for it from your favorite search engine or you can type it directly into the address bar of your browser (**https://zoom.us/freesignup/**).

The first thing you will need to do is enter the email address that you wish to use with Zoom. You might notice that it wants you to enter your work email address, but this is not necessary, and you can use a personal email address such as a Gmail address for your account login.

Figure 2.1

You may also see an option to sign in using other methods such as with your Google or Facebook account (figure 2.2) so this is up to you. I prefer not to link my personal accounts to other services so I will usually just sign up with my email address.

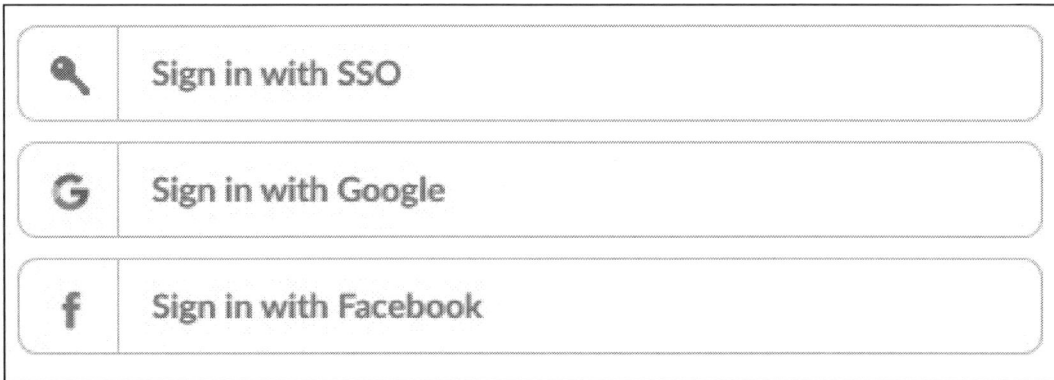

Figure 2.2

Next, you will need to enter your date of birth information. This is probably just to confirm that you are 18 or older and technically you can probably enter anything you like since it says your birth date information won't be stored.

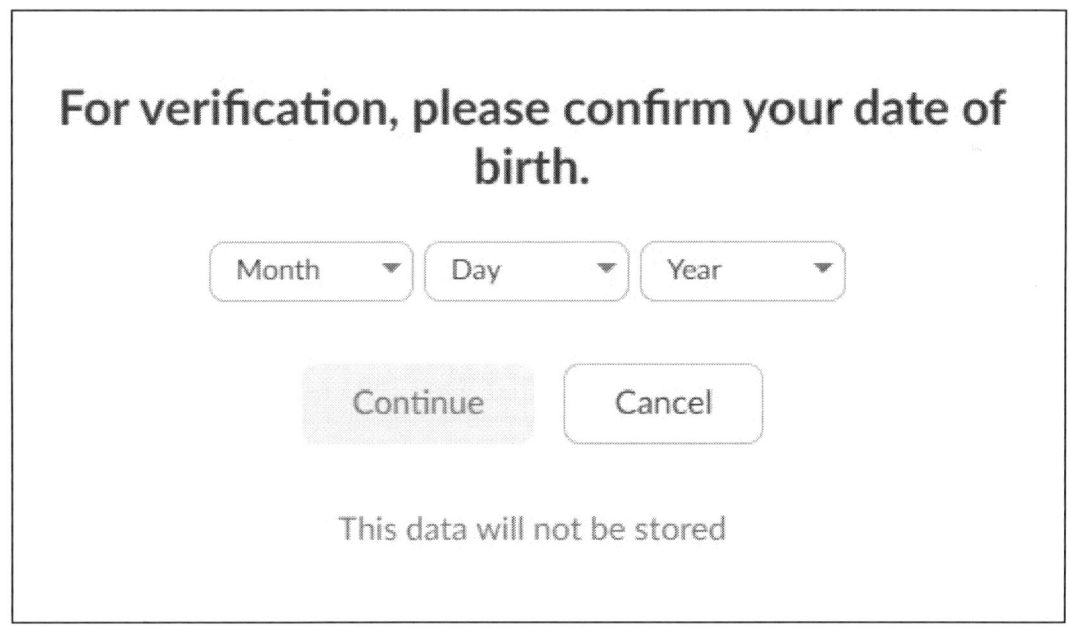

Figure 2.3

Next, you will need to confirm the email address you have entered and click the *Confirm* button which means you also agree to the privacy policy and terms of service that comes with using the Zoom service (figure 2.4). You can click on the links to read more about them if desired.

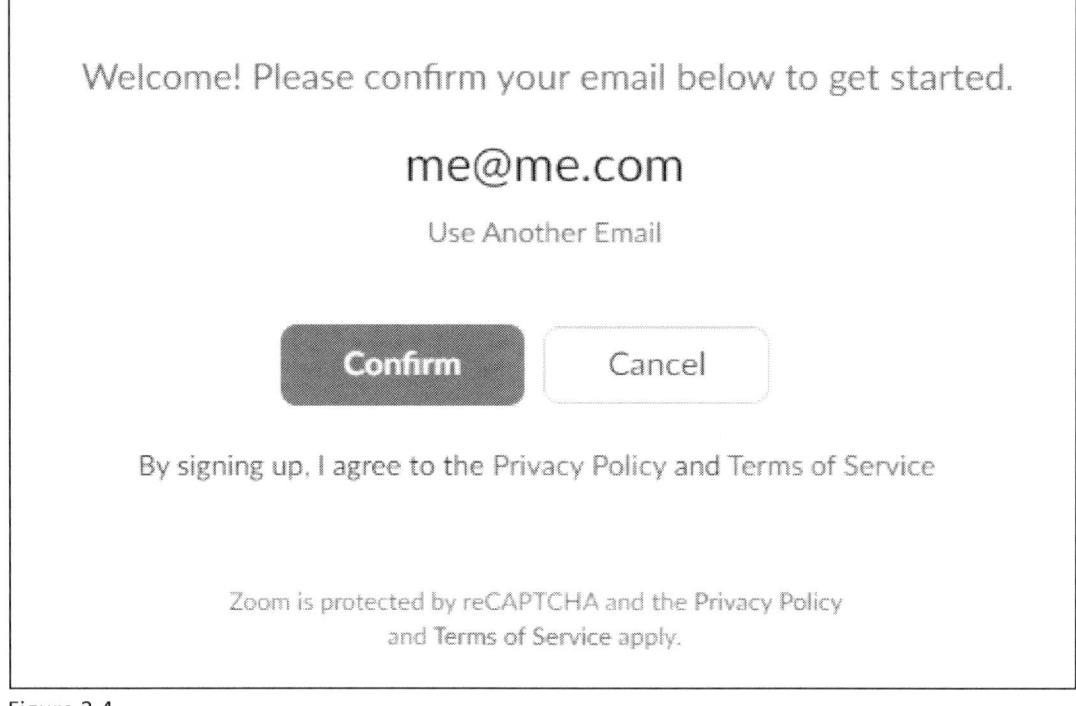

Figure 2.4

After you click on Confirm you will see a message telling you that a confirmation email has been sent to the email address that you used to sign up for Zoom. If you don't see the email in your inbox then check your spam\junk or click the link that says *Resend another email* to have it sent to your email address again.

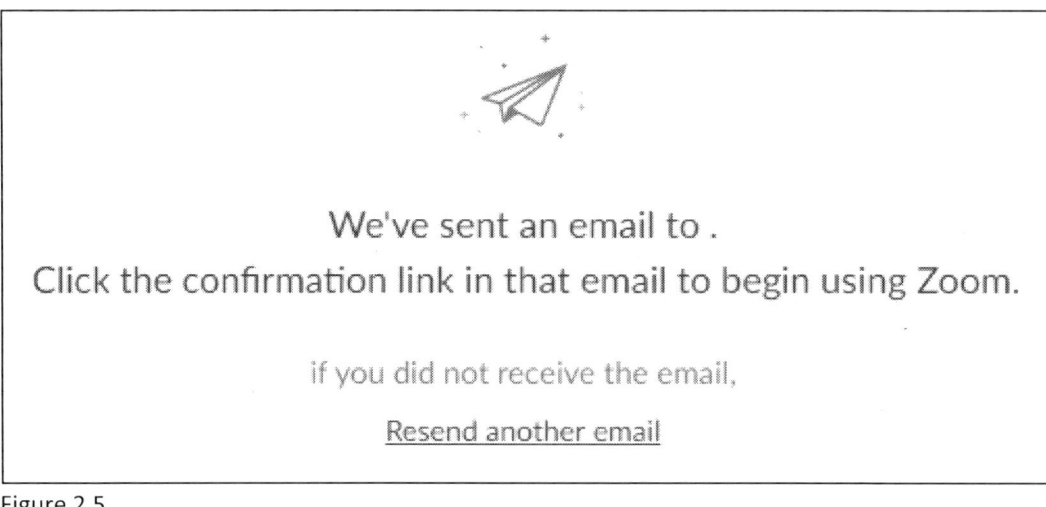

Figure 2.5

Figure 2.6 shows you what the Zoom account activation email will typically look like. All you need to do is click on the Activate Account button to be taken to the Zoom website and have your account activated.

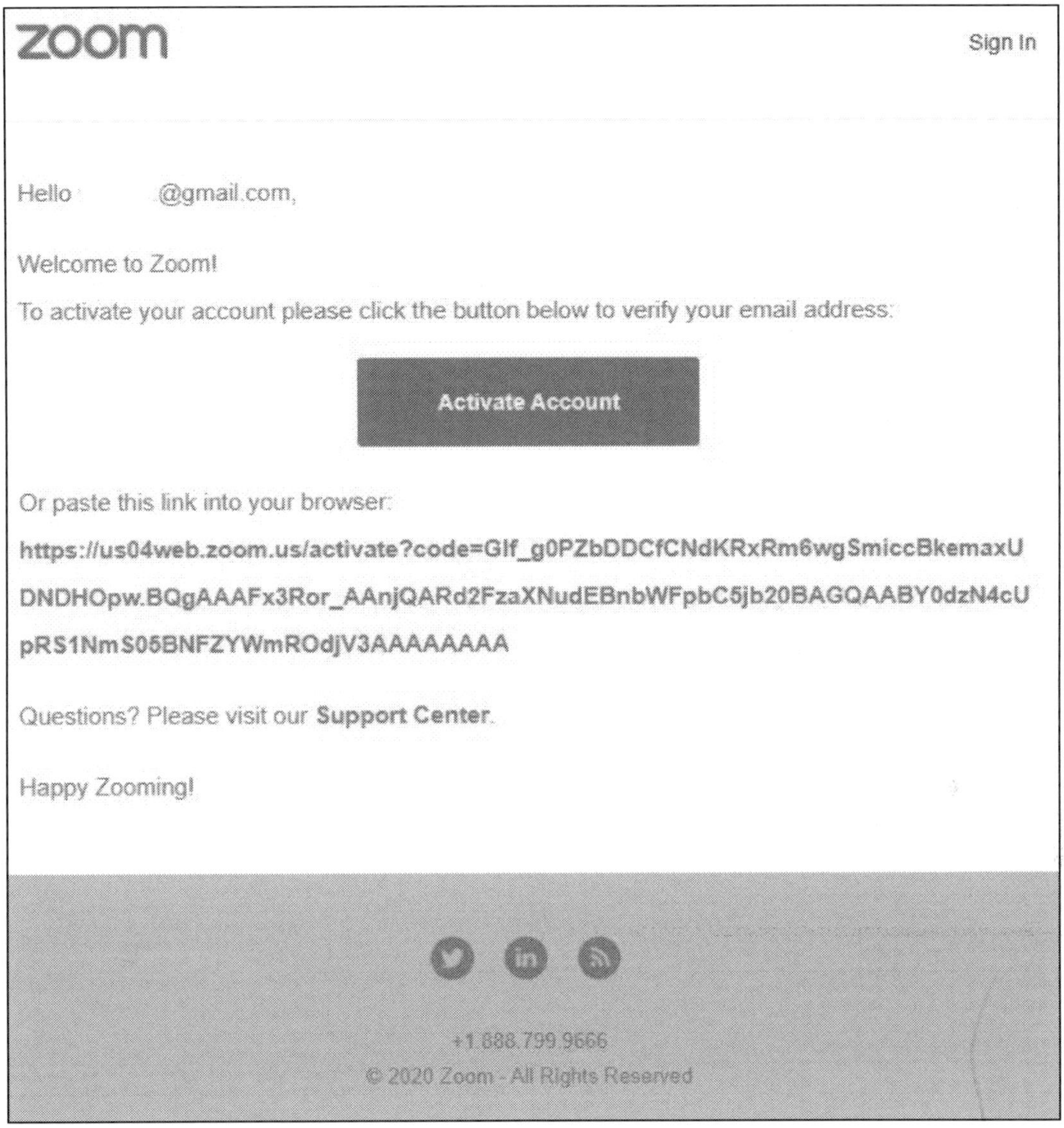

zoom
Sign In

Hello   @gmail.com,

Welcome to Zoom!

To activate your account please click the button below to verify your email address:

Activate Account

Or paste this link into your browser:

https://us04web.zoom.us/activate?code=Glf_g0PZbDDCfCNdKRxRm6wgSmiccBkemaxU

DNDHOpw.BQgAAAFx3Ror_AAnjQARd2FzaXNudEBnbWFpbC5jb20BAGQAABY0dzN4cU

pRS1NmS05BNFZYWmROdjV3AAAAAAAA

Questions? Please visit our **Support Center.**

Happy Zooming!

+1.888.799.9666
© 2020 Zoom - All Rights Reserved

Figure 2.6

Next, you will need to enter the name you wish to use with the Zoom service and then create a password to be used with your account. Try and make a reasonably complex password to prevent your account from being hacked. You will most likely need to include at least an upper case letter, lower case letter, number and special character in your password. Some examples of special characters include *! @ # $ % ^ & *.*

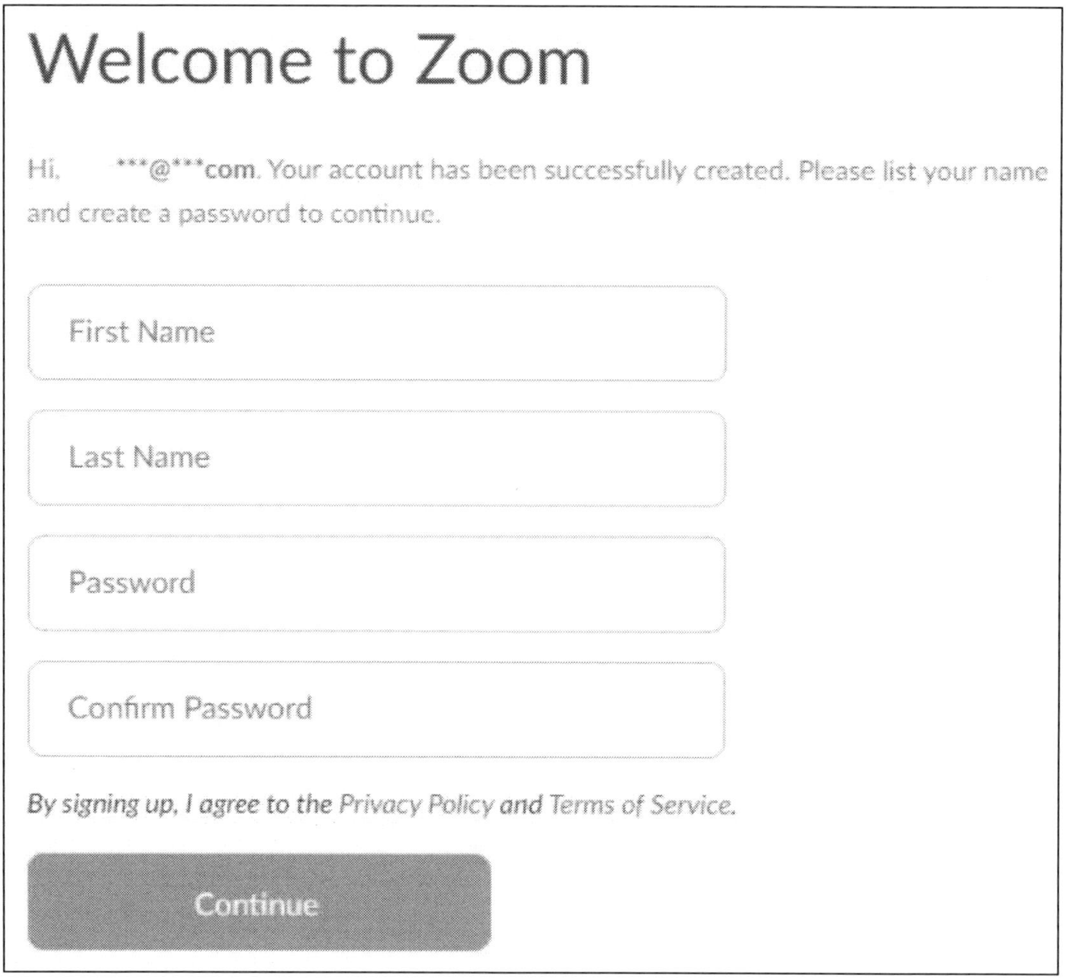

Welcome to Zoom

Hi,   ***@***com. Your account has been successfully created. Please list your name and create a password to continue.

First Name

Last Name

Password

Confirm Password

By signing up, I agree to the Privacy Policy and Terms of Service.

Continue

Figure 2.7

After you enter your name and password information you will have a choice as to whether you want to start a test meeting or go right to your Zoom account.

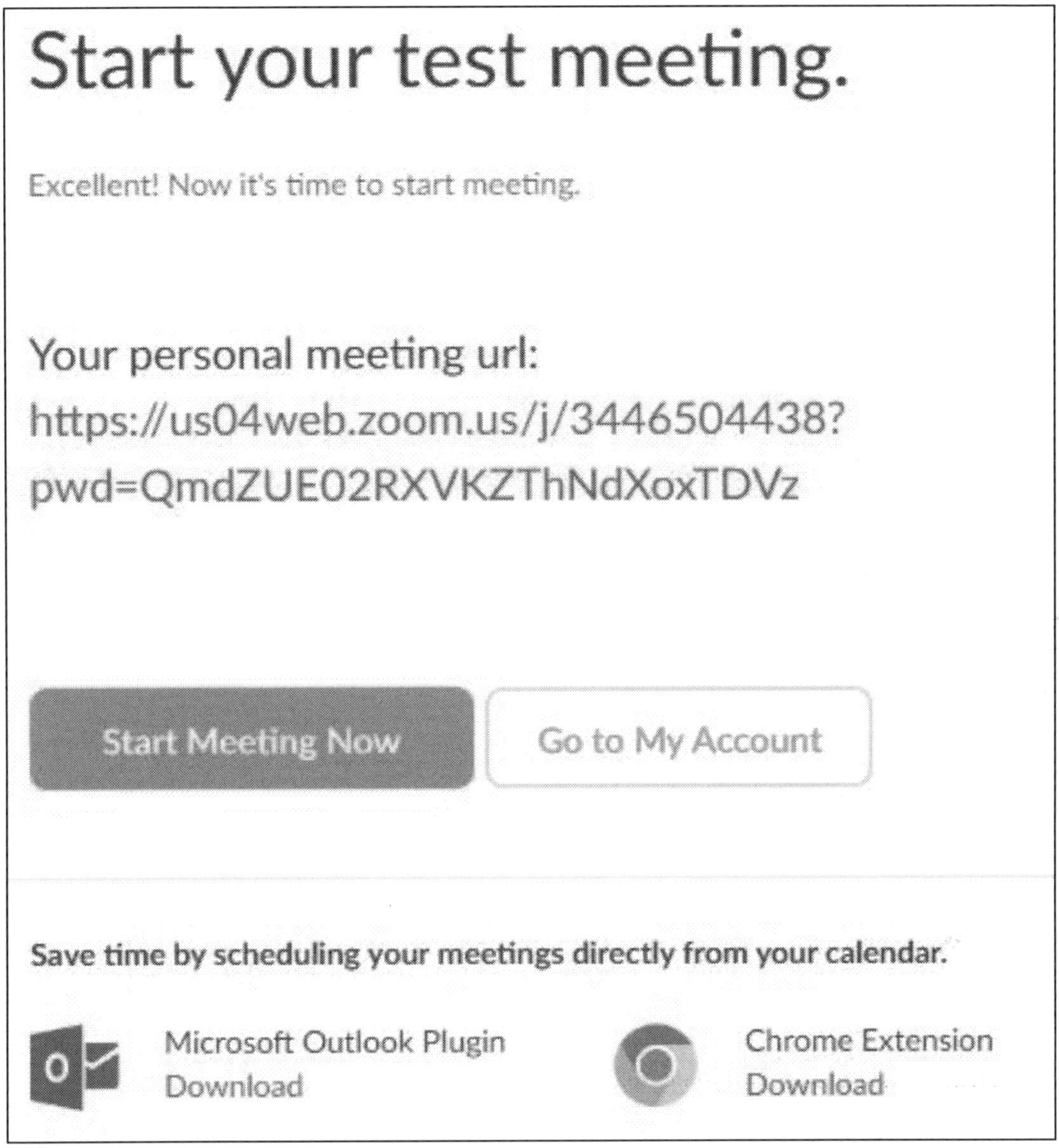

Start your test meeting.

Excellent! Now it's time to start meeting.

Your personal meeting url:
https://us04web.zoom.us/j/3446504438?
pwd=QmdZUE02RXVKZThNdXoxTDVz

Start Meeting Now   Go to My Account

Save time by scheduling your meetings directly from your calendar.

 Microsoft Outlook Plugin
Download

 Chrome Extension
Download

Figure 2.8

Clicking on *Start Meeting Now* will take you to a test meeting that you can run to make sure everything on your computer is up to par when it comes to compatibility with Zoom meetings. If you click on *Go to My Account* then you will be brought to your Zoom profile settings and from here you can do things like start a meeting or webinar or change your Zoom specific settings. I will be discussing the Profile settings in Chapter 3.

You might have noticed the calendar options at the bottom of figure 2.8 for Outlook and Chrome. These can be used to make scheduling meetings easier and I will be going over how to use these in Chapter 3 as well.

Signing Into Zoom

Signing into your Zoom account is very easy and is the same process that you would use to sign into something like your online banking account or email account. Simply go to the Zoom website (zoom.us) and then click on the link that says *Sign In*.

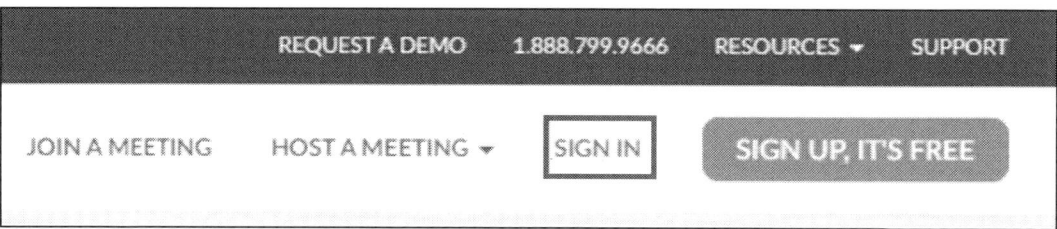

Figure 2.9

Next, you will type in the email address you signed up with and the password you created during the signup process and click the *Sign In* button. If you would like Zoom to keep you logged in and not automatically sign you out then you can check the *Stay signed in* checkbox.

Figure 2.10

If you have forgotten your password then you can click where it says *Forgot password?* and Zoom will send a password reset email to the address you have associated with your account. Then all you need to do is go to your email and click on the link that says *Click here to change your password* and type in a new password to be used with your account.

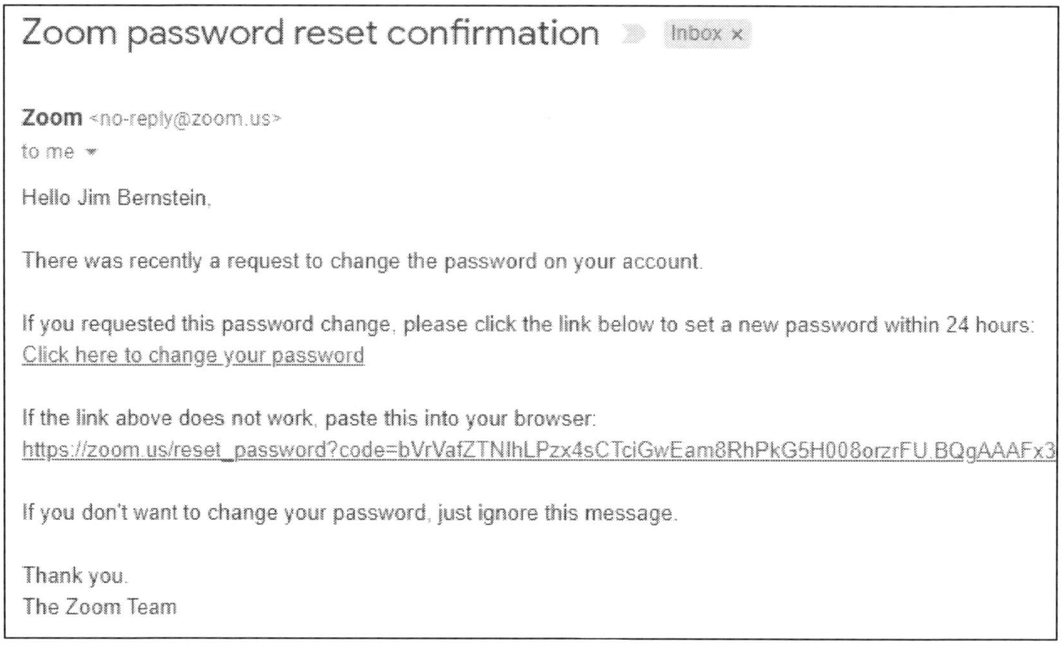

Zoom password reset confirmation ≫ Inbox ×

Zoom <no-reply@zoom.us>
to me ▾

Hello Jim Bernstein,

There was recently a request to change the password on your account.

If you requested this password change, please click the link below to set a new password within 24 hours:
Click here to change your password

If the link above does not work, paste this into your browser:
https://zoom.us/reset_password?code=bVrVafZTNIhLPzx4sCTciGwEam8RhPkG5H008orzrFU.BQgAAAFx3

If you don't want to change your password, just ignore this message.

Thank you.
The Zoom Team

Figure 2.11

Downloading the Zoom Client

When using Zoom on your computer you will need to download the Zoom client that is used to run meetings on your computer. It is also used when you join other people's meetings from your computer. If you are using a tablet or smartphone for Zoom then you will need to download the Zoom app on your device. I will be discussing using mobile devices with Zoom in Chapter 7.

There are a couple of ways you can go about downloading the Zoom client to be used on your computer. If you want to get ahead of the game you can go to the *Zoom Download Center* and then download the Zoom software directly to your computer. This can be found under *Resources* and then *Download Zoom Client* (figure 2.12).

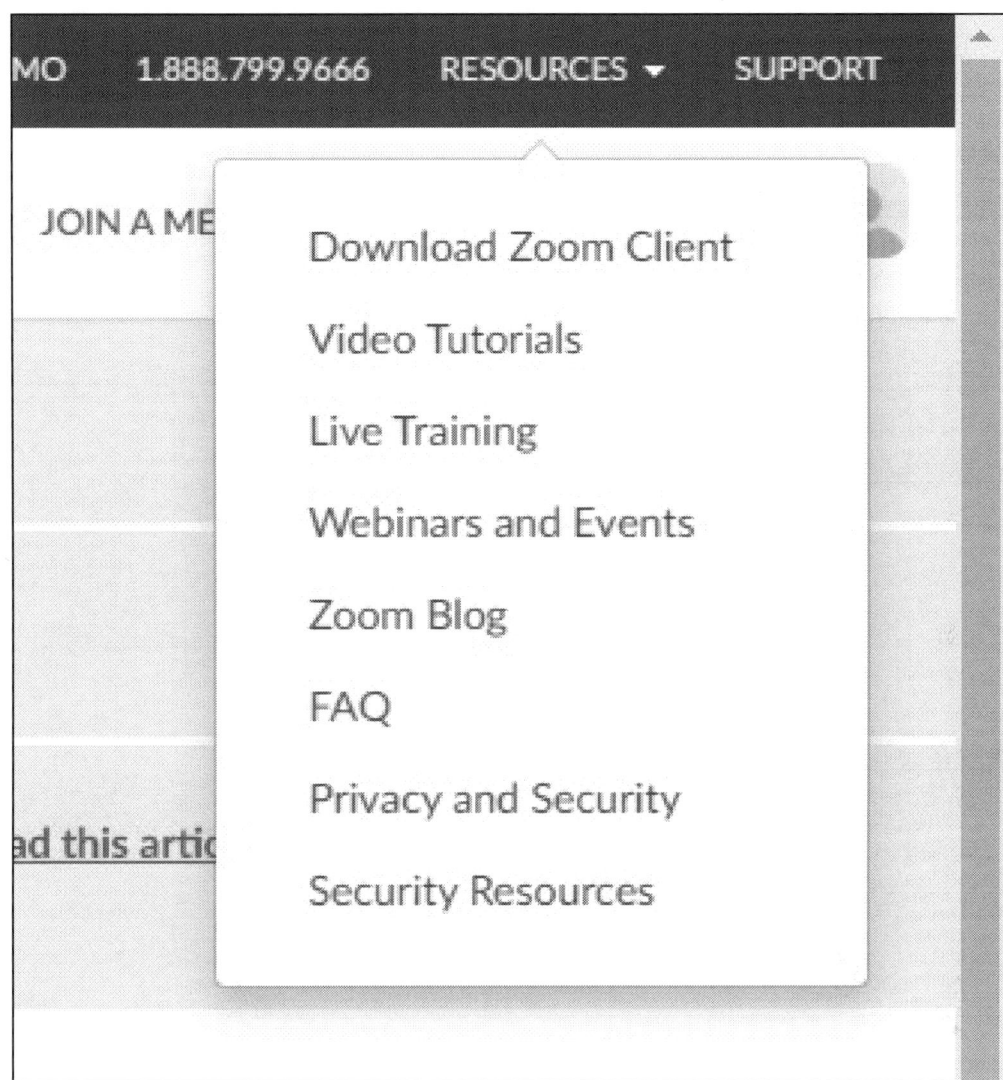

Figure 2.12

The Zoom Download Center will show you all of the download options you have available to you, including the Zoom client.

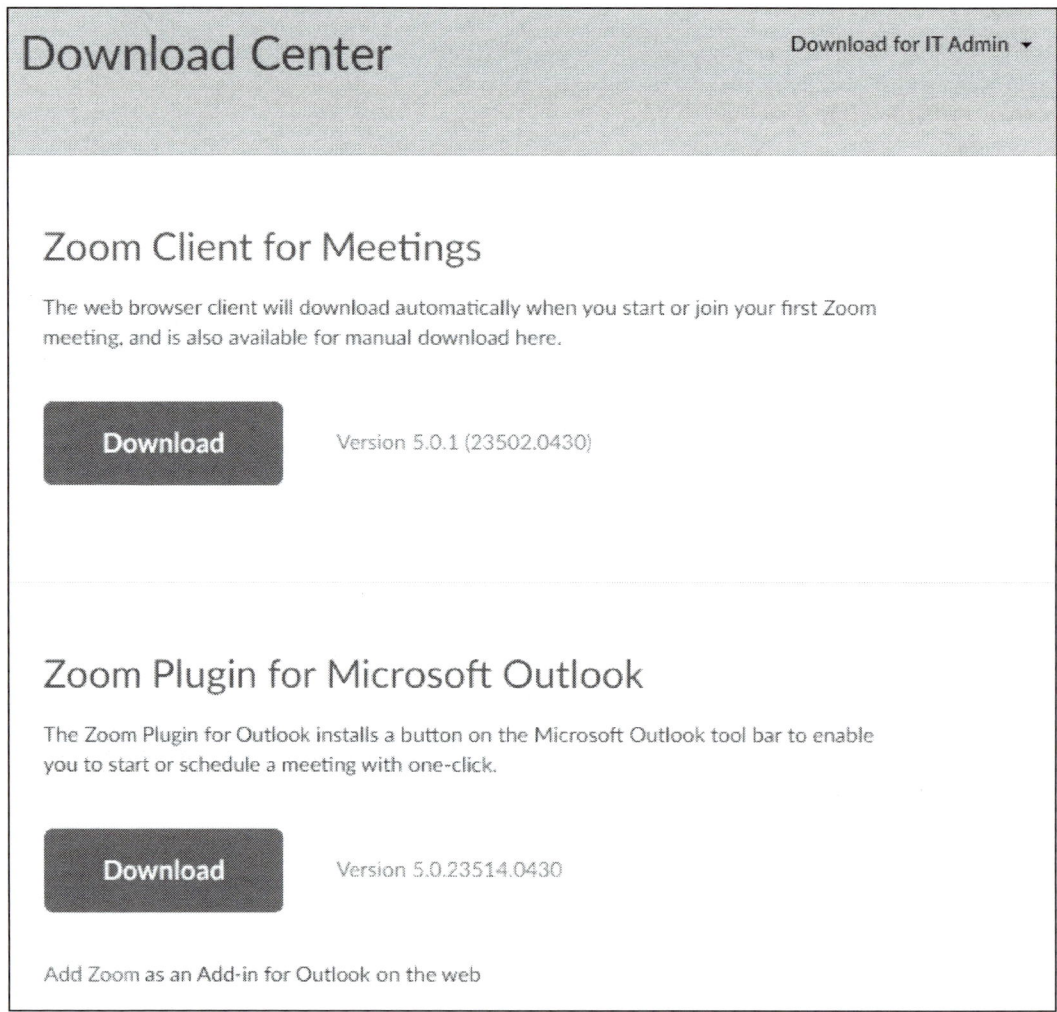

Figure 2.13

All you need to do is click on the *Download* button and save the *ZoomInstaller.exe* somewhere on your computer that you will be able to find. ZoomInstaller.exe is the file for Windows computers and if you have a Mac then it will have a slightly different name (most likely Zoom.pkg). When you double click the file it will do a very quick installation and then bring you to a login screen where you can either join a meeting being hosted by someone else or log into your account.

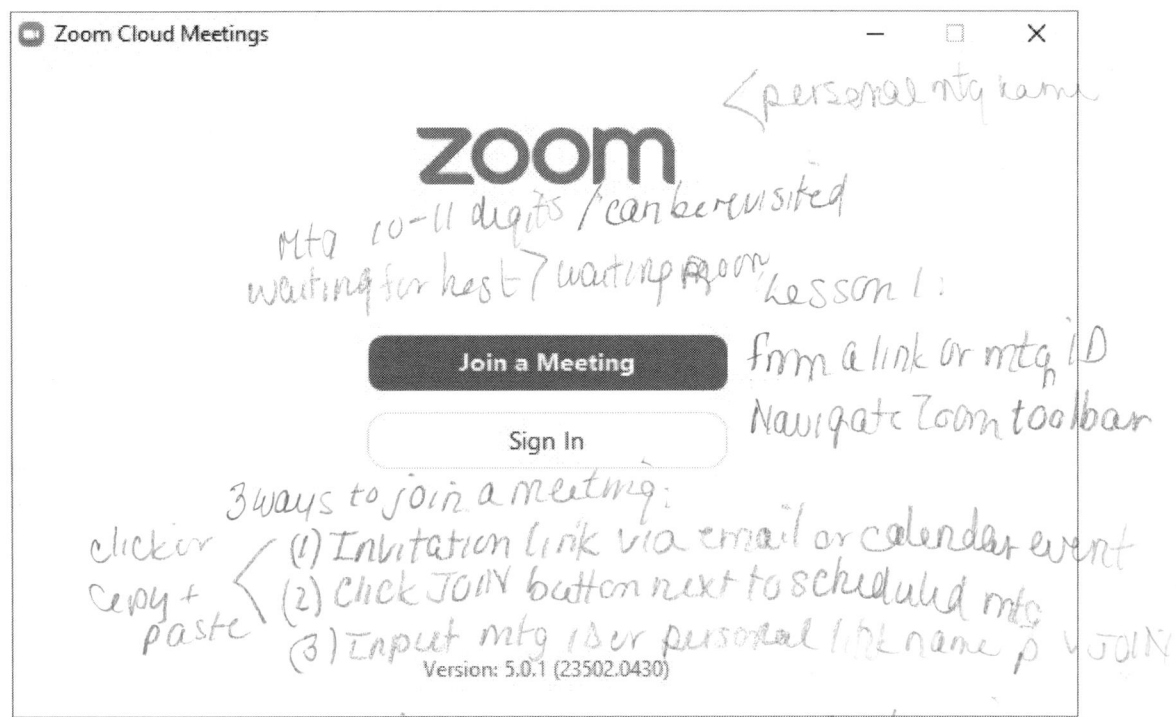

Figure 2.14

If you don't feel like going through this download and installation process then you can wait until you join a meeting before installing the Zoom client and the process will be a lot simpler and involve fewer steps. Just make sure you leave some time to get the client installed before the meeting starts.

One thing that you will notice throughout this book is that I will be using several different Zoom accounts so I can show you how various features work as if I were hosting meetings and webinars with multiple users rather than just myself.

Chapter 3 - The Zoom Interface

In order to use Zoom effectively, you will need to know how to navigate within the Zoom interface to be able to find the tools and settings you need to run your meetings and webinars. Fortunately, the interface is broken down into categories that make things easy to find. Plus there is more than one way to access the Zoom interface giving you even more ways to get things done.

Zoom Client Software Interface
For the most part you will be working with Zoom from your account on their website, but I wanted to show you that you can also use the Zoom client that I discussed in the last chapter to perform the same types of tasks.

After you download and install the client, you will have an icon on your desktop most likely called Zoom which you can double click to open up the Zoom software. As you can see in figure 3.1, the Zoom software is fairly basic looking and easy to navigate. On the main screen from the *Home* section you can do things such as start a new meeting, join an existing meeting, schedule a meeting, or share your screen if you are currently in a meeting.

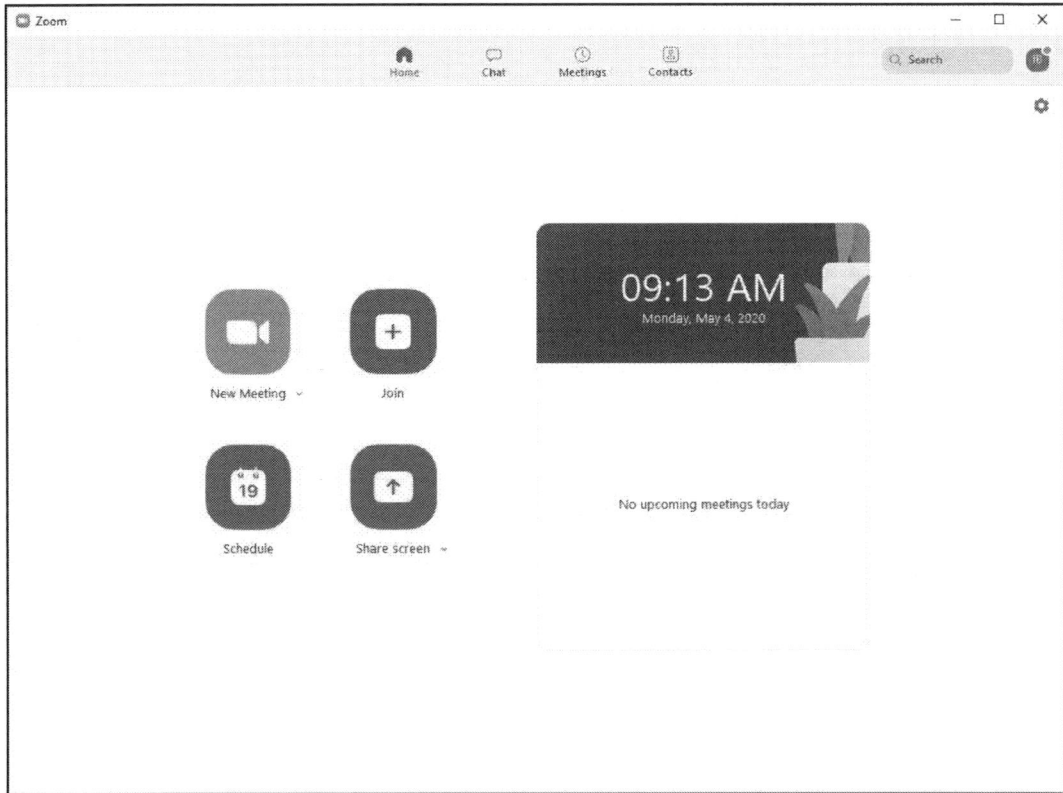

Figure 3.1

The *Chat* section is where you can go to start instant messaging conversations with other people in the meeting. You can either send messages to a particular person or to everyone who is attending the meeting.

The *Meetings* section will show any upcoming or recorded meetings that you have within your Zoom account. You can start your meeting from here or copy the meeting invitation information to send out to others if needed.

The *Contacts* section is where you can keep the names and email addresses of other Zoom users making it easy to invite them to future meetings or webinars.

I will be discussing all of these sections in more detail throughout this book once we start setting up meetings and webinars.

Zoom Website Interface

When you sign into your Zoom account online, you will be taken to the Zoom website where you can perform all of the same tasks that you did with the Zoom client and then some. The only thing to really be aware of is that things will look a little different between the website and the client, but it should be pretty easy to navigate around one if you have used the other.

Figure 3.2 shows the main sections from the Zoom website and you can see that it is broken down into five main sections that you will use for your meeting and webinar purposes as well as four sections for administrative tasks which will be discussed in Chapter 6 along with how to manage your Zoom settings.

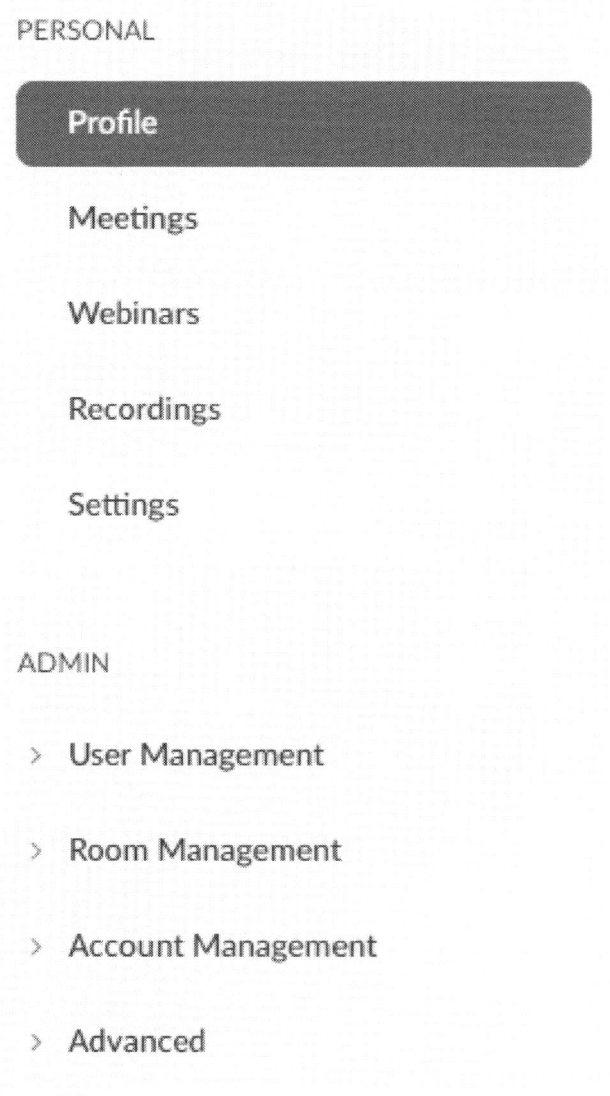

Figure 3.2

Clicking on any one of these categories will take you to their respective areas where you can perform the tasks associated with that section. As I move along and create meetings and webinars I will go into more details about each one of these sections but for now I just wanted to show you where things are located.

At the top right of the Zoom website you will also see some similar choices which are shortcuts to do things such as schedule, join, or host a meeting.

Figure 3.3

The Resources drop down menu can be used to get more information and even some training on how to use Zoom.

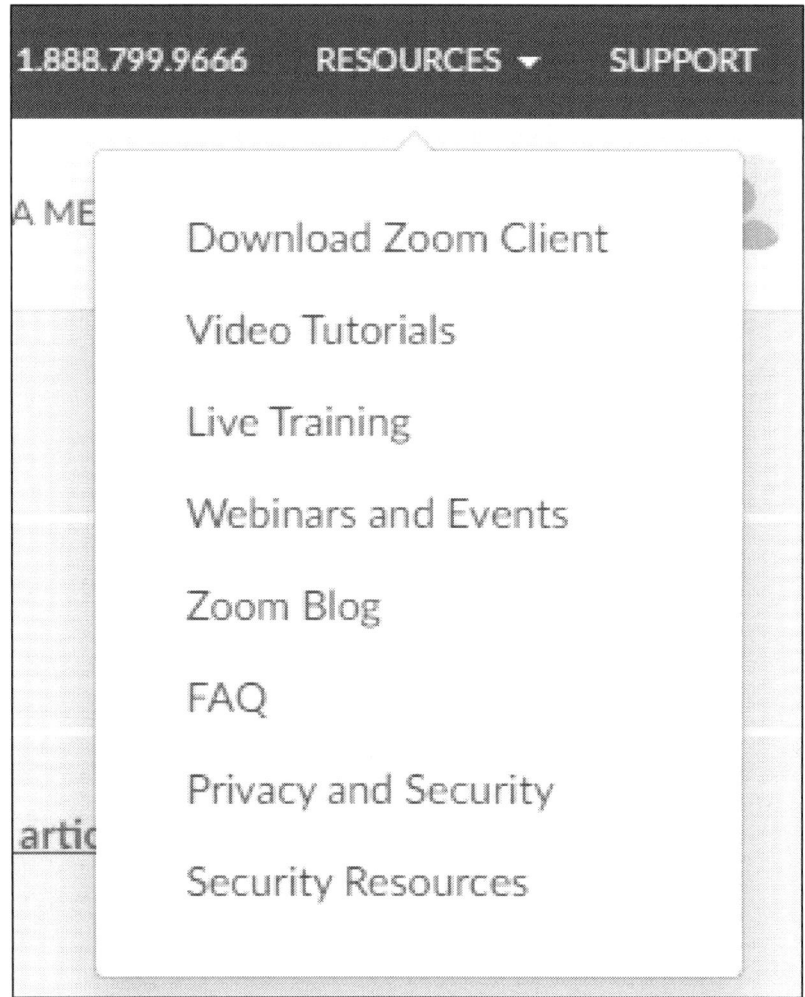

Figure 3.4

The Support section can be used to get help with Zoom if you have any questions on how to perform a specific task or if you are having technical difficulties with the software. Just keep in mind that the type of support you will receive will depend on which plan you are using. So if you are using the Basic\free plan then you will most likely be limited to searching the help section or watching training videos. If you have one of the pay for plans then you should be able to contact a real person for help.

Profile Settings
One of the first things you should configure when signing up for your Zoom account is to check your profile settings to make sure they are correct and make

any changes that might be required. To do this simply log into the Zoom website with your credentials and click on the *Profile* button.

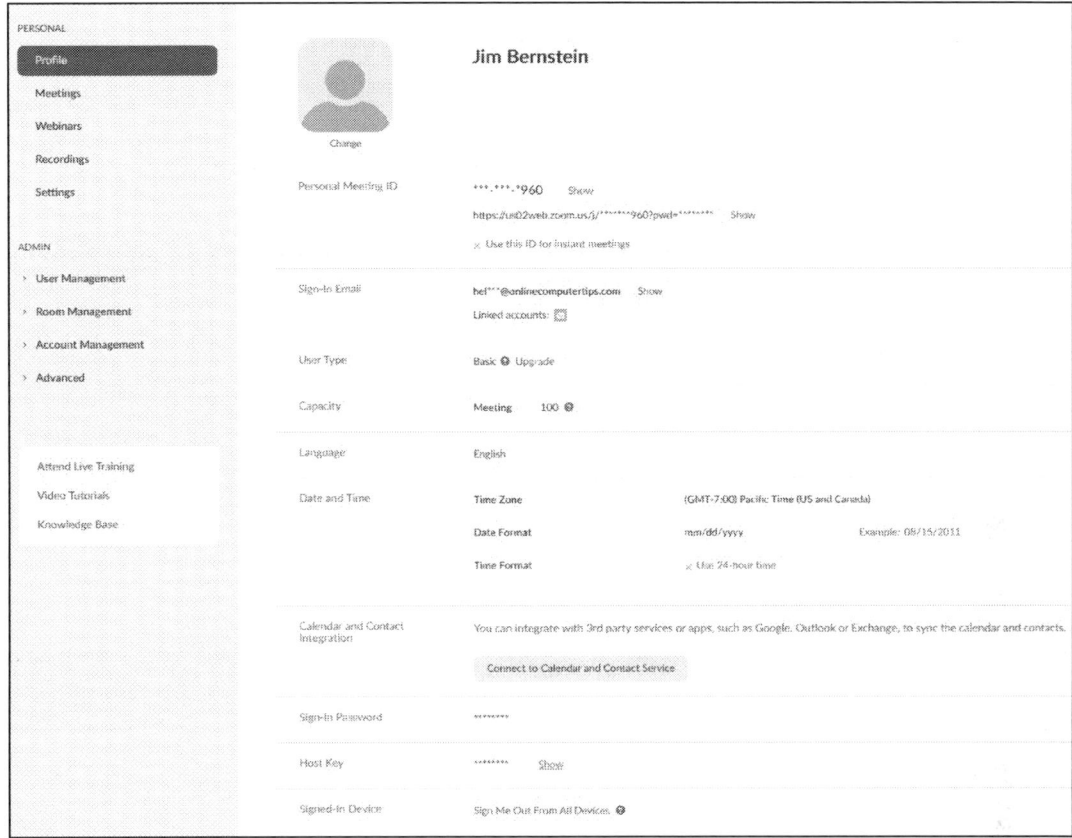

Figure 3.5

Here you will see your Zoom display name and various information about your account and have the option to make changes to most of it.

- **Personal Meeting ID** - This is your own dedicated meeting ID number that you can use over and over again for your meetings. You will also see your Zoom URL (address) that you can send to others as a quick way for them to join your meeting.

- **Sign-In Email** – Here you can change the email address that you use with your Zoom account.

- **User Type** – This shows the account type or plan that you have signed up for.

31

- **Capacity** – This will show how many people you can have participate in one of your meetings at one time.

- **Date and Time** – Here you will see the time zone you are located in as well as the date and time format that your account is set to use.

- **Calendar and Contact Integration** – Configuring these options makes it easier to schedule meetings. I will be discussing this in the next section.

- **Host Key** – This is a password that grants you as the host controls during a meeting. There are some situations that you might encounter that require you to use your host key such as after joining a meeting by phone or after joining a meeting using the Zoom client and join before the host is enabled.

- **Signed-In Device** – If you think you have left your account logged in on someone else's computer or have lost your computer or phone you can use this option to log out of all the devices that your account is logged in on.

If you need to change any of these settings you can click on the *Edit* link to the right of the option and make your changes. For example, if I want to change my time zone or the way the date and time are displayed in my meetings I can click on Edit and make my changes as needed.

Figure 3.6

Calendar and Contact Integration

By integrating your Zoom account with your calendar you can easily keep track of your meetings and webinars and get notifications from your calendar service like you would for all of your usual appointments.

To set this up you will need to go into the Calendar and Contact Integration settings within the *Profile* section and click on the button that says *Connect to Calendar and Contact Service.*

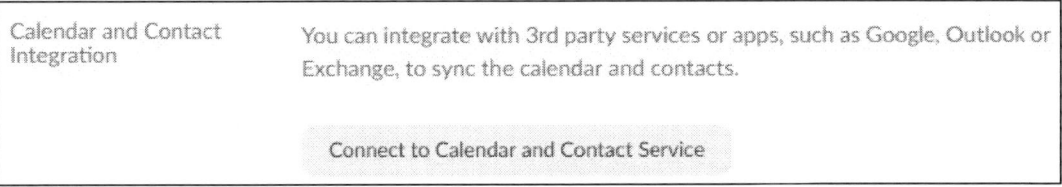

Figure 3.7

Next, you will be prompted as to what type of calendar service you wish to use. Your options will be Google, Exchange, or Office 365. I suppose there could be a chance that Zoom will add other calendar services to this list by the time you are reading this book.

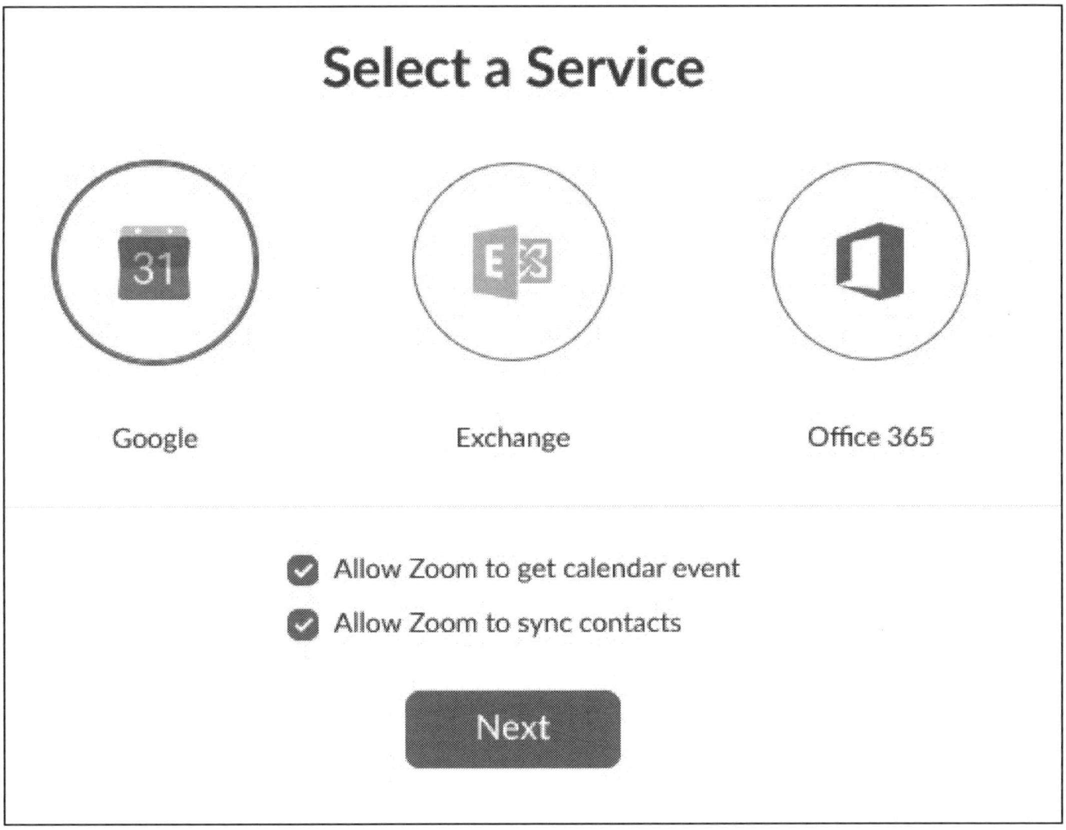

Select a Service

Google	Exchange	Office 365

✅ Allow Zoom to get calendar event
✅ Allow Zoom to sync contacts

Next

Figure 3.8

For my example, I will be using the Google calendar and contact integration option. Then I will be brought to my Google sign in page where I will sign in with the Google account I wish to use with Zoom. When I configure this I will be prompted by Google to allow Zoom the various permissions it needs to set this up as shown in figure 3.9 through 3.11.

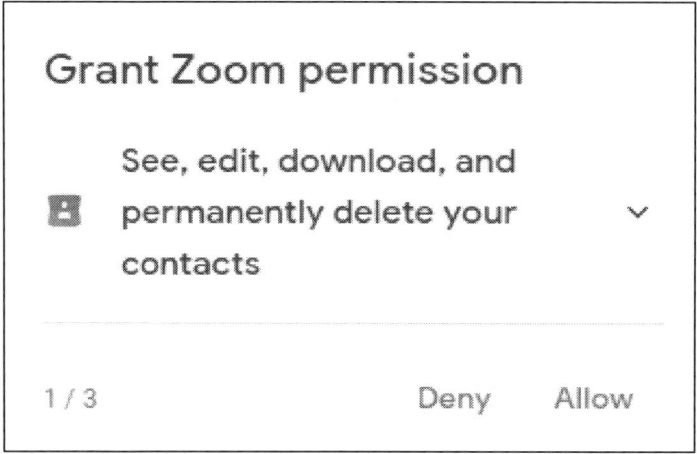

Figure 3.9

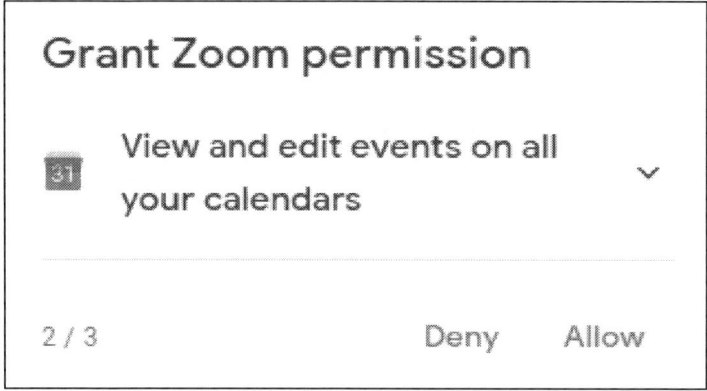

Figure 3.10

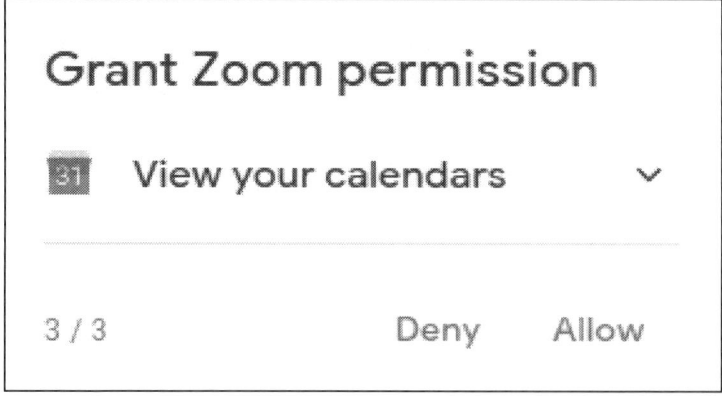

Figure 3.11

When I go back to the Calendar and Contact Integration section I can see that it has been configured to access the calendar and contacts associated with my Google\Gmail account.

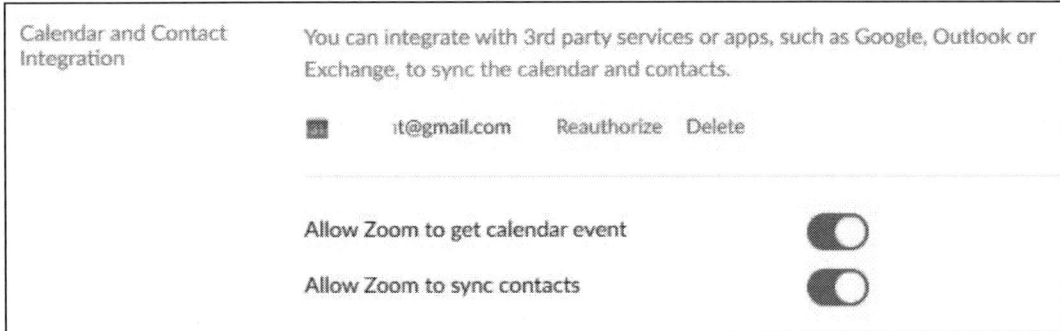

Figure 3.12

Now that I have my calendar and contact integration configured I will be able to take advantage of this when scheduling meetings and webinars by having Zoom add the meeting to my calendar for me with all the pertinent information.

Contacts
Before I get into creating meetings, I would like to show you how to add other Zoom users as contacts so when you create your meetings you will be able to see how it helps speed up the process.

From the Zoom client you will go to the Contacts section and click on the + button and choose *Add a Contact*.

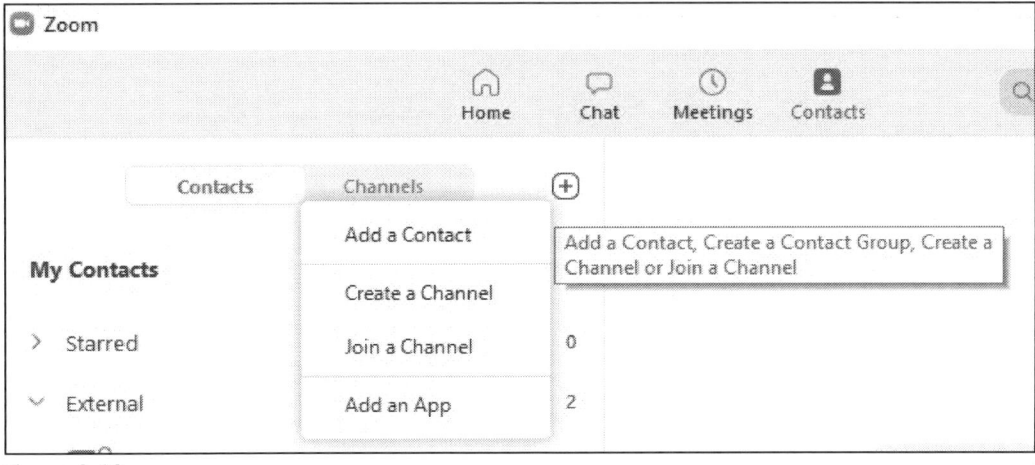

Figure 3.13

Next, you will enter the email address of the Zoom user you want to add to your contact list and then click the *Add Contact* button. I will enter the email address for Jim Brown (jimb@onlinecomputertips.com).

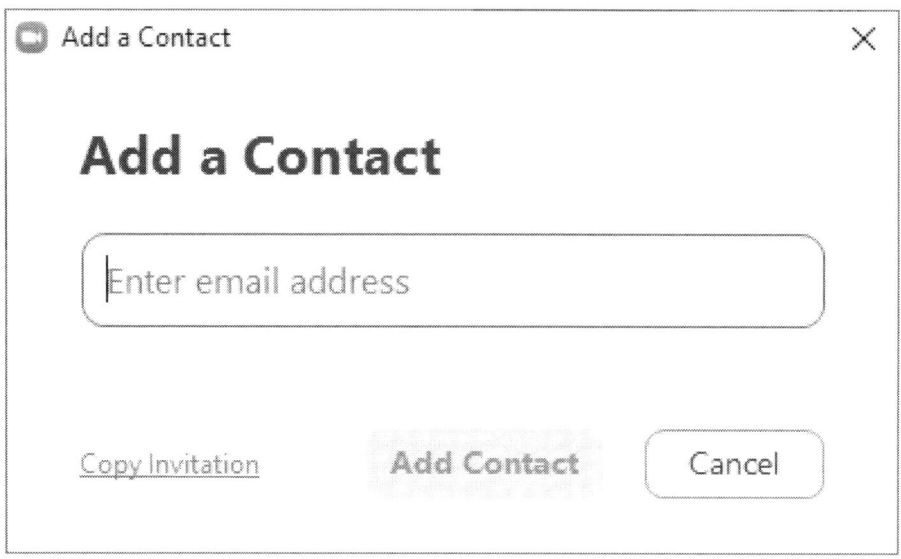

Figure 3.14

Then Jim Brown will get an email saying that you want to add them as a contact for your Zoom address book. They will need to click on the *Approve* button to allow you to add them to your contacts.

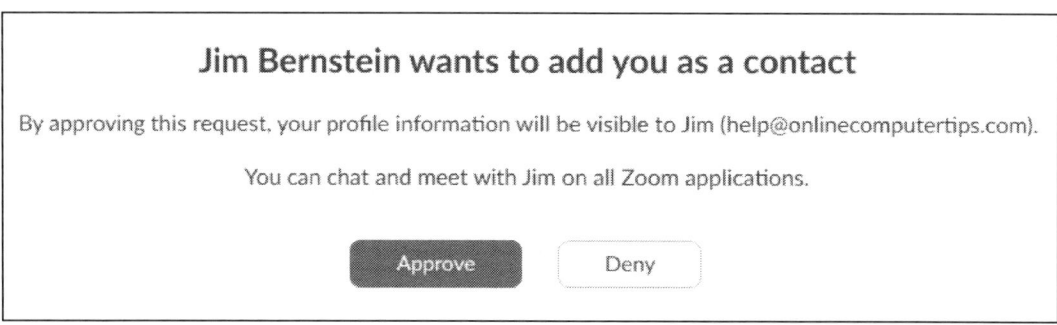

Figure 3.15

Now I have Jim Brown as a contact in my Zoom client. I also added one of my other email accounts to my contacts, so I had more than one.

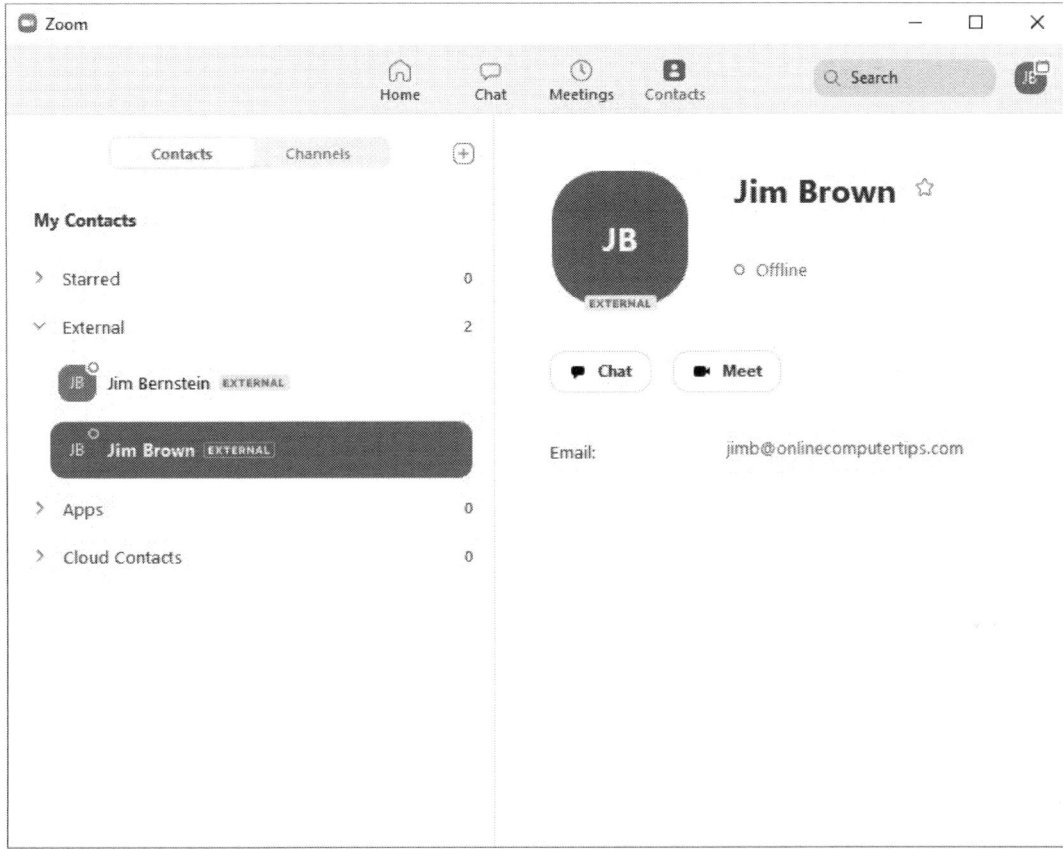

Figure 3.16

Google Chrome Extension

Google's Chrome web browser is one of the most popular web browsers that you can use on almost any device from your computer to your tablet to your smartphone. Chrome uses what they call extensions that are small pieces of software that can be installed into the browser to enhance its functionality. You most likely already have several installed if you are a Chrome user. You can see your installed extensions by clicking the three vertical dots up at the top right hand corner of the Chrome window and then choose *More Tools > Extensions*. You can also disable and remove extensions from here.

To install the Chrome extension, go to the Meetings section of your Zoom account in your web browser while using Chrome and click on *Download* under Chrome Extension. Then you will be taken to the Chrome web store where you can click the button that says *Add to Chrome* for the *Zoom Scheduler* extension.

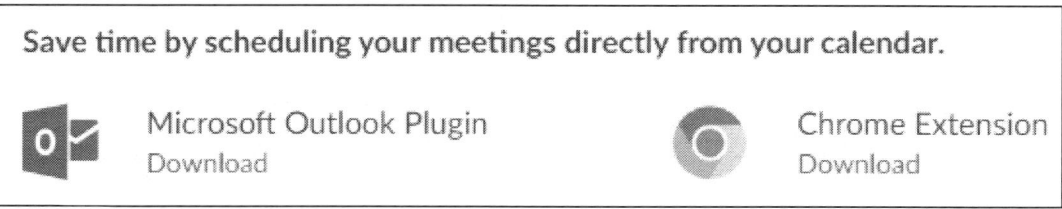

Save time by scheduling your meetings directly from your calendar.

Microsoft Outlook Plugin
Download

Chrome Extension
Download

Figure 3.17

chrome web store   ⚙   it@gmail.com ⌄

Home > Extensions > Zoom Scheduler

Zoom Scheduler   Add to Chrome

Offered by: zoom.us

★★★★☆ 643 | Productivity | 👤 5,000,000+ users

Figure 3.18

You will then have a shortcut in Chrome that you can use to quickly schedule or start a Zoom meeting.

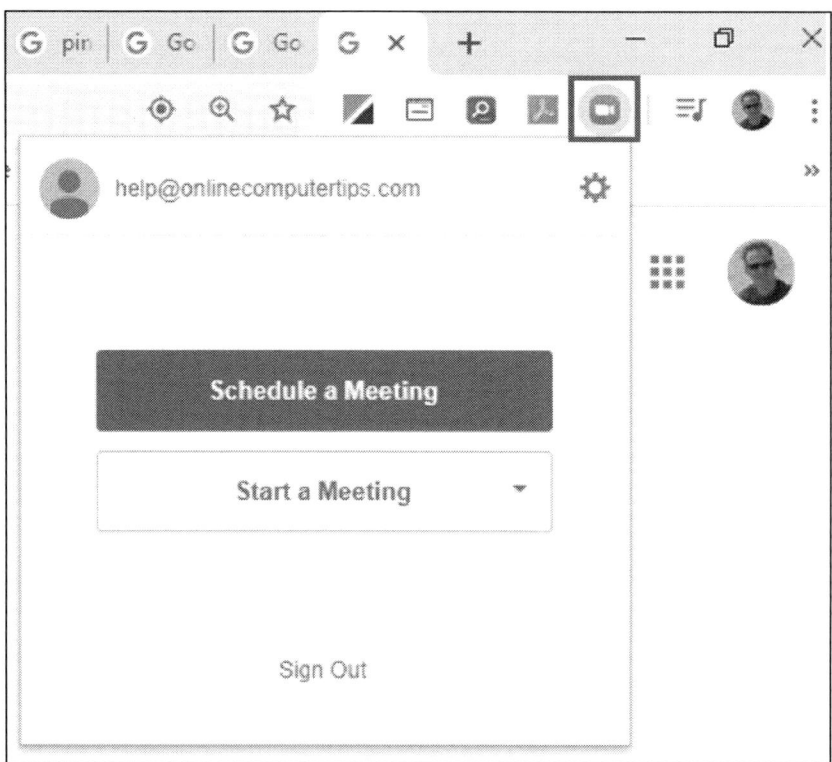

Figure 3.19

Checking Your Microphone and Webcam Setup
In order to use audio and video for your meetings and webinars, you will need to have some sort of microphone and camera configured on your computer that can be used with Zoom. If you are using a tablet or smartphone then you can use the built in camera that comes with your device.

Most laptops will also come with a built in webcam which should be located at the top of the screen when you have the laptop lid open. It might be a little hard to see because they tend to be very small. Your laptop should also have a built in microphone as well.

To test your video capabilities you can go into the Zoom client and click on the gear icon under your initials which will take you into the Zoom settings.

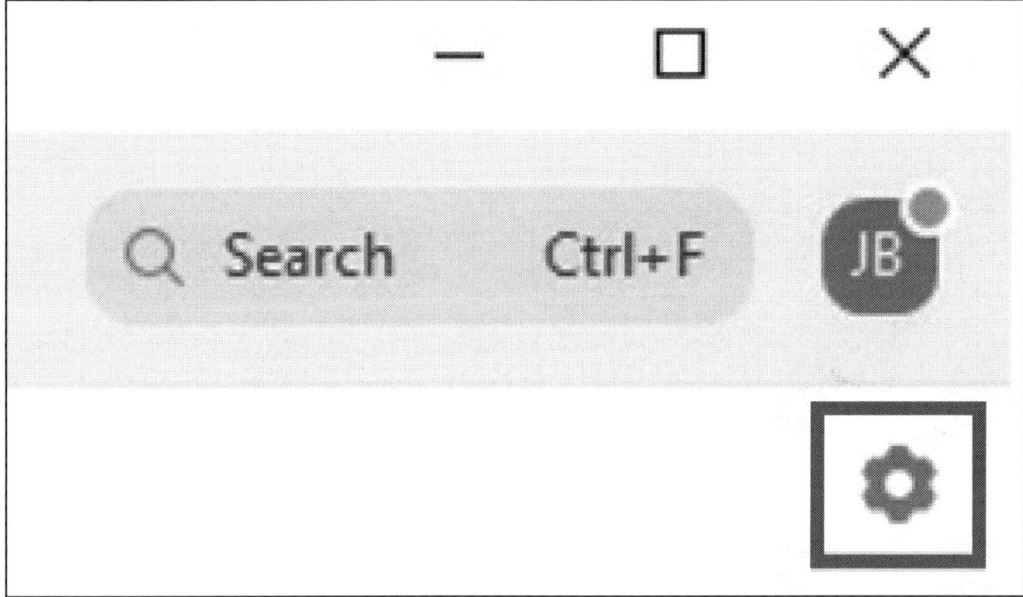

Figure 3.20

From there you will click on Video and you should then see a shot of what your camera is seeing if you have one. As you can see in figure 3.20, mine is a gray box because I don't have a camera configured on my desktop computer but rather only on my laptop.

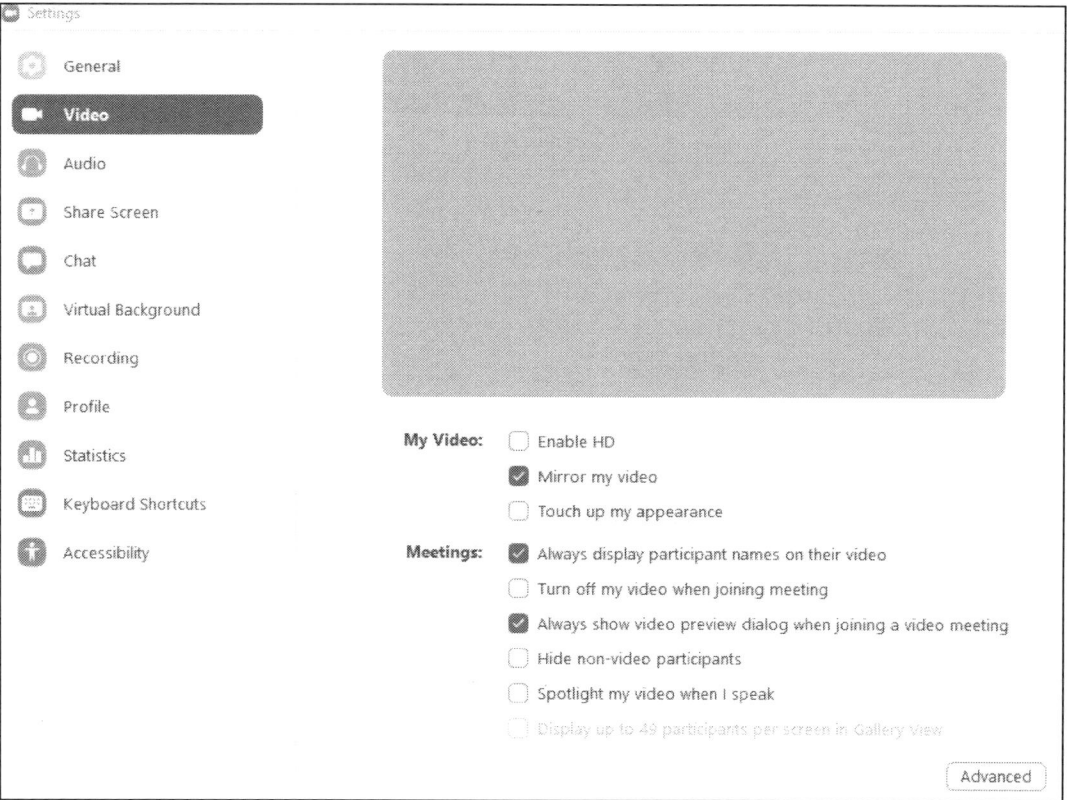

Figure 3.21

If you don't see yourself there then you know that you have some type of camera issue with your device that you will need to troubleshoot before starting your meeting. It's better to find out now than after your meeting starts and you realize nobody can see you!

To test your microphone you can run a test meeting with a friend to make sure they can hear you. When you start the meeting simply choose the option that says Join with Computer Audio (figure 3.22) to make sure that Zoom will configure the meeting to use your microphone.

Figure 3.22

You should also be given the option to test your speakers and microphone before starting the meeting as shown in figures 3.23 and 3.24 but I would suggest you test it in an actual test meeting to be sure a real person can hear you.

Testing speaker...

Do you hear a ringtone?

| Yes | No |

Speaker 1: Speakers (Realtek High Definition Au... ⌄

Output Level: ▬▬▬▬

Figure 3.23

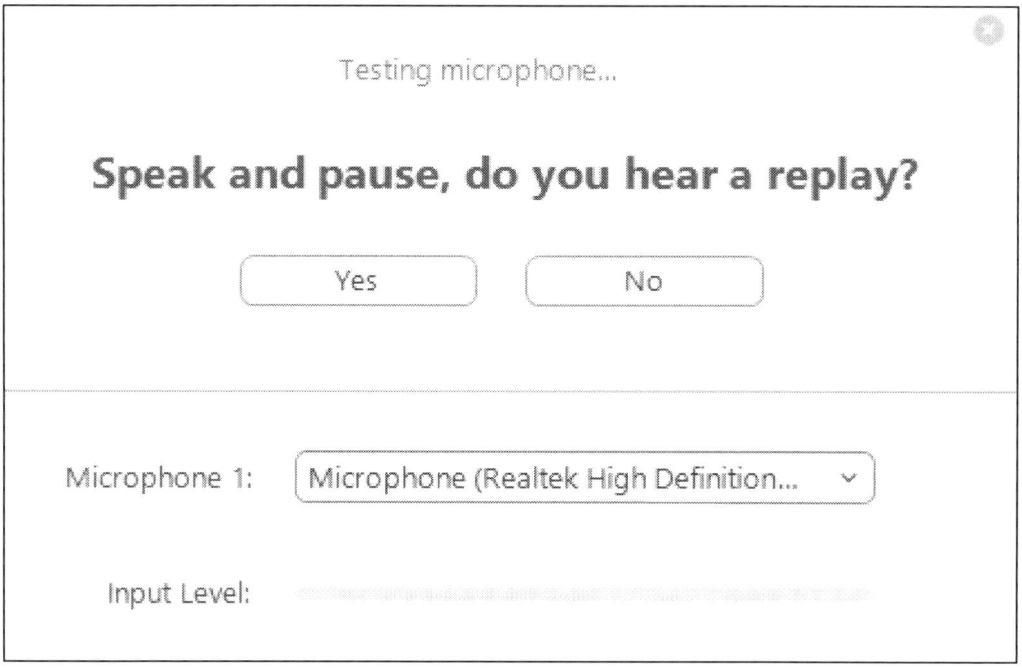

Testing microphone...

Speak and pause, do you hear a replay?

Yes   No

Microphone 1:   Microphone (Realtek High Definition... ⌄

Input Level:

Figure 3.24

If you still don't see any video or hear any audio then you will have to check the settings on your computer to make sure that your hardware is recognized properly. There can be many reasons for this and it's beyond the scope of this book so hopefully you are the techy savvy type or know someone who is!

Chapter 4 - Zoom Meetings

Now that we have all of the account setup and initial configuration out of the way, it's time to start scheduling and running some meetings! There are a few ways to go about this using both the web interface and Zoom client so I will cover all you need to know to get your meetings started and your guests connected.

Creating and Scheduling a Meeting
In order to host your own meeting you will first need to create one and allow other people to join by sending them an invitation or link that allows them to connect to your meeting. When you go to the Meetings section of the web interface you will see any upcoming meetings and have the option to schedule a meeting by clicking on the *Schedule a New Meeting* button.

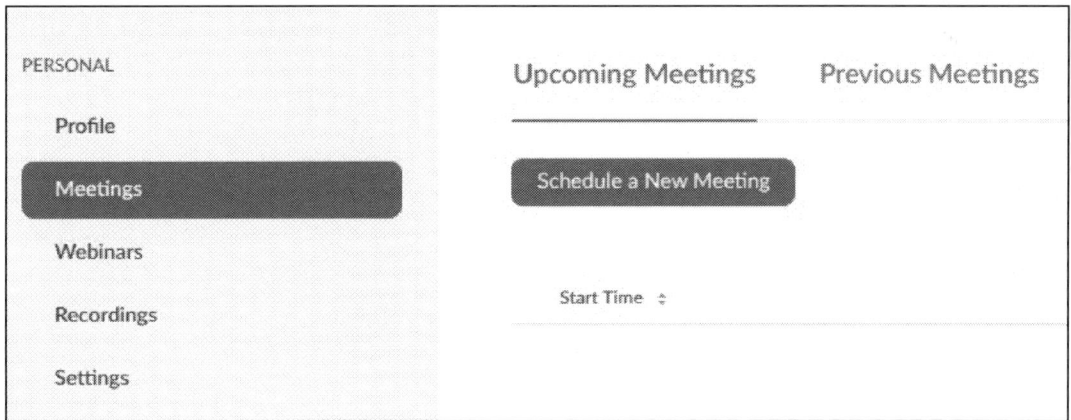

Figure 4.1

When you click on the Schedule a New Meeting button you will see a screen similar to figure 4.2. I realize it might be a little hard to see so you may want to schedule a meeting on your own computer so you can follow along.

Schedule a Meeting

Topic   [My Meeting]

Description (Optional)   [Enter your meeting description]

When   [05/04/2020] 📅   [7:00 ∨]   [PM ∨]

Duration   [1 ∨] hr [0 ∨] min

                               Your Zoom Basic plan has a 40-minute time limit on meetings with 3 or more
                               participants.
                               Upgrade now to enjoy unlimited group meetings.Upgrade Now
                               ☐ Do not show this message again

Time Zone   [(GMT-7:00) Pacific Time (US and Canada) ∨]

                               ☐ Recurring meeting

Meeting ID   ⦿ Generate Automatically   ◯ Personal Meeting ID 683

Meeting Password   ☑ Require meeting password   [5NSqa4]

Video   Host   ◯ on   ⦿ off

                               Participant   ◯ on   ⦿ off

Audio   ◯ Telephone   ◯ Computer Audio   ⦿ Both
                               Dial from   Edit

Meeting Options   ☐ Enable join before host

                               ☐ Mute participants upon entry ☑

                               ☑ Enable waiting room

                               ☐ Record the meeting automatically on the local computer

                               [Save]   [Cancel]

Figure 4.2

I will now go over all of the configuration settings you can change for a new meeting.

- **Topic** – Here is where you can type in the name of the meeting and is what others will see when they get the invitation and join.

- **Description** – If you want to type in a description of what the meeting is about you can do so here.

- **When** – This is the date and time that the meeting takes place.

- **Duration** – This is how long the meeting is scheduled to run although it can be finished earlier if needed. As you can see in figure 4.2, the free version of Zoom only allows you to hold 40 minute meetings when you have three or more participants and will automatically disconnect you after that 40 minute time period.

- **Time Zone** – Here you will see the time zone configured on your computer, but you can change it if you are in a location with a different time zone as to not confuse people.

- **Meeting ID** – The unique ID assigned to your meeting. You can either have Zoom generate a random ID for you or you can use your own personal ID. Just keep in mind that if you use your personal ID and someone remembers it then they can potentially join your meeting next time you are using that ID.

- **Meeting Password** – If you want to force others to type in a password to join your meeting you can check the box here and also change the password from the one Zoom suggests for you. Most people don't require a password for their meetings.

- **Video** – If you choose the *on* option for host or participant video then when you or they join, your video will be enabled by default. You can disable your video after the meeting has started if you desire.

- **Audio** – Here you can decide what type of audio will be used for the meeting. You can either force participants to use their phones or computer audio or give them a choice as to what they want to use by selecting both.

- **Meeting Options** – There are four main options in this section you can configure to further customize your meeting.

  o **Enable join before host** – If you want people to be able to join the meeting before you get then you can check this box.

  o **Mute participants upon entry** – Checking this box prevents your participants from communicating with each other until you allow it.

  o **Enable waiting room** – This option forces the participants to wait in a virtual waiting room until you bring them into the meeting either one at a time or all at once.

  o **Record the meeting automatically on the local computer** – If you want your meetings recorded without any intervention from you then you can choose this option.

For my meeting I will name it *Getting to Know Zoom* and set it for 30 minutes starting at 7 PM. Figure 4.3 shows that my new meeting is set up and ready to start. I can then add it to my Google calendar by clicking the *Google Calendar* button in the *Time* section.

If I simply want to send a link to the people who will be joining the meeting I can copy the *Join URL* and paste it into an email or text message to send out to the participants. Or I can click on *Copy the invitation* which will provide me with some additional information that I can paste into an email as shown in figure 4.4.

Chapter 4 - Zoom Meetings

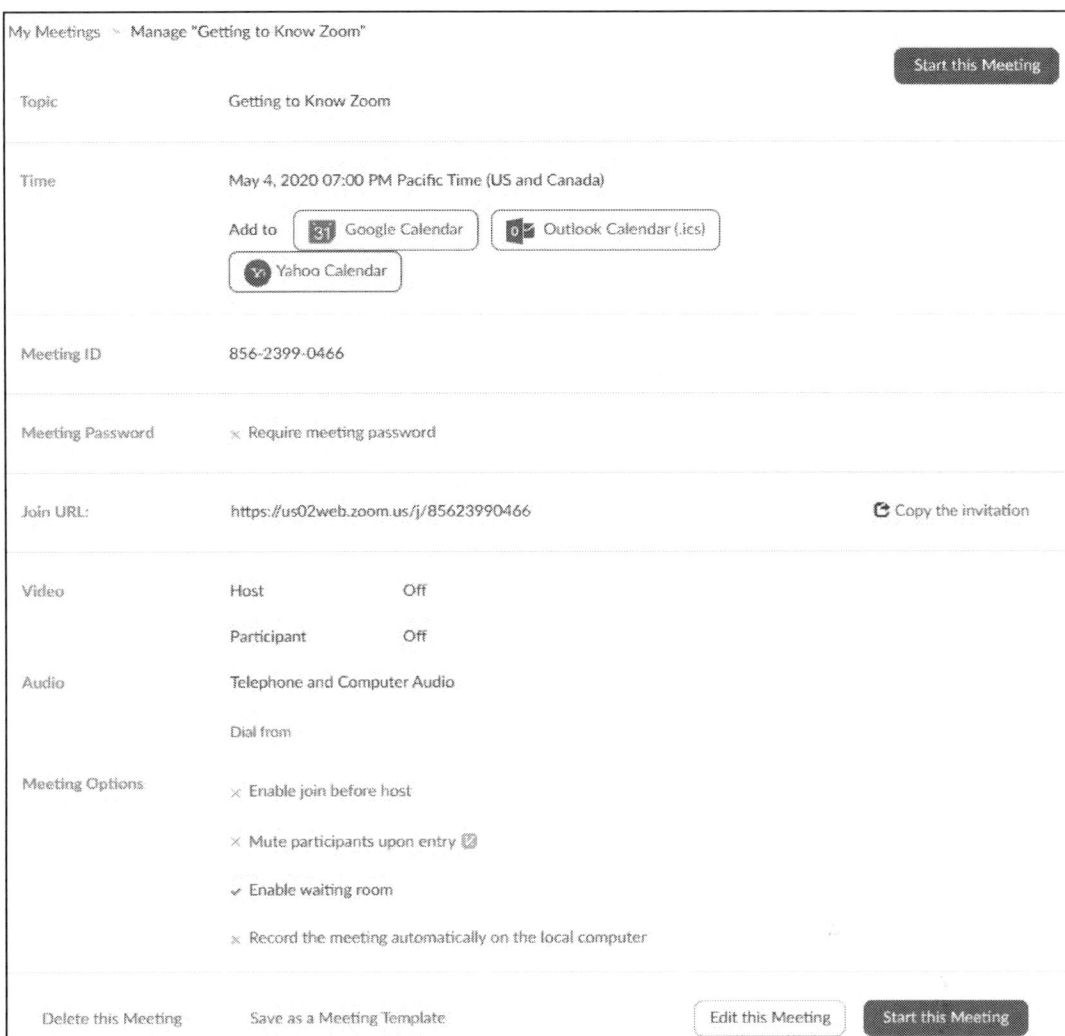

My Meetings > Manage "Getting to Know Zoom"

		Start this Meeting
Topic	Getting to Know Zoom	
Time	May 4, 2020 07:00 PM Pacific Time (US and Canada)	
	Add to [31] Google Calendar [O] Outlook Calendar (.ics) [Y!] Yahoo Calendar	
Meeting ID	856-2399-0466	
Meeting Password	× Require meeting password	
Join URL:	https://us02web.zoom.us/j/85623990466	↻ Copy the invitation
Video	Host Off	
	Participant Off	
Audio	Telephone and Computer Audio	
	Dial from	
Meeting Options	× Enable join before host	
	× Mute participants upon entry 🖉	
	✓ Enable waiting room	
	× Record the meeting automatically on the local computer	
Delete this Meeting Save as a Meeting Template		Edit this Meeting Start this Meeting

Figure 4.3

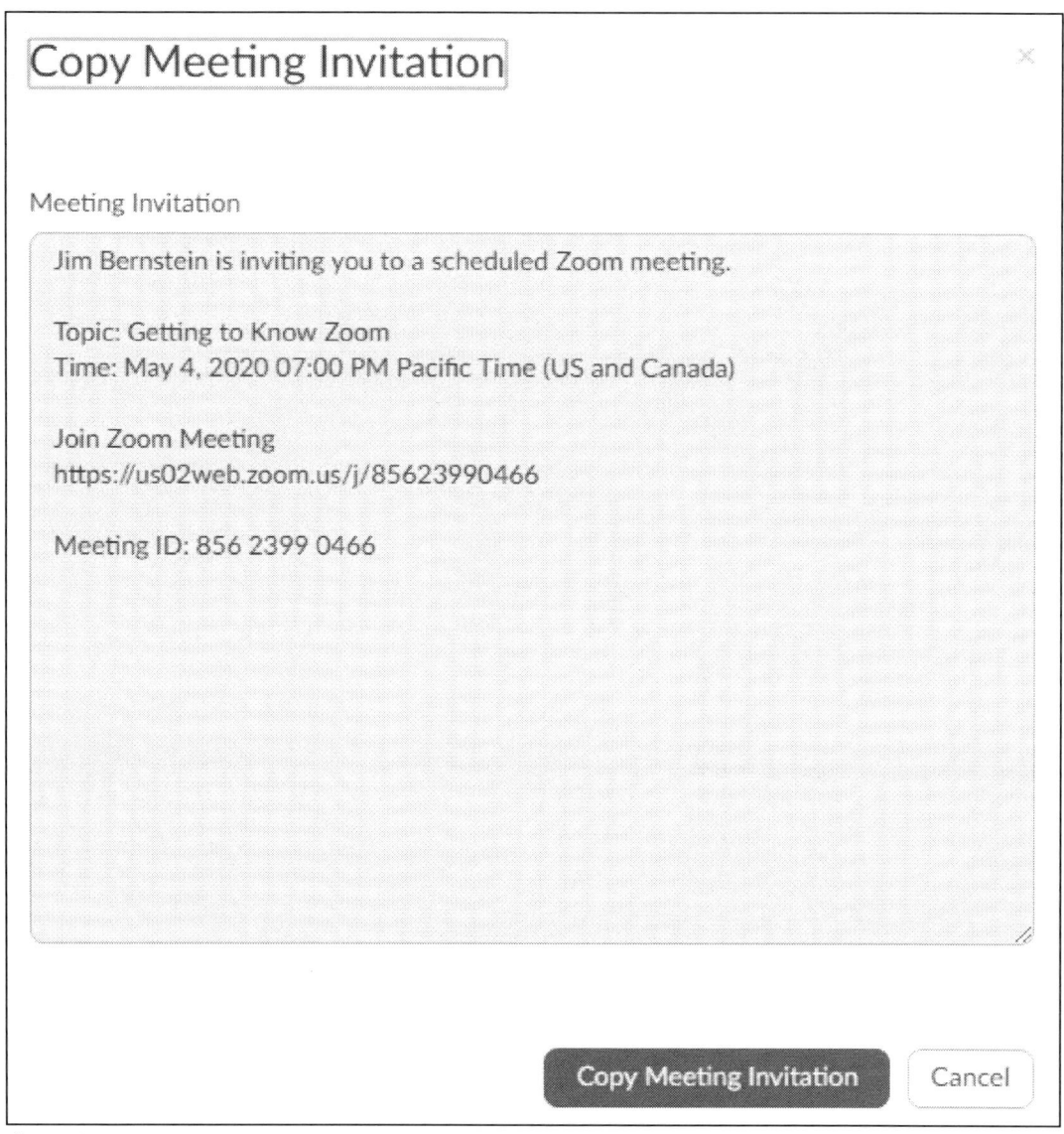

Figure 4.4

Starting a Meeting

After I make sure all of my meeting settings look good and I am ready to go I can simply click on the *Start this Meeting* button and the Zoom client will open up and my meeting will begin (figure 4.5). Since nobody has joined my meeting yet, it's pretty much just me sitting in an empty room waiting for others to arrive. If needed I can invite more people by clicking on the Invite Others icon and either add people from my Zoom contacts or send out an email invitation to these other people.

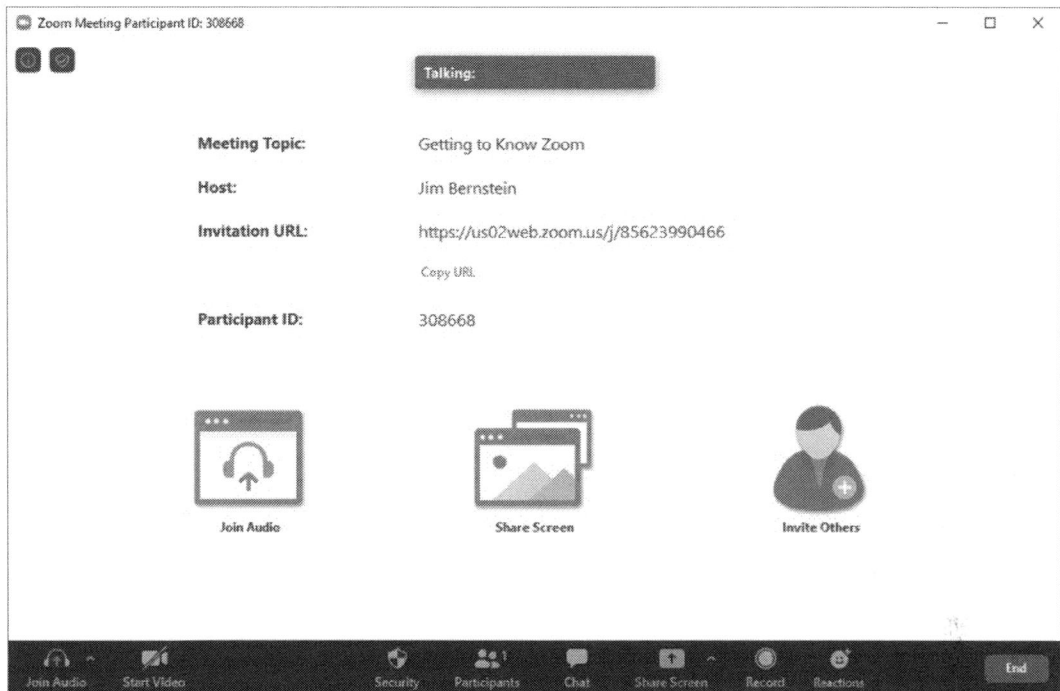

Figure 4.5

Before getting into how to join a meeting I would like to go over the buttons seen from the Zoom meeting interface in figure 4.5. I will be going over some of these options in more detail later in the chapter.

- **Join Audio** – Here is where you can choose to join the meeting with either your microphone or your telephone.

- **Share Screen** – This option allows you to share items on your computer screen with your participants. I will be going into this in more detail later in this chapter.

- **Invite Others** – I just mentioned how you can invite additional people while your meeting is running.

- **Start Video** – If you want to enable the camera on your computer or device so others can see you speaking then you can do so from here.

- **Security** – Here you can do things such as lock the meeting, turn off chat capabilities and disable screen sharing.

- **Participants** – Clicking on Participants will show you a listing of everyone who is attending your meeting. You can do things such as mute certain people and allow participants to rename themselves if they desire.

- **Chat** – If you want to send a message to everyone in the meeting or just to a particular person you can do so from here.

- **Share Screen** – If you would like your participants to see what you are doing on your computer then you can share your entire screen or just a certain window.

- **Record** – Recording your meetings allows you to review it later on so you can see how it went or get any useful information out of it that you might need.

- **Reactions** – If you want to give a thumbs up or some applause to someone who is speaking you can do so from here.

- **End** – Clicking on End will allow you to leave the meeting or end the meeting for everyone that is participating.

Joining a Meeting

Joining a Zoom meeting is very easy to do assuming you have an invitation or the meeting URL (address) from the meeting host. Once you click on the link to join the meeting you will be prompted to download and install the Zoom client if you don't already have it installed on your computer from a previous meeting.

You might see something similar to figure 4.6 in your browser depending on which web browser you use. It will tell you to click on the downloaded Zoom installer file to start the Zoom client installation process.

Figure 4.6

Then you should see a status box similar to figure 4.7 where it will be preparing your computer to join the Zoom meeting.

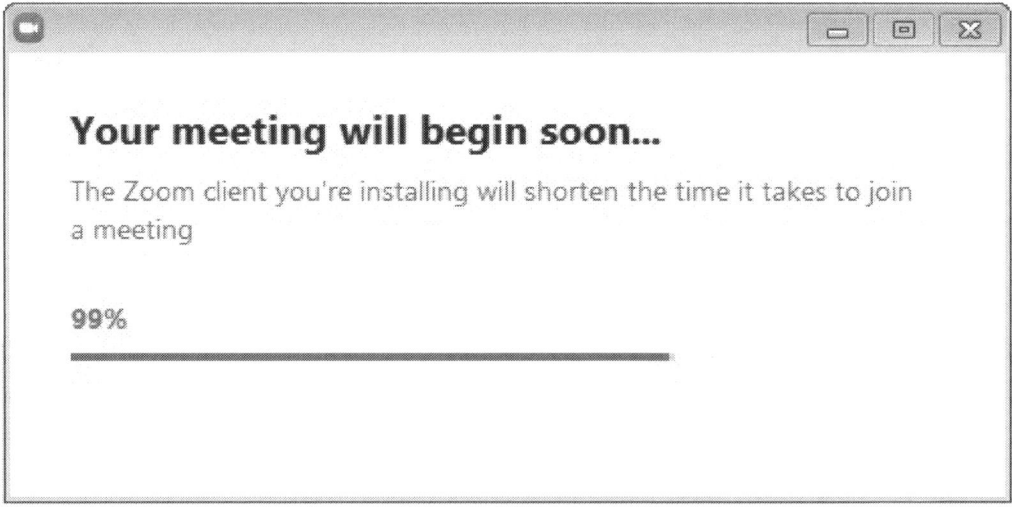

Figure 4.7

Next, you will be asked for your name which will appear to everyone else in the Zoom meeting so don't put anything you might think is funny because it might not be to everyone else!

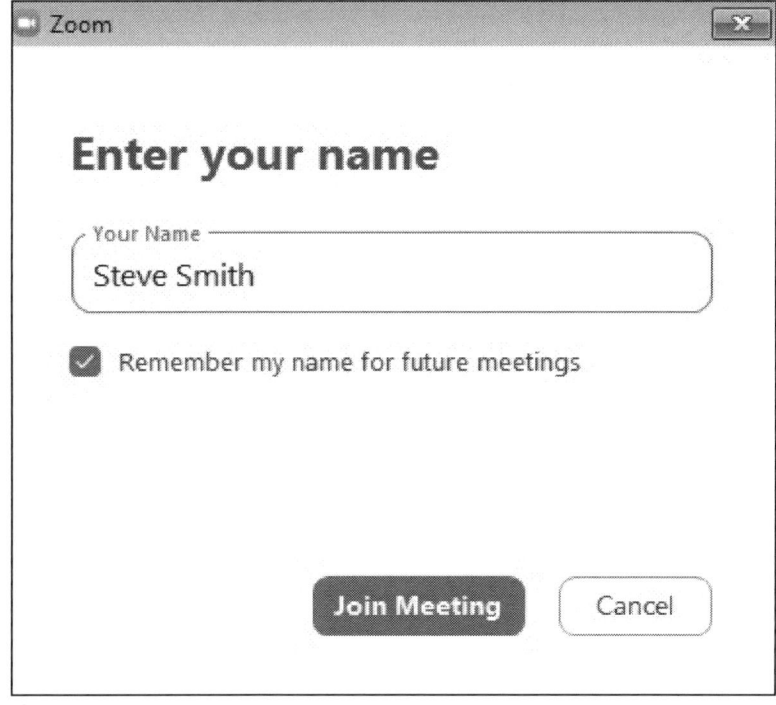

Figure 4.8

Since I kept the Enable Waiting Room checked, Steve Smith will not be allowed in until I let him in and will see the message from figure 4.9.

Please wait, the meeting host will let you in soon.

Getting to Know Zoom

5/4/2020

Figure 4.9

Back in my Zoom client I will see a message that Steve Smith is waiting to join, and I will have the option to Admit him to my meeting.

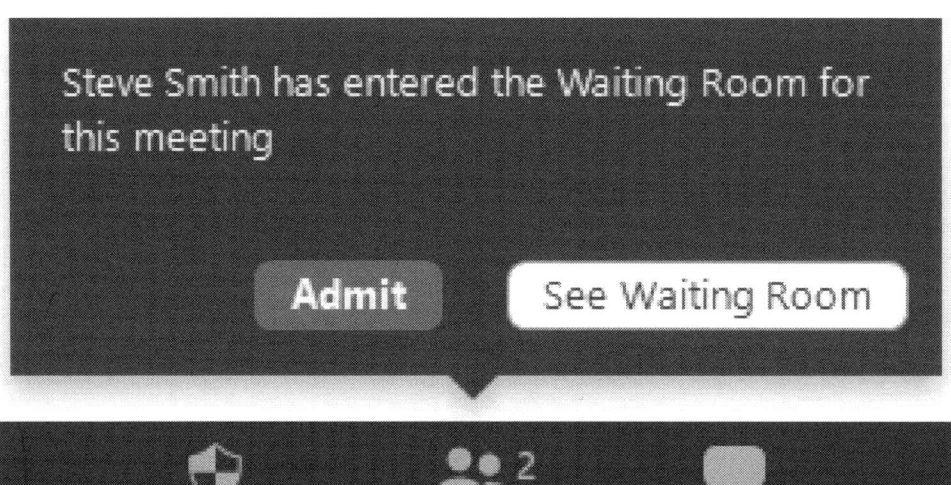

Figure 4.10

If I click on the *See Waiting Room button* I will see everyone who is waiting to be admitted to my meeting. I will also have the option to send Steve a message without letting him into my meeting. I can also admit him from here or remove him if I decided I don't want him to join my meeting.

Participants (1)

1 person is waiting   **Message**

SS   Steve Smith

1 participant in the meeting

JB   Jim Ber... (Host, me, participant ID: 308668)

Figure 4.11

Once Steve has joined he will have a similar screen to me as seen in figure 4.12. He will then be able to do things such as share his screen, chat with others, invite others to the meeting etc. Just keep in mind that he will need the appropriate permissions to do many of these things which will be determined by how you set up the meeting options.

When Steve is done with the meeting he can click the *Leave* button to disconnect from the meeting and you will be able to see that he has disconnected because you will have one less person in your participant list.

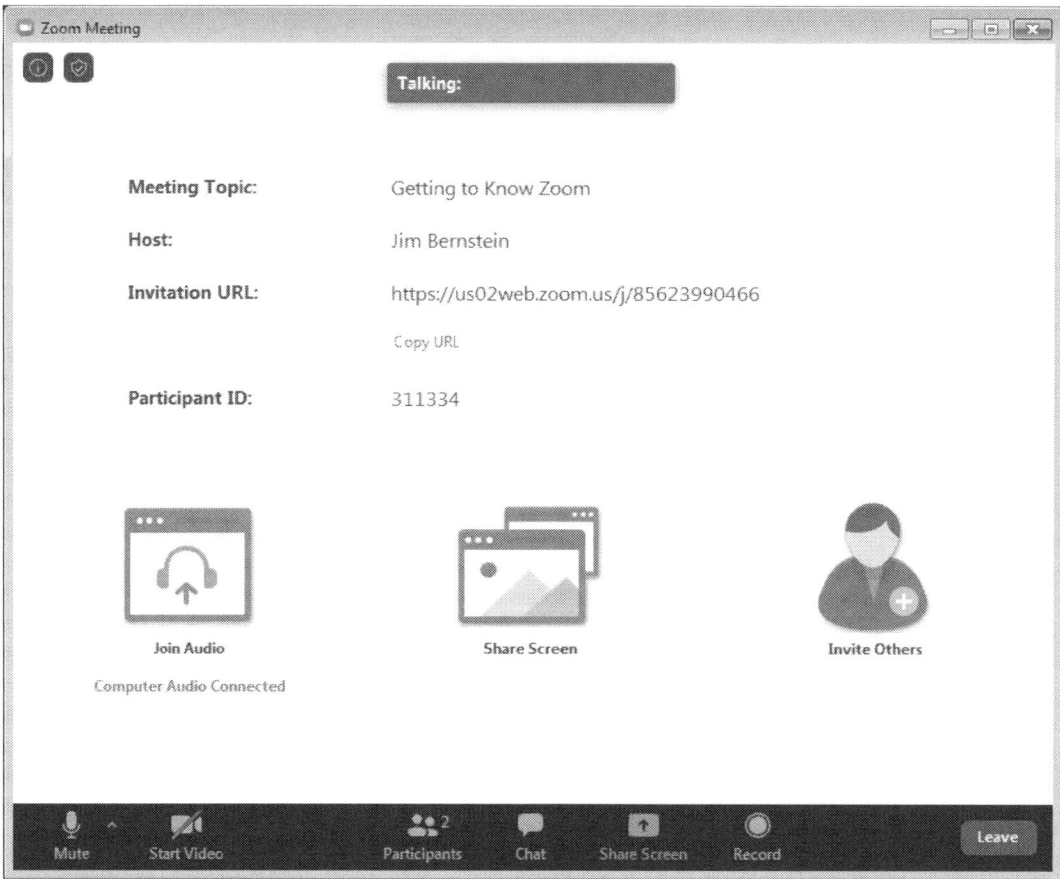

Figure 4.12

Making Calls via Zoom Numbers vs. Using Computer Audio

You might have noticed when starting a Zoom meeting that it asks you if you want to join with your computer audio meaning the built in microphone on your laptop or mobile device or some sort of microphone or headset you have connected to your computer.

Sometimes connecting with computer audio is not an option and you need another way to be able to "call in" to the meeting. Fortunately, Zoom offers a way to call in using your phone and still be able to talk to others who are using their computer audio.

Zoom offers several phone numbers you can use to call in via your phone but if you are using the Basic\free plan you might not have that option depending on when you are reading this book and if Zoom decided to bring back the phone call option for the Basic plan.

If you are using one of the pay for plans then you will have the option to provide a call in number when setting up your meeting and also when people join your meeting. Then when the call connects the participants will enter the meeting ID provided by you and possibly a password if you have configured the meeting to use one. If you are the one setting up the meeting with the dial in number just make sure it's a toll free number before handing it out, so your participants don't get any surprises later on when they get their phone bill.

Of course you can always use your own phone number for your meeting if you only have two or three people on the call assuming you know how to make conference calls on your phone.

Screen Sharing
One of the great features of Zoom and many other online meeting services is the ability to share your screen and show the other participants what you are working on rather than trying to explain it to them verbally. This works great for showing presentations or spreadsheets for work meetings or webinars and you can also share pictures and videos for personal calls.

Screen sharing is an easy process and once you have your meeting running you will notice the *Share Screen* option in the middle of the Zoom client as well as in the toolbar at the bottom.

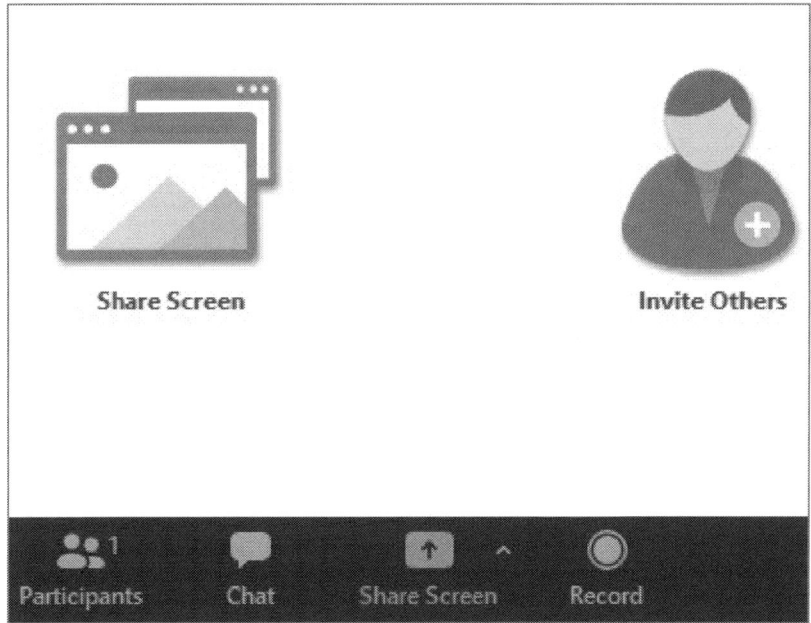

Figure 4.13

If you click the up arrow next to the Share Screen option at the bottom of the screen you will get some additional sharing options that you can configure such as allowing only one participant to share their screen at a time or allowing multiple participants to share their screen at the same time.

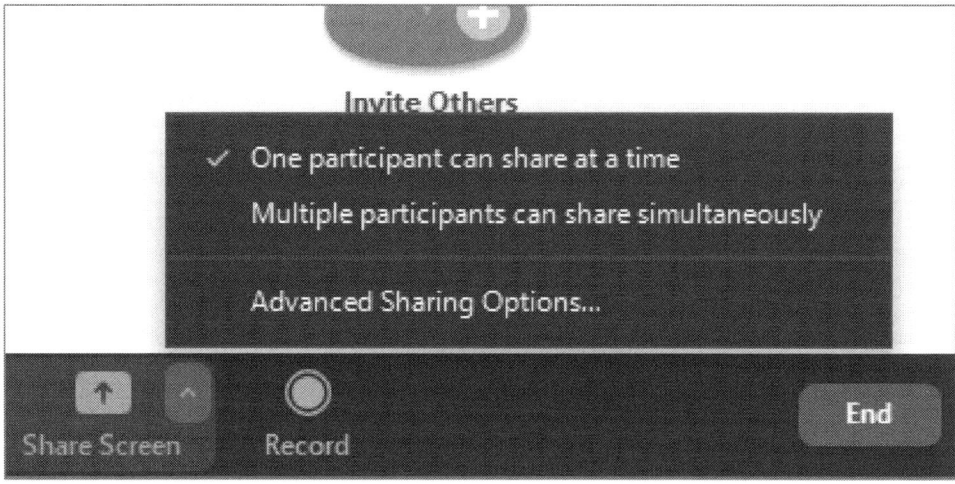

Figure 4.14

When it comes time to share your screen you will have several options as to what you want to share. When you click on either Share Screen button you can either choose the *Screen* option which will share your entire desktop and everything you have open on it or you can choose just to share one program such as PowerPoint for your presentation (figure 4.15). If you are planning to show various items such as documents, spreadsheets and pictures for example, then you should use the Screen option.

You can also start a shared whiteboard from here or share your iPhone or iPad screen if it's connected to your computer. I will be going over the Whiteboard and smartphone setup later in this book.

Take a look at the bottom of figure 4.15 and you will see that there is a checkbox that says *Share computer sound*. If you are planning on sharing videos then you should check this box so the sound from your computer can be heard by the participants in your meeting. It's also a good idea to check the box for *Optimize Screen Sharing for Video Clip* as well if you plan on sharing videos to improve video performance.

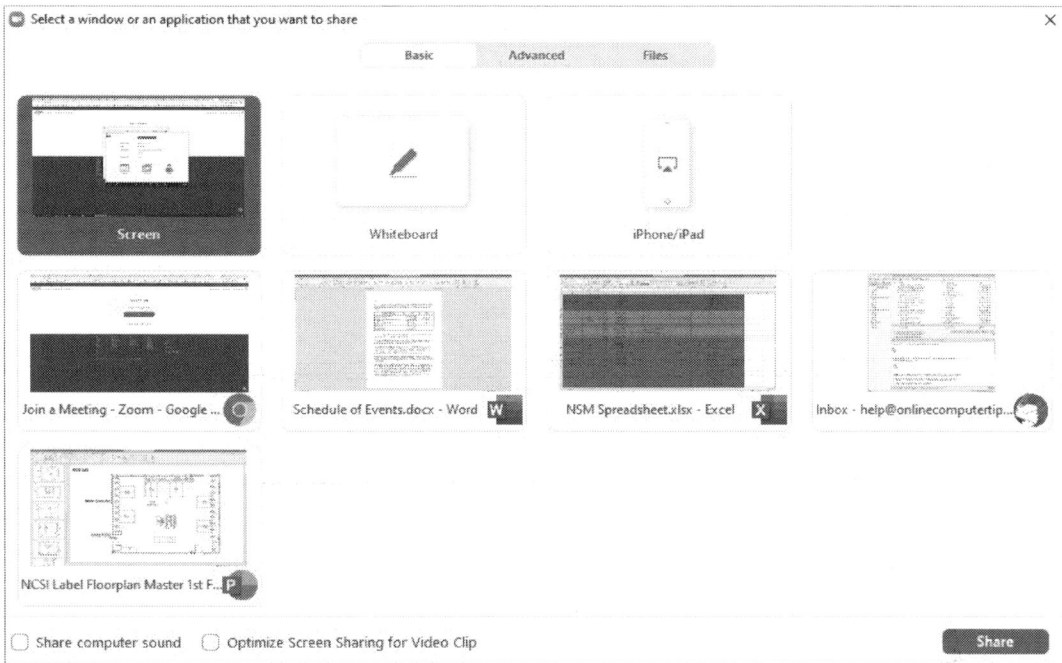

Figure 4.15

Figure 4.16 shows the *Advanced* section of the Screen Sharing feature where you can use a movable and resizable box to share just a particular area of your screen or share just the audio from your computer.

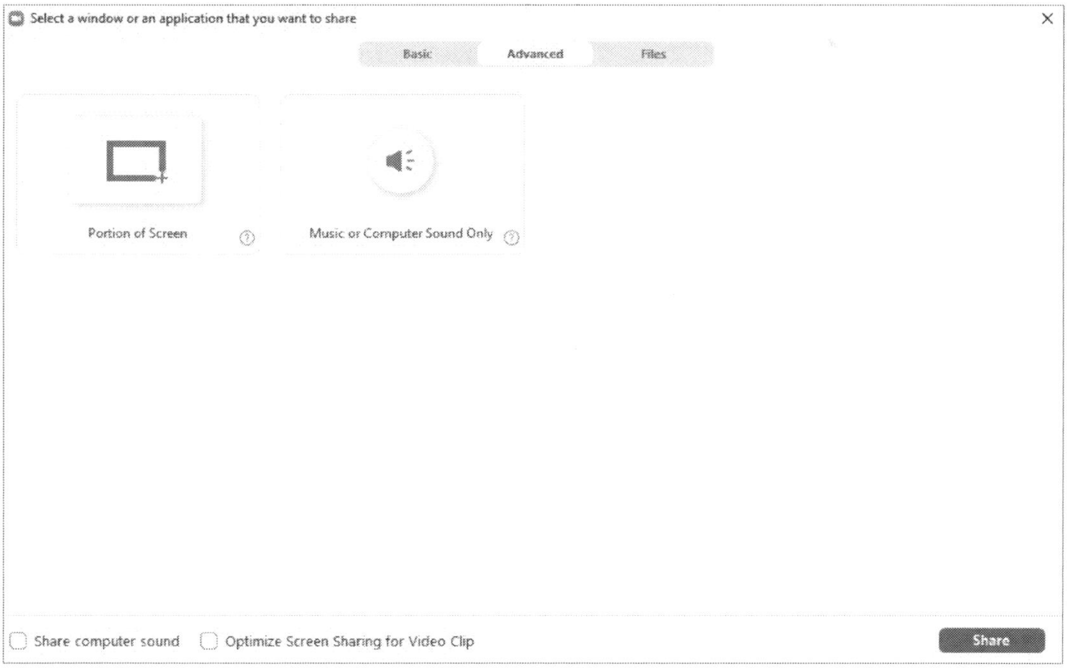

Figure 4.16

If you use any online\cloud storage services and want to share files from them then you can do so from the *Files* section of the Screen Sharing feature. As of this writing, you can use Microsoft OneDrive, Google Drive and box files.

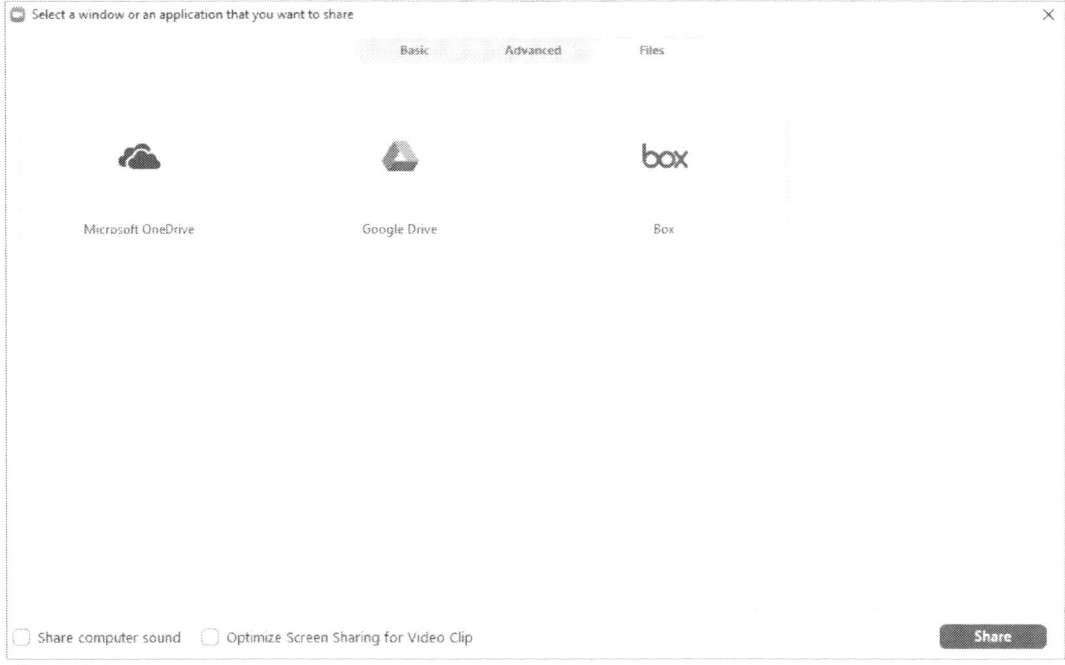

Figure 4.17

Once you share your screen you will obviously need a way to stop sharing your screen when you are finished. If you hold your mouse at the top of your screen you should get a toolbar that drops down that will have a red button that says *Stop Share* that you can click on to end your screen sharing. There will also but a button that says *Pause Share* in case you want to pause the screen sharing and then continue where you left off later.

Figure 4.18

Whiteboard Feature

I mentioned how you can use a whiteboard when discussing the Screen Sharing feature and now I would like to go into a little more detail about how to use it and what you can do with it.

To access the whiteboard simply click on Screen Sharing and this time choose *Whiteboard* as seen in figure 4.15. Then you will be presented with a blank whiteboard and a toolbar with various tools you can use to mark up your new whiteboard. You can do things such as add text and shapes as well as draw freehand images if you like. Plus you can change the colors of your text and shapes and erase anything you don't want to be shown in the whiteboard.

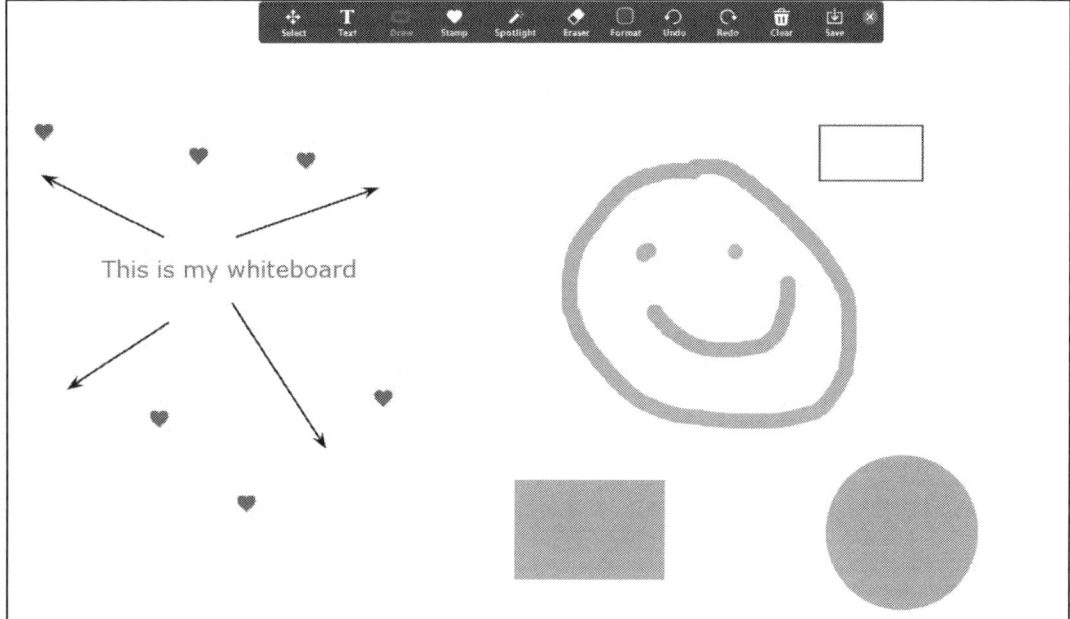

Figure 4.19

If you want to remove everything on the whiteboard simply click on the *Clear* icon to start over again. You also have *Undo* and *Redo* buttons just like you do in other software such as Microsoft Word.

If you wish to save the work you have done on the whiteboard simply click the *Save* button and Zoom will automatically save it to your computer as a PNG image file and name it according to the name of your meeting. The image will be saved In a folder called Zoom in your Documents folder.

Making Annotations
When sharing your screen you might have the need to make some annotations or notes to point out certain things on the screen that you feel your audience should be aware of. Fortunately, Zoom makes this very easy to do.

If you look at the drop down toolbar you get when sharing your screen you will see that there is an *Annotate* button that you can click on to start the process.

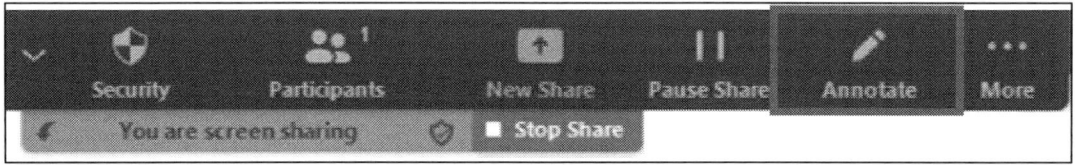

Figure 4.20

Clicking on this button will give you the same markup tools that you had for the whiteboard except you will be able to mark up whatever you are sharing on your screen as shown in figure 4.21.

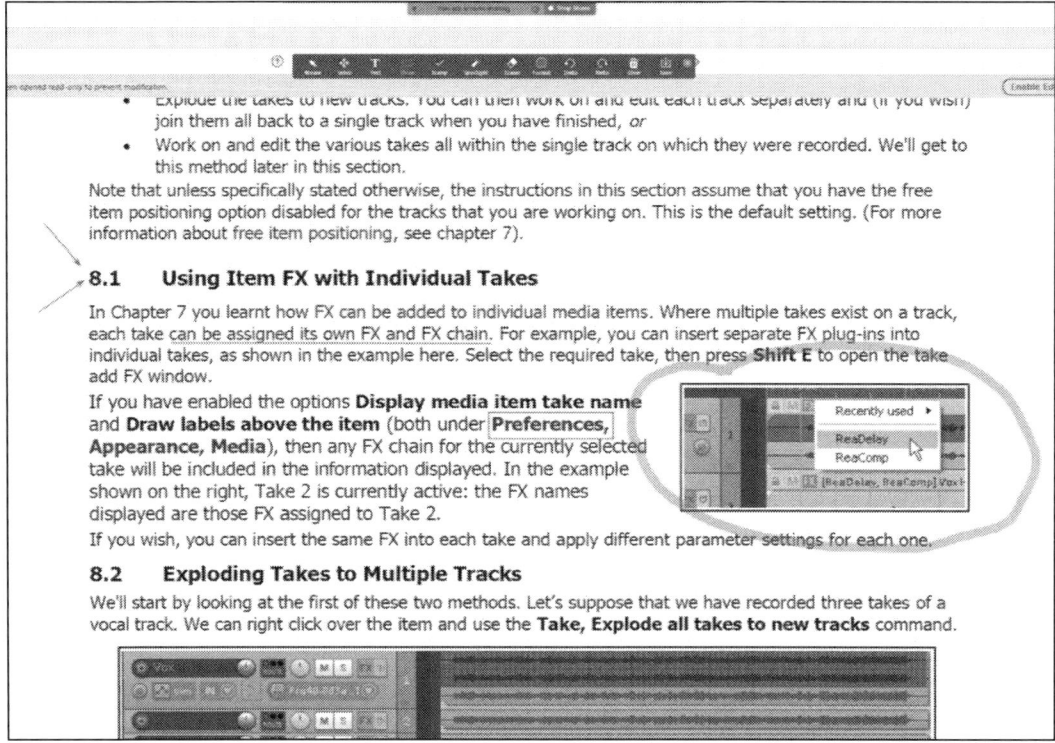

Figure 4.21

One thing to keep in mind is that your annotations will stay in the same place on your screen if you move things around or switch to a different window so you will need to erase them to avoid things getting messy.

Chatting

Even though you will most likely have some sort of audio call going on when hosting your meetings you can still use the Chat feature to make comments or communicate with others without disrupting the meeting.

You can get to the chat feature a couple of different ways. If you click on *Participants* you will see everyone in your meeting and then the chat option will be below their names.

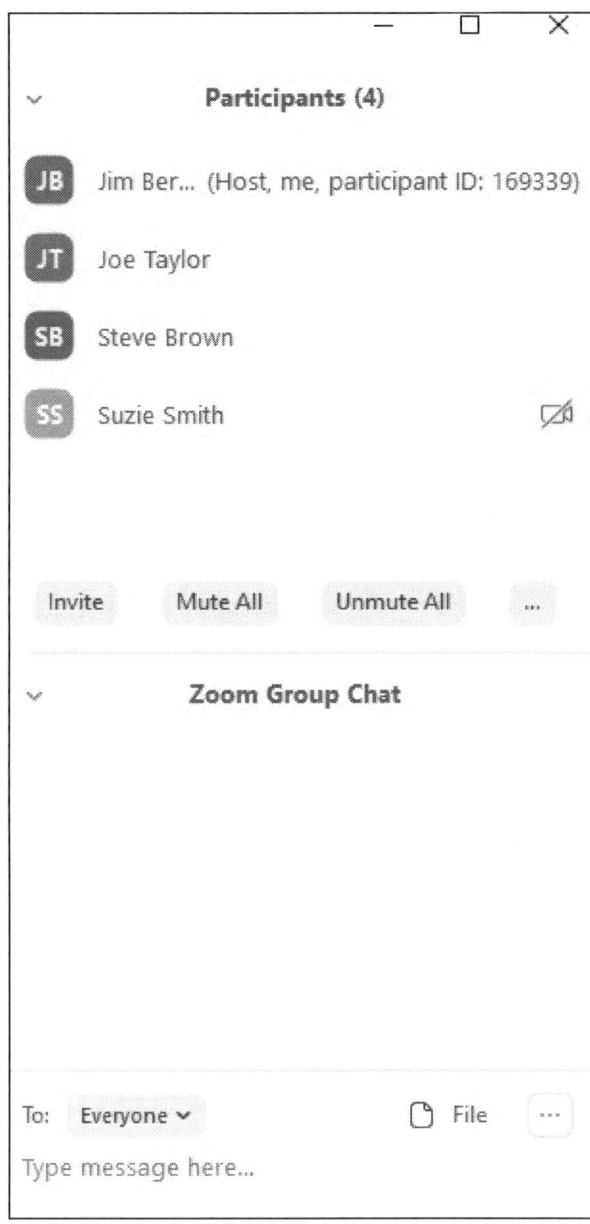

Figure 4.22

You can also just click on the *Chat* button in the Zoom client to bring up the chat window by itself.

The default setting is to send messages to everyone who is in your meeting but if you want to send one to a specific person then you can choose that person from the dropdown list in the chat window.

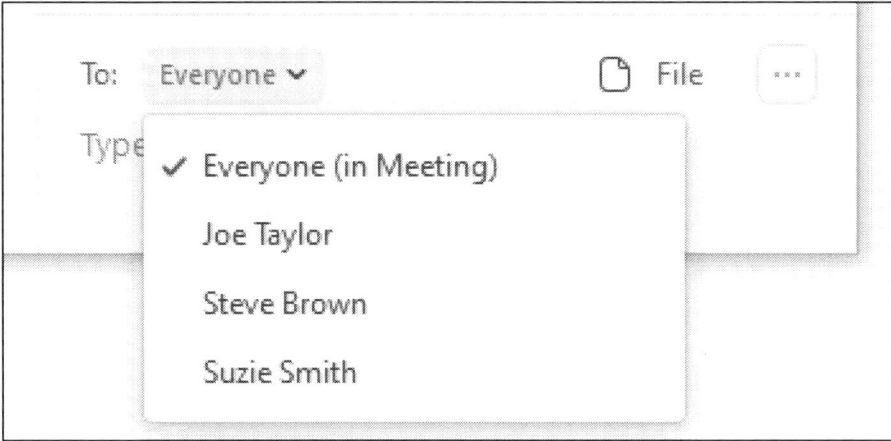

Figure 4.23

Figure 4.24 shows a message sent from me to everyone and then Suzie replying with a message to everyone. Then the final message from Suzie is sent just to me and you can see that because it says (Privately) next to it.

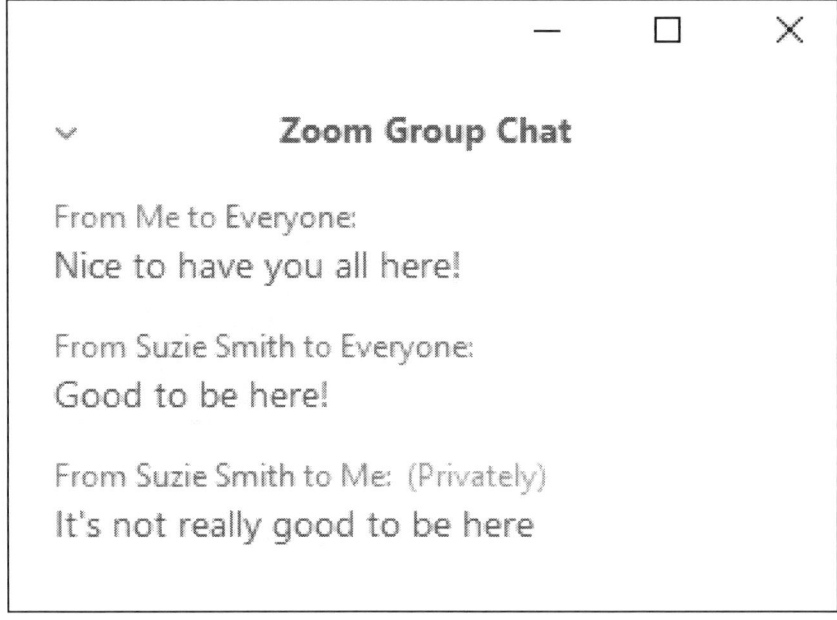

Figure 4.24

If you click on the ellipsis on the right of the chat window you will see your chat options. You can save the chat if you would like to review it later and also change chat permissions for your participants.

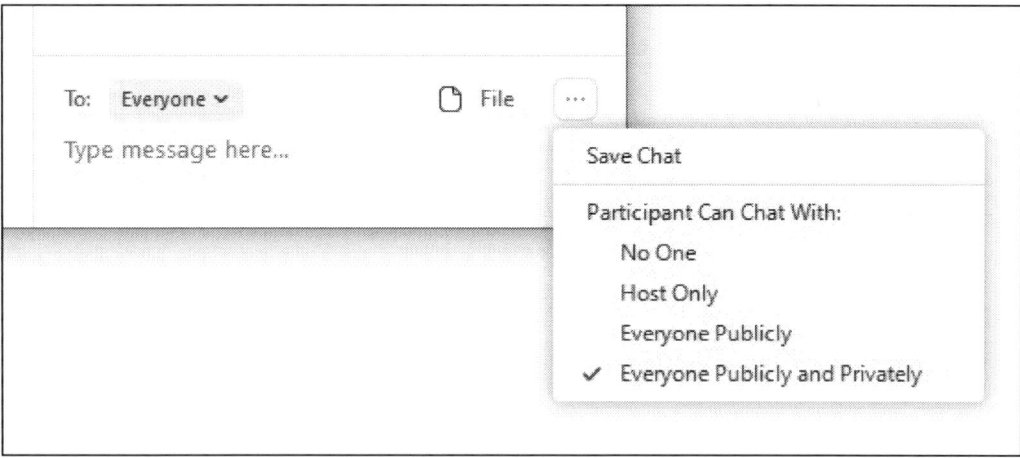

Figure 4.25

The File option will let you send a file from your computer or your cloud\online storage service to people within the chat. So if you would like to send a document or picture etc. for people to keep then you can attach it to the chat just like you would attach a file to an email.

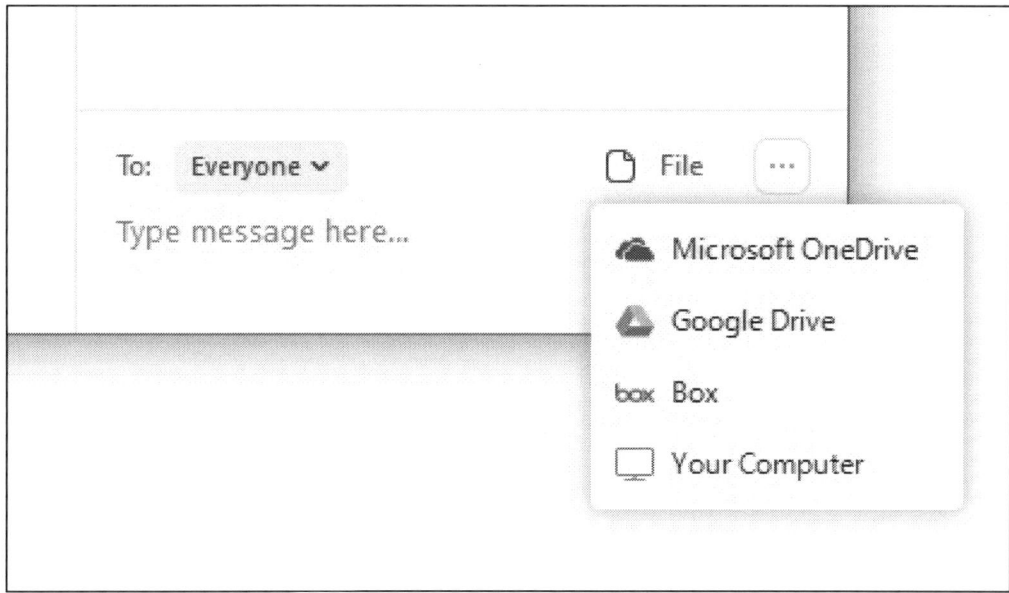

Figure 4.26

The file will show up in the chat window as seen in figure 4.27 and the users can view or save it from there.

Figure 4.27

Background Effects

When you are using your video camera to show yourself during your meetings you might not be in the most ideal spot such as in your kitchen or a messy room. This type of situation may deter you from using your camera during your meetings.

Zoom has a cool feature that allows you to disguise your surroundings so you can be holding your meeting from any virtual location you can imagine. You can take a picture or video that you have saved on your computer and use it as your background during your meeting.

Figure 4.28 shows an example taken from the Zoom website of the Golden Gate Bridge being used as a background image for a meeting and you can see that Zoom does a pretty good job of making it look like you are there.

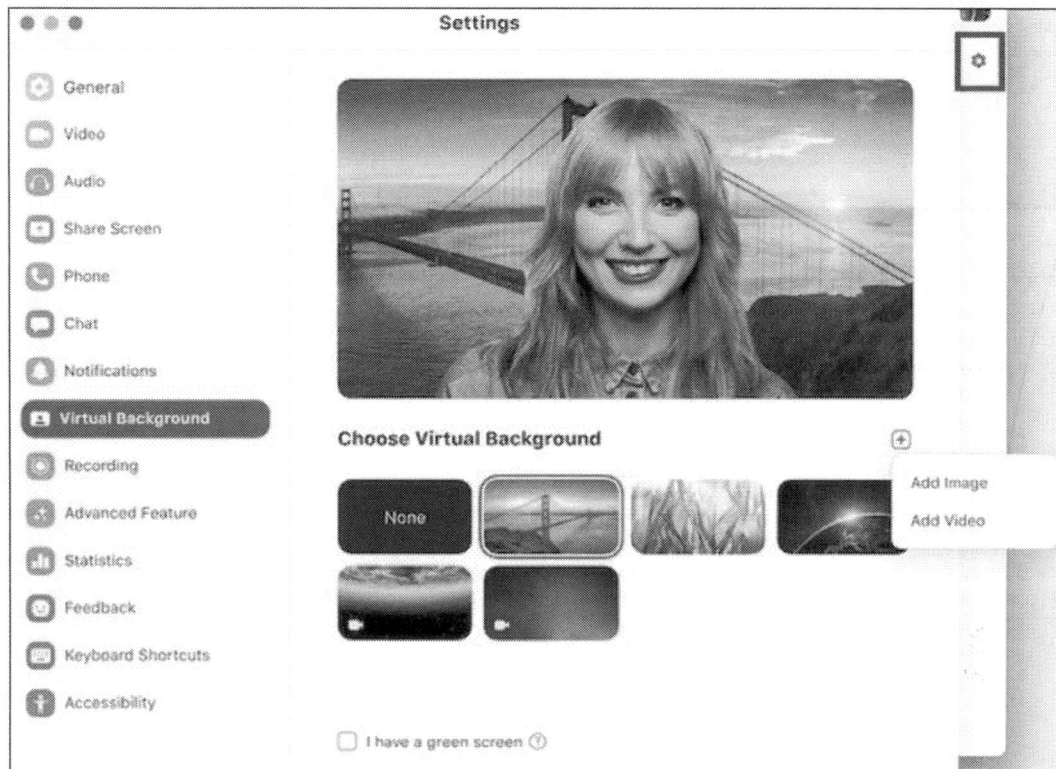

Figure 4.28

To configure a background effect you will need to go to the Zoom client and then the settings by clicking the gear icon at the top right of the window. Next, you will click on *Virtual Background* and then choose a photo or video. If you don't have anything to choose from or you want to use something different you will need to click on the + sign to choose an image or video file from your computer.

After doing this your new background will be applied to your live video and everyone who is in the meeting will be able to see your new "location".

Zoom Outlook Plugin
I had previously discussed the Zoom Google Chrome web browser extension back in Chapter 3 but now I would like to discuss the Microsoft Outlook plugin for those of you who use Outlook as their email client.

The Outlook plugin is a piece of software that gets installed and integrated into the Outlook client making it easy to schedule and start your Zoom meetings right from Outlook itself.

To download the Outlook plugin simply log into the Zoom website and go to the *Meetings* section and you will see the download link at the bottom of the page next to the Chrome extension link.

Figure 4.29

Once you download and install the plugin (with Outlook closed) it will then add a new group to your Outlook software called Zoom with a *Schedule a Meeting* option and a *Start Instant Meeting* option.

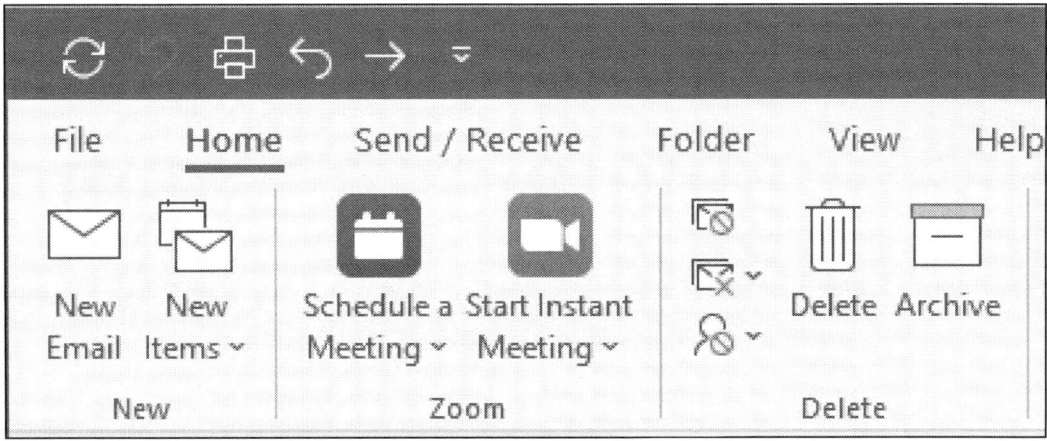

Figure 4.30

If you click on Schedule a Meeting it will open the Zoom scheduler (figure 4.31) where you can enter in all the details of your new meeting just like you would from the Zoom website but then when you are finished it will add it to your Outlook calendar.

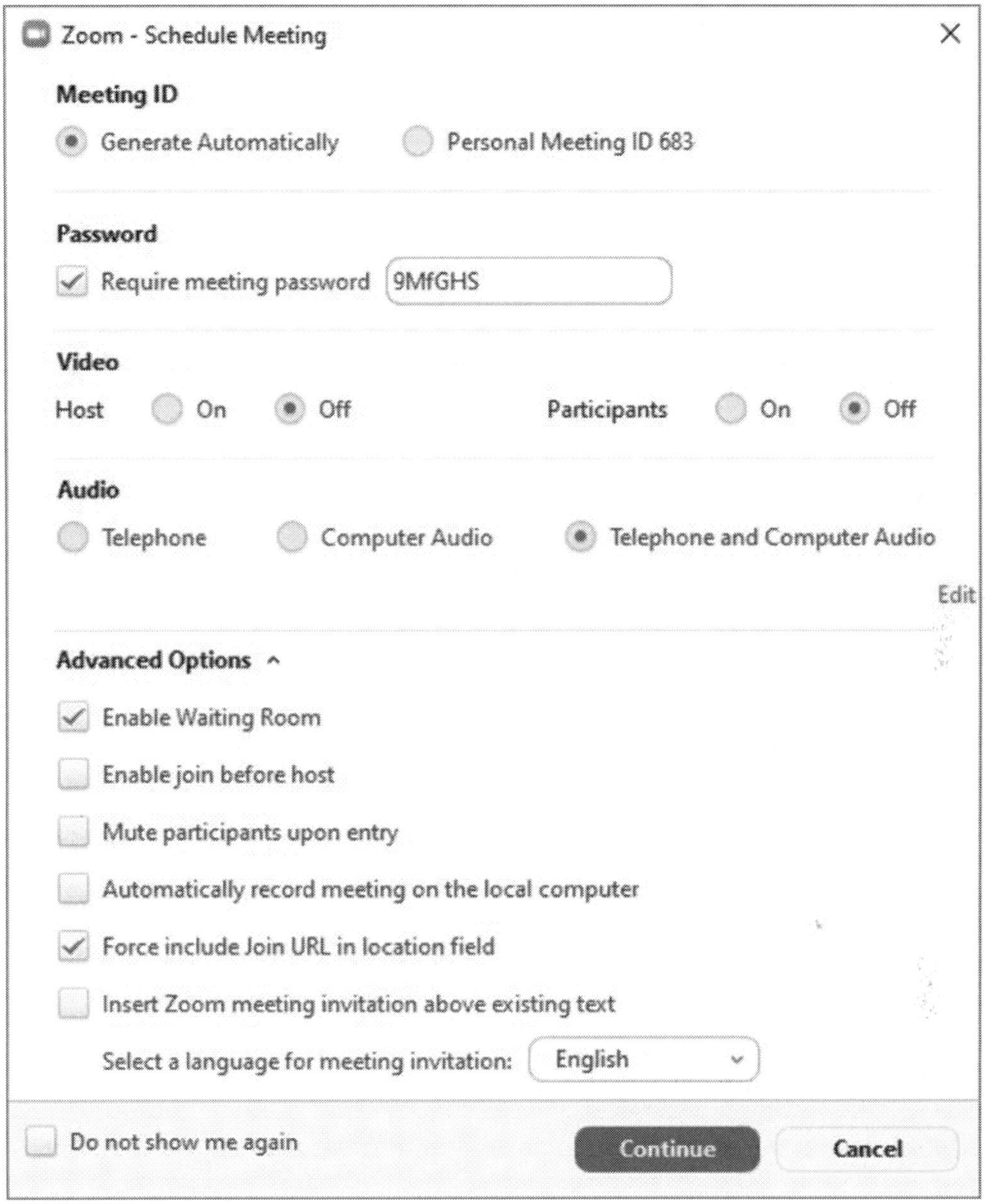

Figure 4.31

Clicking on Start Instant Meeting will start a meeting on the spot and open the Zoom client. Then you can do things such as invite participants and all the other things you can do with the client.

Changing Video Views

Zoom has a couple of different view options when your participants are using their video cameras to show themselves while in your meeting. You can configure the client to use *Speaker View* which will take whoever is talking and make their video the main focus of the meeting while keeping the other participants in smaller video windows. The way this displays on your screen will depend on how many participants you have in your meeting. Figure 4.32 was taken from the Zoom website and shows the Speaker View with the person on the bottom having a larger view because she is the one currently speaking.

Figure 4.32

The Gallery view (figure 4.33) will show everyone in the meeting with equal size video boxes and try and fit everyone on the screen at once.

Figure 4.33

If you click on the ellipsis that shows up when you hover over a person's video box there will be an option to chat with that person and also an option to hide all participants that are not using video in the meeting.

Muting and Spotlighting a Participant

You might run across a situation where someone in your meeting is getting too chatty or has a lot of background noise going on and you find yourself needing to quiet them down.

This can be done by muting that specific person from the Participants list. This can only be done if they have their audio turned on of course and you will see that because they will have a microphone icon next to their name like me (the host) does in figure 4.34.

To mute the person simply hover over their name and then click the Mute button to prevent them from being heard in your meeting. When you do this, the audio icon in their Zoom client will show a red line going through their microphone as seen in figure 4.35.

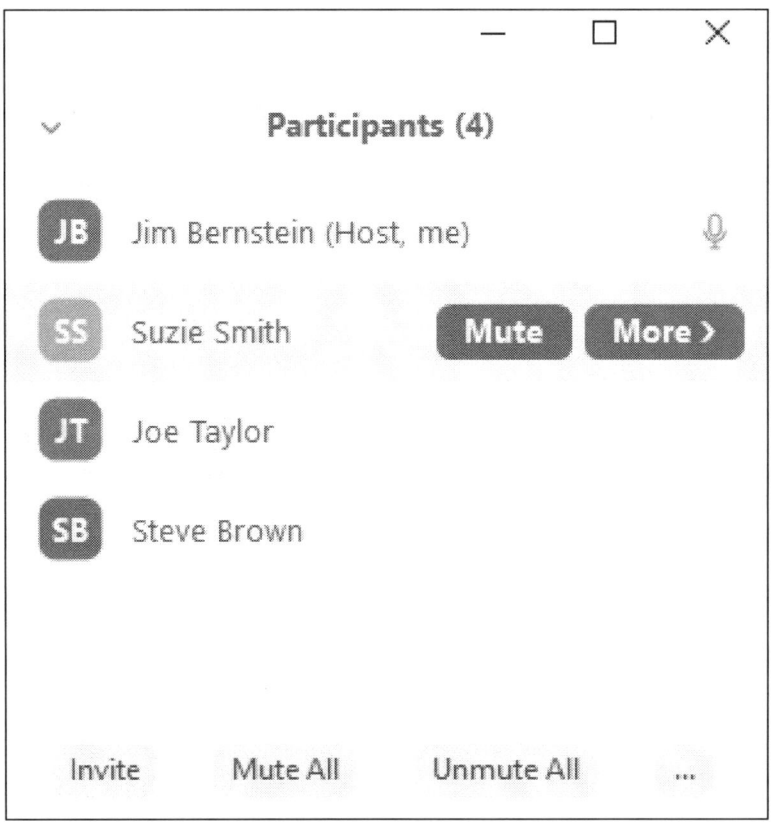

Figure 4.34

Figure 4.35

Just keep in mind that if you have users set to be able to unmute themselves in your settings then those people can easily do so from their Zoom client.

If you want to highlight a certain participant's video feed then you can go to that person in the participant list, click on the More button and then choose *Spotlight Video*. This will make that participant's video be the main focus of the meeting and will display it in a larger box compared to all of the other participants. To turn off this spotlight feature, simply go back to the More menu and choose *Cancel the Spotlight Video*.

Recording Your Meetings

You might have noticed a *Record* button on the toolbar of the Zoom client and wondered what you can do with this feature. Well, the answer is pretty simple; you can record your meeting so you can view it later and even share it with others that were not in the meeting to begin with.

If you haven't set your meeting to automatically record when it starts then all you need to do is click on the Record button to start recording at any time during the meeting.

Figure 4.36

You will then notice that the Record button turns into a Pause/Stop Recording button. So if you want to pause the recording, you would click on the left button as seen in figure 4.37 and then then the button will change as seen in figure 4.38 and if you want to resume your recording, simply press it again.

Figure 4.37

Figure 4.38

To stop the recording you will need to press the button with the square in the middle of it on the right.

When the meeting has ended, Zoom should automatically convert your recording into an MP4 video that you can play on your computer.

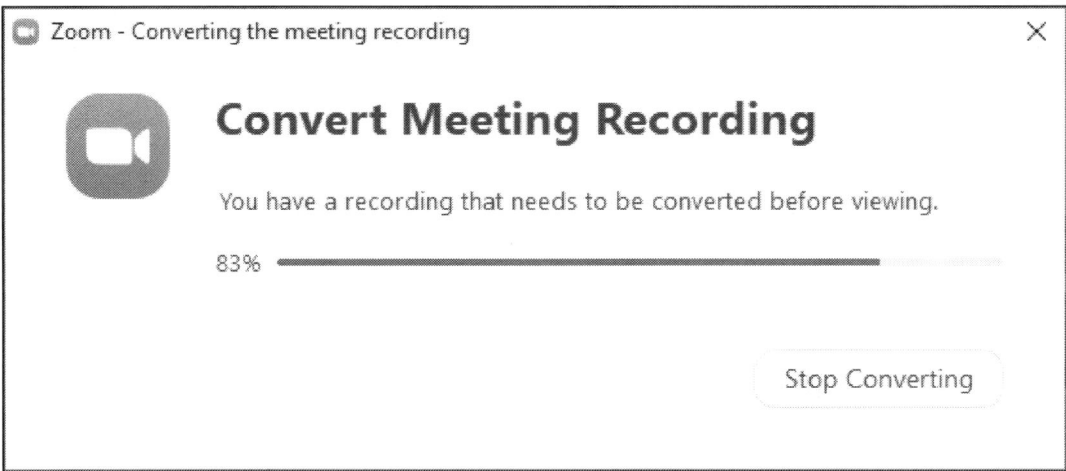

Figure 4.39

If it doesn't then you can try and convert the recording yourself by navigating to your Zoom folder within your Documents folder. Here you should see a file similar to the one shown in figure 4.40. Then you can double click the file and see if Zoom converts it for you.

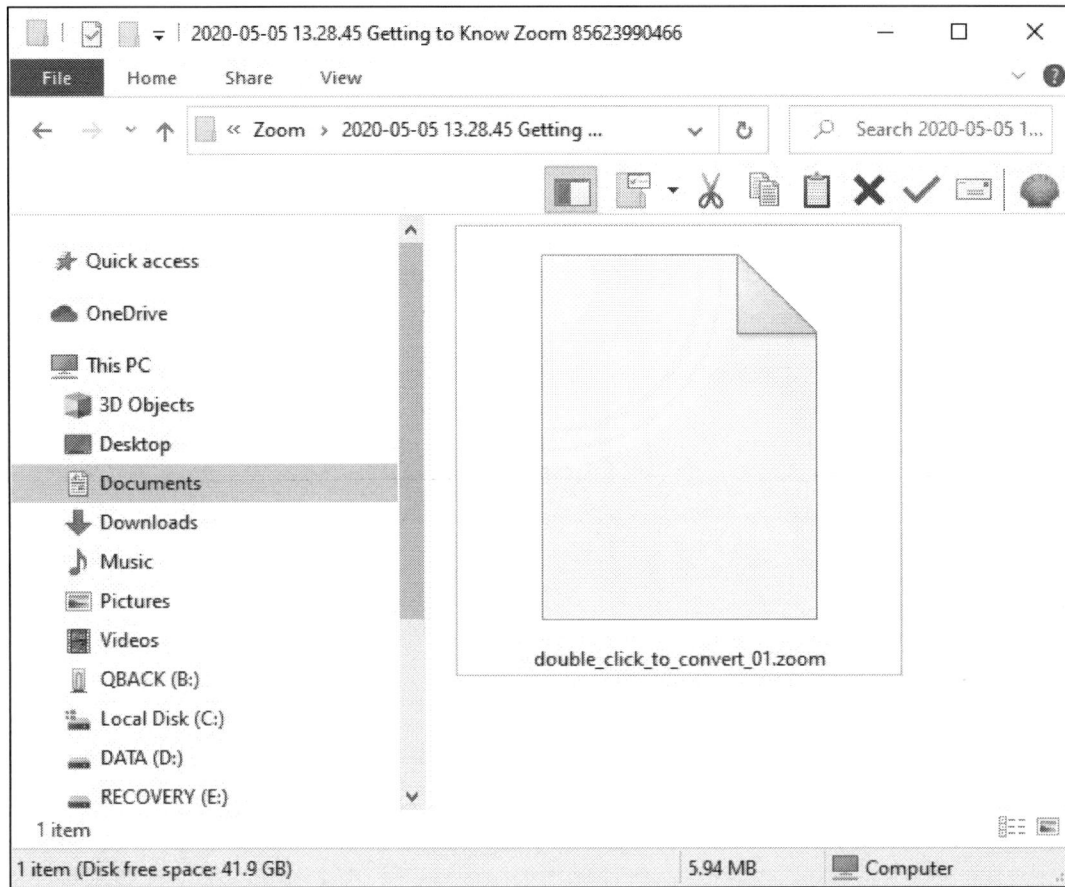

Figure 4.40

You can also go back to the Zoom client and go to the Meetings section and see if it's listed in the Recordings area. You can then try to open the video or have Zoom convert it from here.

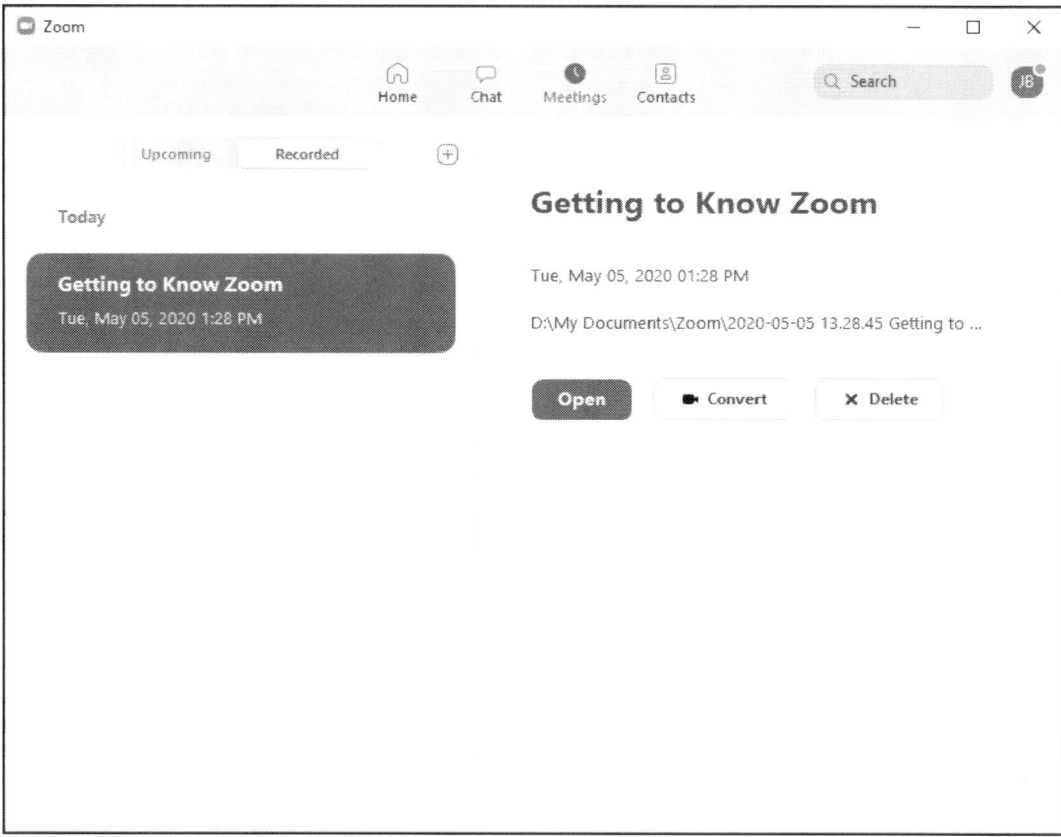

Figure 4.41

If you have one of the pay for plans then you will have the option to save your video files online (in the cloud) so you don't need to worry about taking up hard drive space on your local computer or other device. It will also make it easier to share your recordings with other people.

Meeting IDs
I discussed meeting IDs earlier in this book but wanted to take a minute to go into a little more detail and show you how you can use them to make things easier for you.

Each Zoom user is assigned their own unique meeting ID that they can use over and over for their meetings. So if you have a group of people that you have regular meetings with then they can just use that same meeting ID each time they want to join your meeting. But like I mentioned before, this might mean that they can join your meeting any time they like, even if they are not invited. You can prevent this by making participants wait to be invited into the main meeting room when they join and if you see any unwanted guests, you can simply kick them out of the waiting room.

To find and use your personal meeting ID you can go into the Zoom client and click on the arrow next to *New Meeting* and then check the box that says *Use My Personal Meeting ID (PMI)* and the meeting ID will be shown under this checkbox.

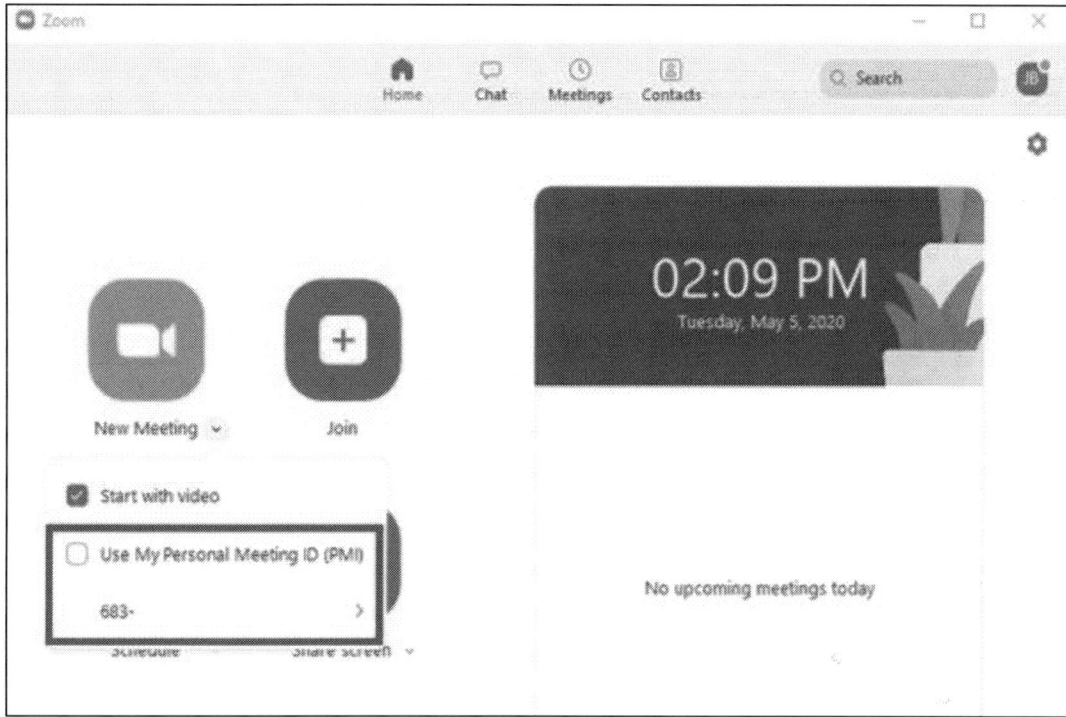

Figure 4.42

This can also be done from the web interface from your Profile page and in the *Personal Meeting ID* section.

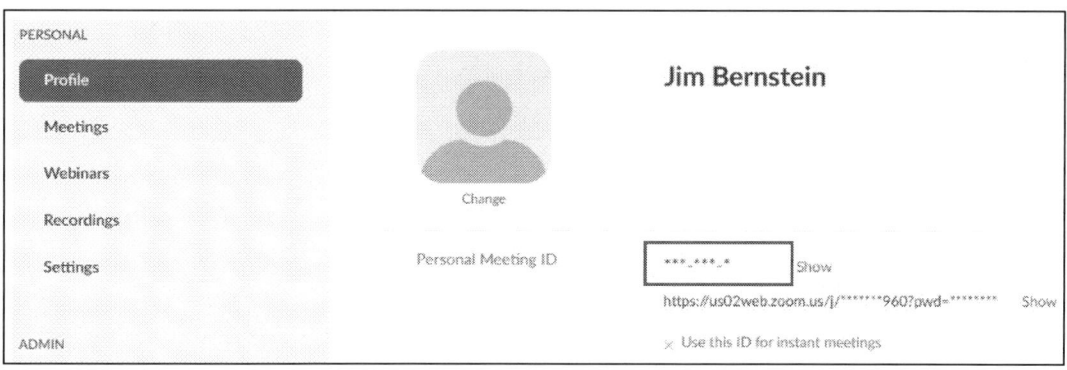

Figure 4.43

If you don't enable the usage of your Personal Meeting ID then Zoom will generate a random meeting ID each time you start a meeting and you will need to give that to the participants in the form of a link or invitation.

Chapter 5 - Zoom Webinars

Most Zoom users will be using the service for meetings but there will be other users who will use the webinar feature of Zoom for personal or business reasons. And if you think you might be one of those people then this is the chapter for you!

The main difference between a meeting and a webinar is that with webinars, the focus is on the presenter and the rest of the participants are there to watch and learn rather than participate. Sure they can participate if you allow them to but for the most part they are just there to hear what you have to say and see what you are going to show them.

Many people use webinars to demonstrate products that they are selling or things they are promoting such as maybe a book or movie. You can host a webinar for any topic you like and invite whoever you want to come and watch.

One of the most important things to know about Zoom webinars is that you need to have one of the pay for plans to enable this feature. You will have to select one of the pay for plans PLUS buy the additional add-on plans to enable the video webinar feature. You can purchase a monthly plan or a yearly plan which will cost you less per month.

Figure 5.1 shows the optional add-ons that come with the Pro plan and you would need to purchase the one that says *Add video webinars*.

Optional Add-on Plans

Extra Cloud Recording Storage (starting at $40/mo)

H.323/SIP Room Connector (starting at $49/mo)

Join by Zoom Rooms (starting at $49/mo)

Join by Toll-free dialing or Call Me (starting at $100/mo)

Add Video Webinars (starting at $40/mo)

Figure 5.1

Scheduling a Webinar

To schedule a Zoom webinar you will need to sign into the web interface and then go to the Webinars section and click on *Schedule a Webinar*.

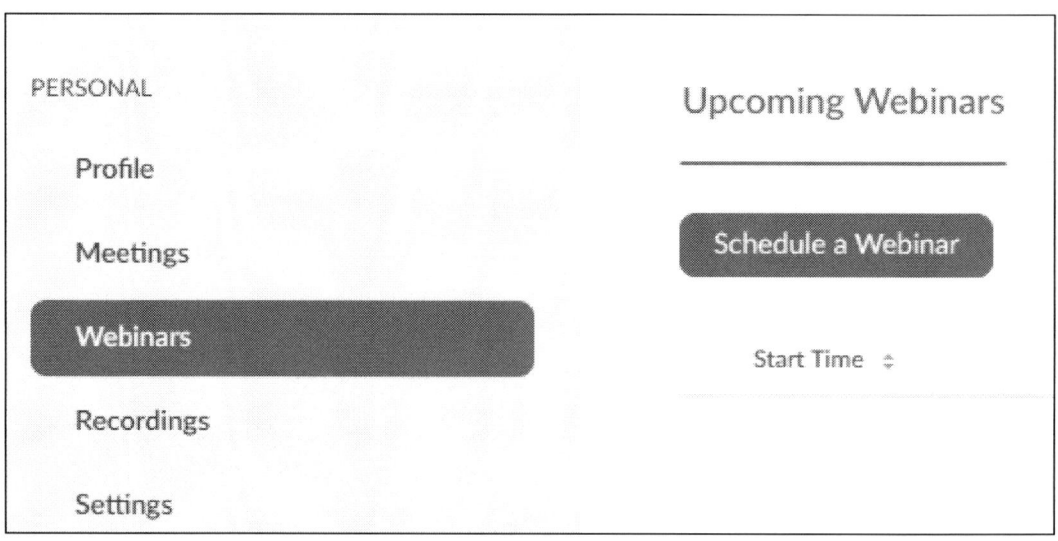

Figure 5.2

Figures 5.3 and 5.4 show all the options you have to choose from when scheduling a webinar and they look very similar to the options you get for meetings.

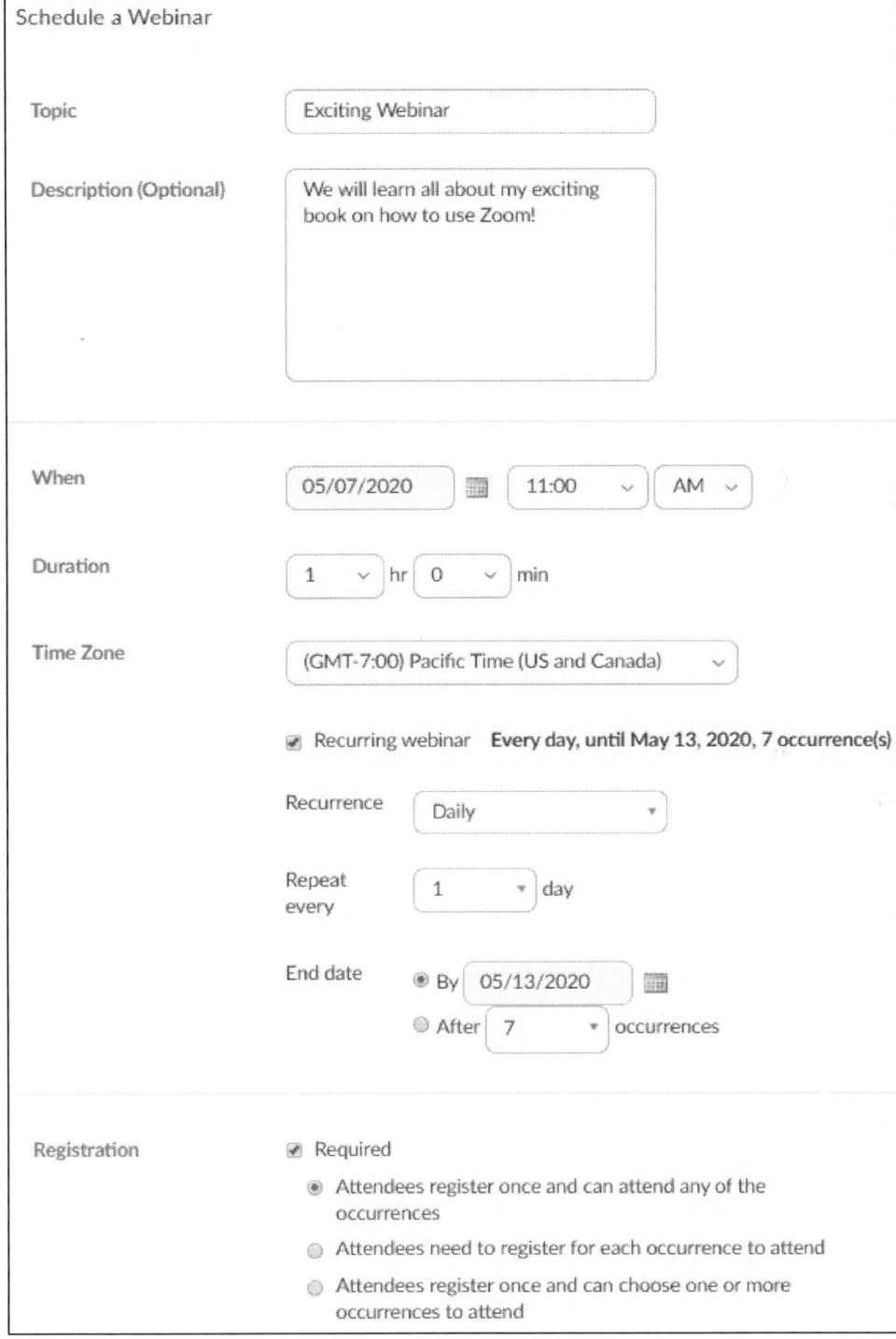

Figure 5.3

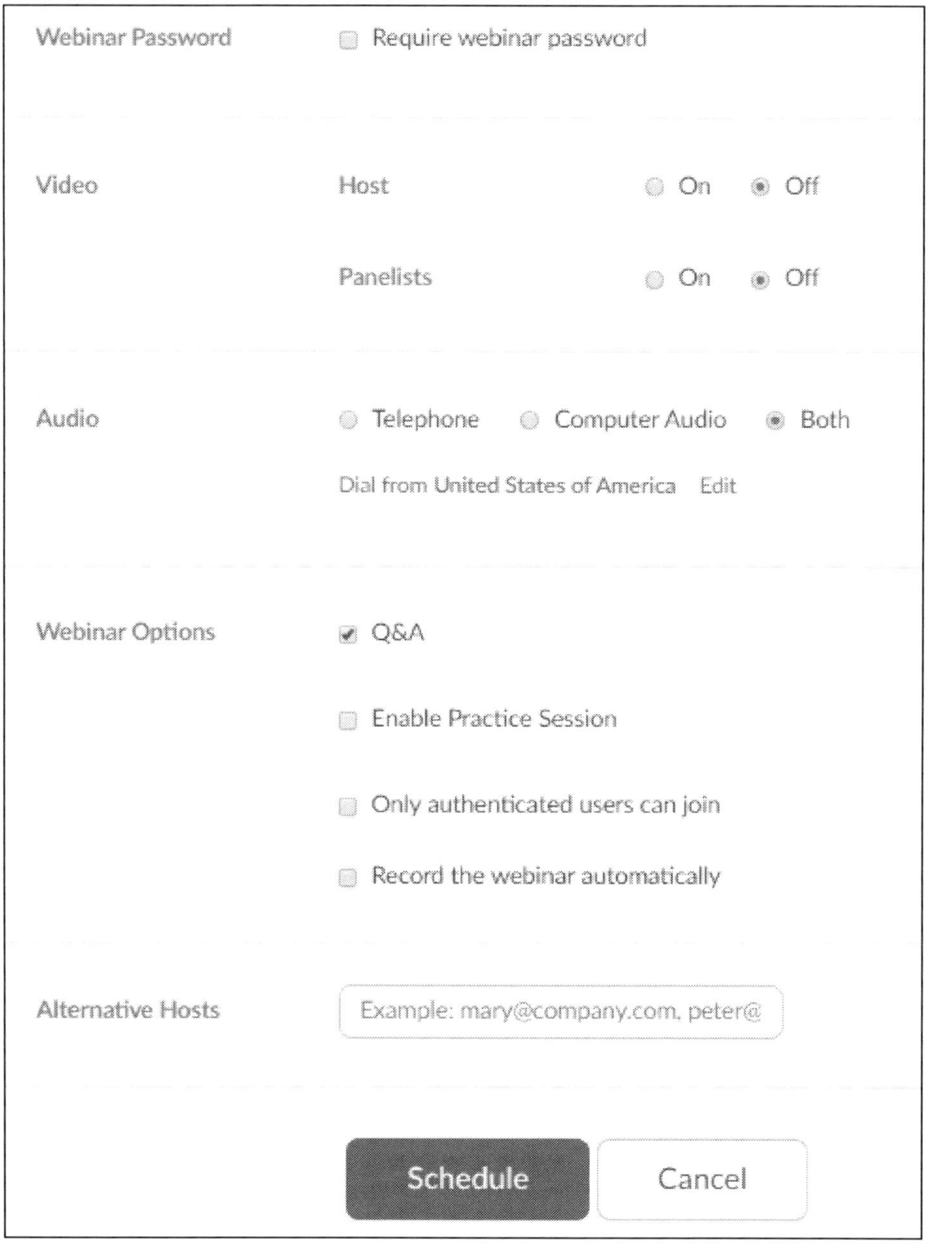

Webinar Password	☐ Require webinar password		
Video	Host	○ On	◉ Off
	Panelists	○ On	◉ Off
Audio	○ Telephone ○ Computer Audio ◉ Both		
	Dial from United States of America Edit		
Webinar Options	☑ Q&A		
	☐ Enable Practice Session		
	☐ Only authenticated users can join		
	☐ Record the webinar automatically		
Alternative Hosts	Example: mary@company.com, peter@		

Schedule   Cancel

Figure 5.4

I will now go over what they all do even though most of them are fairly obvious.

- **Topic** – This is the name for your webinar and is what will show up on the invitation and when you are running the webinar.

- **Description** – If you want to add a description of what your webinar will be covering then you can do so here.

- **When** – This is the start date of the webinar.

- **Duration** – This is how long the webinar is scheduled to run. You can end it early or have it run longer if needed.

- **Time Zone** – If you need to change the time zone to something different than what your computer is set to then you can do so here. If you check the box for *Recurring webinar* then you will be able to schedule your webinar to re-run at specific times using the same webinar ID.

- **Registration** – If you want your participants to register for your webinar then you will want to have this box checked and then you can choose from one of the three selections under this section.

- **Webinar Password** – You can require your participants to enter a password to get into your webinar if you are concerned about security.

- **Video** – Here you can decide if you want your participant's video to automatically start when they enter your room.

- **Audio** – Here you can decide if you want your participants to be able to use only computer audio, only phone audio, or both with your webinar.

- **Webinar Options** – There are several additional options you can choose from here to fine tune your webinar experience.

  o **Q&A** – This allows attendees to ask questions during the webinar that can be answered by the panelists, co-hosts and the host.

  o **Enable Practice Session** – This allows you and your panelists to get set up and familiarized with the Zoom webinar controls before you go live with your webinar.

  o **Only authenticated users can join** – If you want to make your account more secure then you can setup authenticated users in your account management and then only those who have been configured will be able to join your webinars.

o **Record the webinar automatically** – Use this option if you want Zoom to record your webinar automatically without you needing to start it manually.

- **Alternative Hosts** – This option allows you to schedule meetings and assign other licensed users on your account to start the meeting on your behalf.

Once you have configured all of your webinar options then click the Schedule button to have the webinar listed in your upcoming webinars. Figure 5.5 shows my new webinar and you can see that its listed multiple times because it's a recurring webinar.

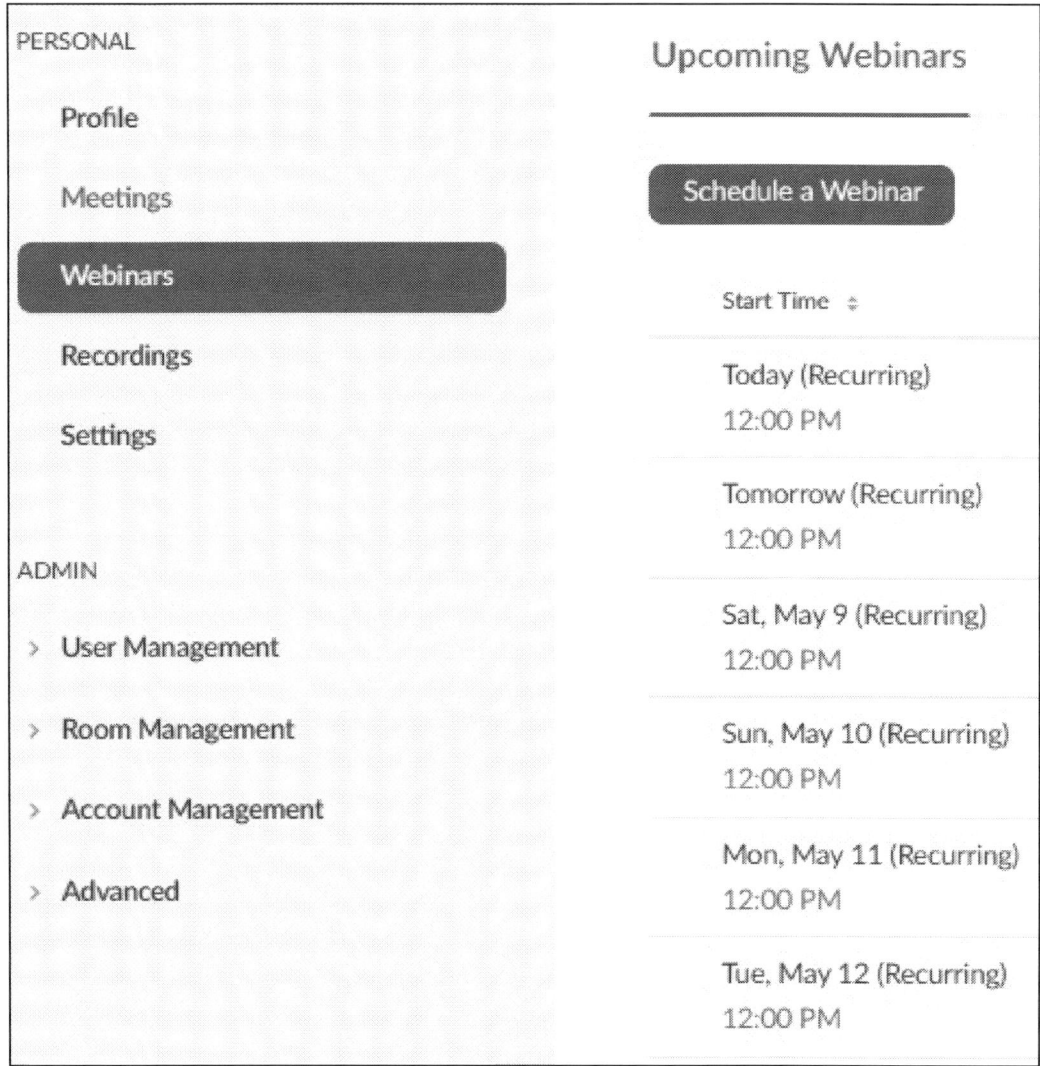

Figure 5.5

Templates

If you have spent some time configuring your webinar to get it just the way you like it then you might want to consider saving it as a template so you can use it over again for another webinar.

To save a current webinar as a template simply go to the settings for that webinar and click on the link that says *Save this webinar as a template*. Then you can give the template a name and decide if you would like to save the recurrences of the webinar within the template. Once you name the template click on the *Save as Template* button to have it saved to your Zoom account.

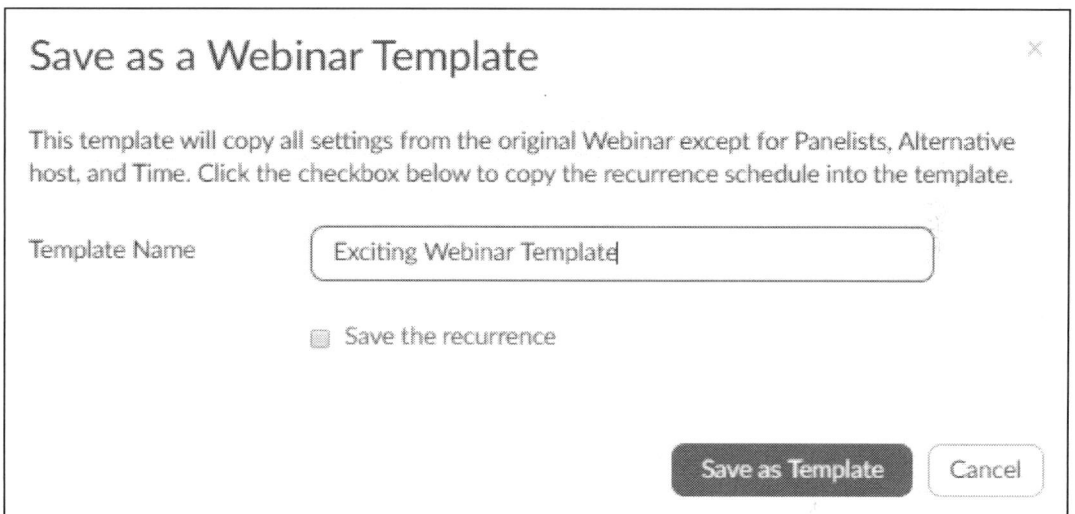

Figure 5.6

Now when you go to your *Webinar Templates* under Webinars in the web interface you will see your newly saved template that you can then click on and use to schedule a new webinar using its saved settings.

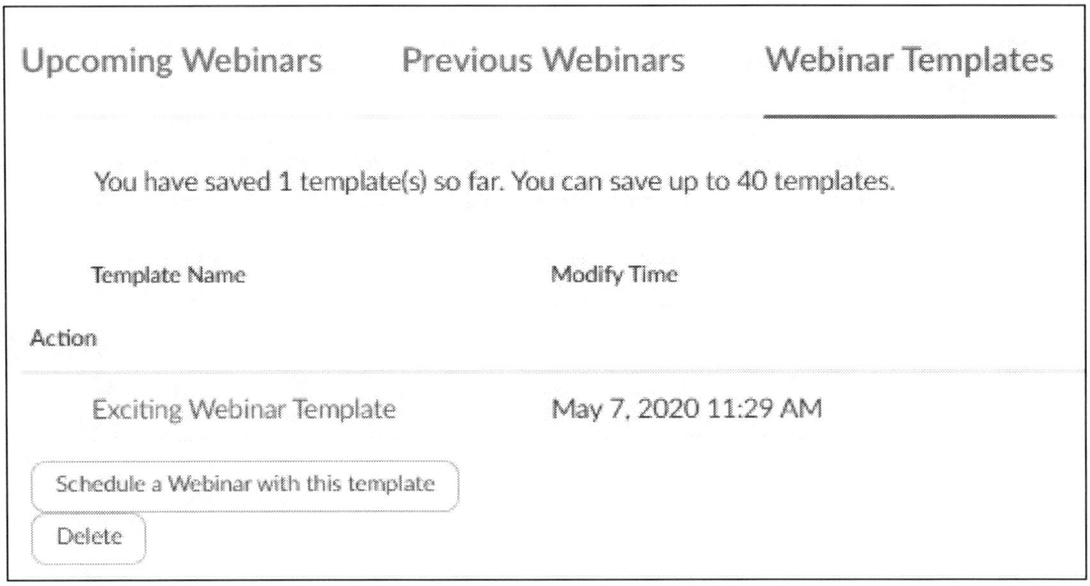

Upcoming Webinars	Previous Webinars	Webinar Templates

You have saved 1 template(s) so far. You can save up to 40 templates.

Template Name	Modify Time
Action	
Exciting Webinar Template	May 7, 2020 11:29 AM

Schedule a Webinar with this template

Delete

Figure 5.7

Branding

Branding is a way to customize your webinar experience by adding things such as banners, logos and themes to your webinar that enhance the overall look and feel of your presentation.

You can start the branding process by going to the webinar section, selecting a webinar and then clicking the Branding section.

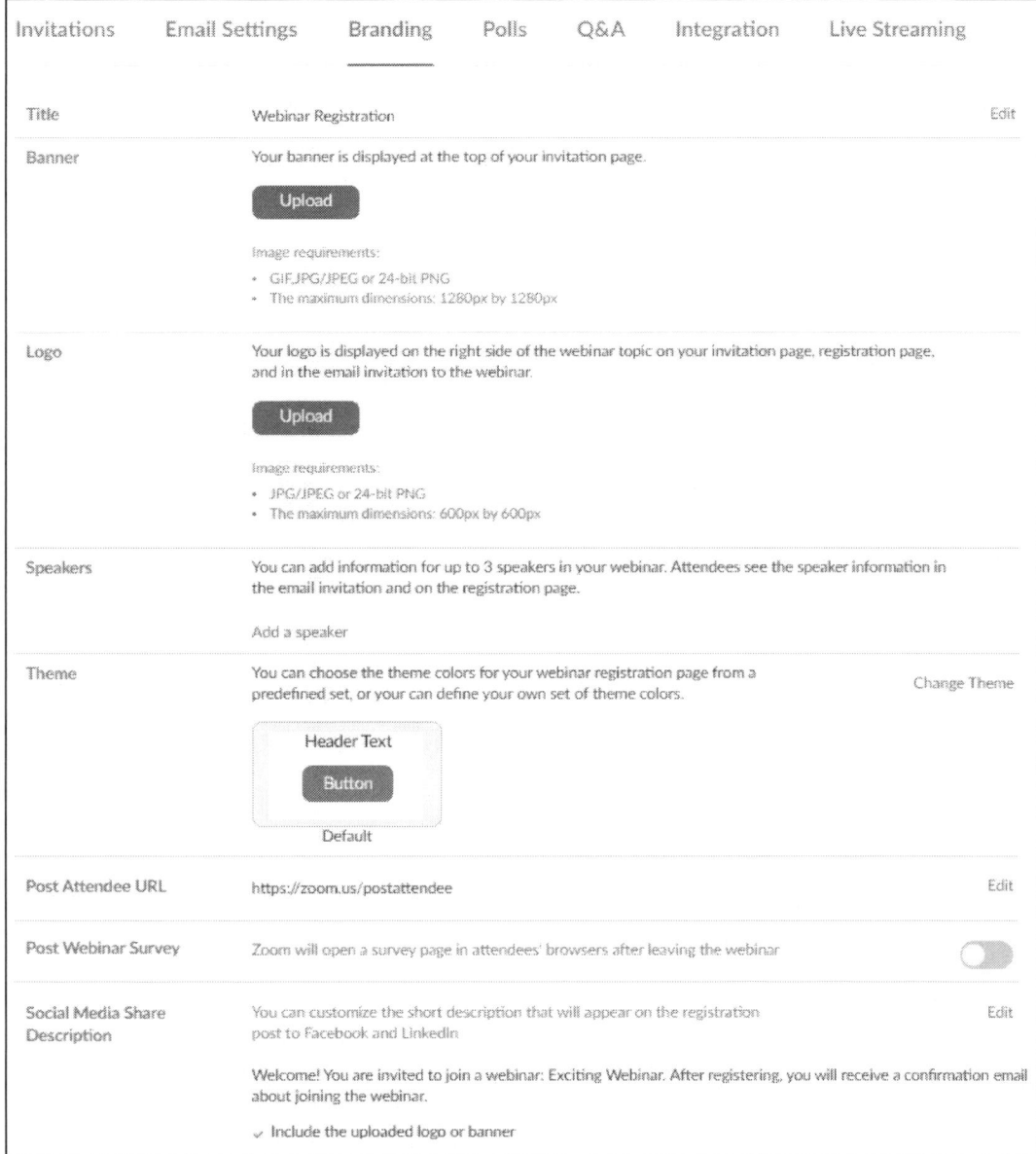

Figure 5.8

I will now go over the various options in the Branding section and then show some examples.

- **Title** – This information will be displayed at the top middle section of the page.

- **Banner** – You can create your own custom banner and save it as an image file to be used in your webinar.

- **Logo** – If you have a company logo that you want to have displayed during your webinar then you can upload it from here.

- **Speakers** – Many times you will have additional people who will be speaking during your webinar. You can upload their photo and add information about these people in this section.

- **Theme** – Zoom offers several different color schemes that you can choose from if you want to change the way your overall webinar looks.

- **Post Attendee URL** – This section can be used to add a website for your company or that your attendees to go to for additional information about whatever you might be discussing in your webinar.

- **Post Webinar Survey** – If you use any type of survey site and have setup a survey about your webinar then you can add the site address here.

- **Social Media Share Description** – Here you can enter the description that you would like to be included when the webinar is shared on Facebook or LinkedIn and also decide if you want to include your uploaded logo or banner.

I have gone through the above settings and did things such as add a banner, logo, speaker and post attendee URL, and figures 5.9 and 5.10 show the results. You will see how these apply to my webinar when it's time to start it.

| Invitations | Email Settings | Branding | Polls | Q&A | Integration | Live Streaming |

Title   Zoom Made Easy

Banner   Your banner is displayed at the top of your invitation page.

Image requirements:
- GIF,JPG/JPEG or 24-bit PNG
- The maximum dimensions: 1280px by 1280px

Logo   Your logo is displayed on the right side of the webinar topic on your invitation page, registration page, and in the email invitation to the webinar.

Image requirements:
- JPG/JPEG or 24-bit PNG
- The maximum dimensions: 600px by 600px

Figure 5.9

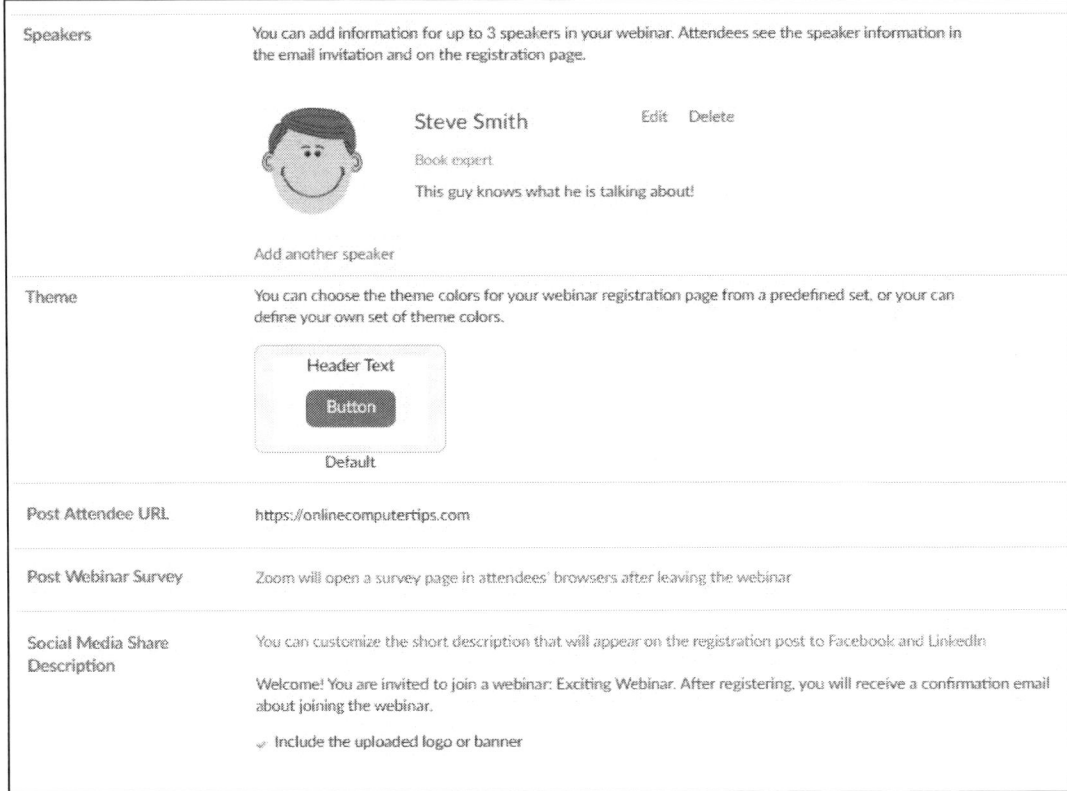

Figure 5.10

Configuring Polls

Polls are a great way to get information from your attendees by asking them a question or series of questions about your webinar. You can choose from a single choice answer or a multiple choice answer.

To get to the poll settings, simply go to your webinar and then the *Polls* section and click the *Add* button and add a question. Next, you will need to select if you want to use a single choice question or a multiple choice question. I will use a multiple choice question for my example and ask if anyone is interested in buying my book after hearing about it in my webinar and give them three answers to choose from. Figure 5.11 shows how I configured the question.

If you want your attendees to be able to answer anonymously then you can check the box that says *Anonymous* otherwise you will be able to see who gave what answer.

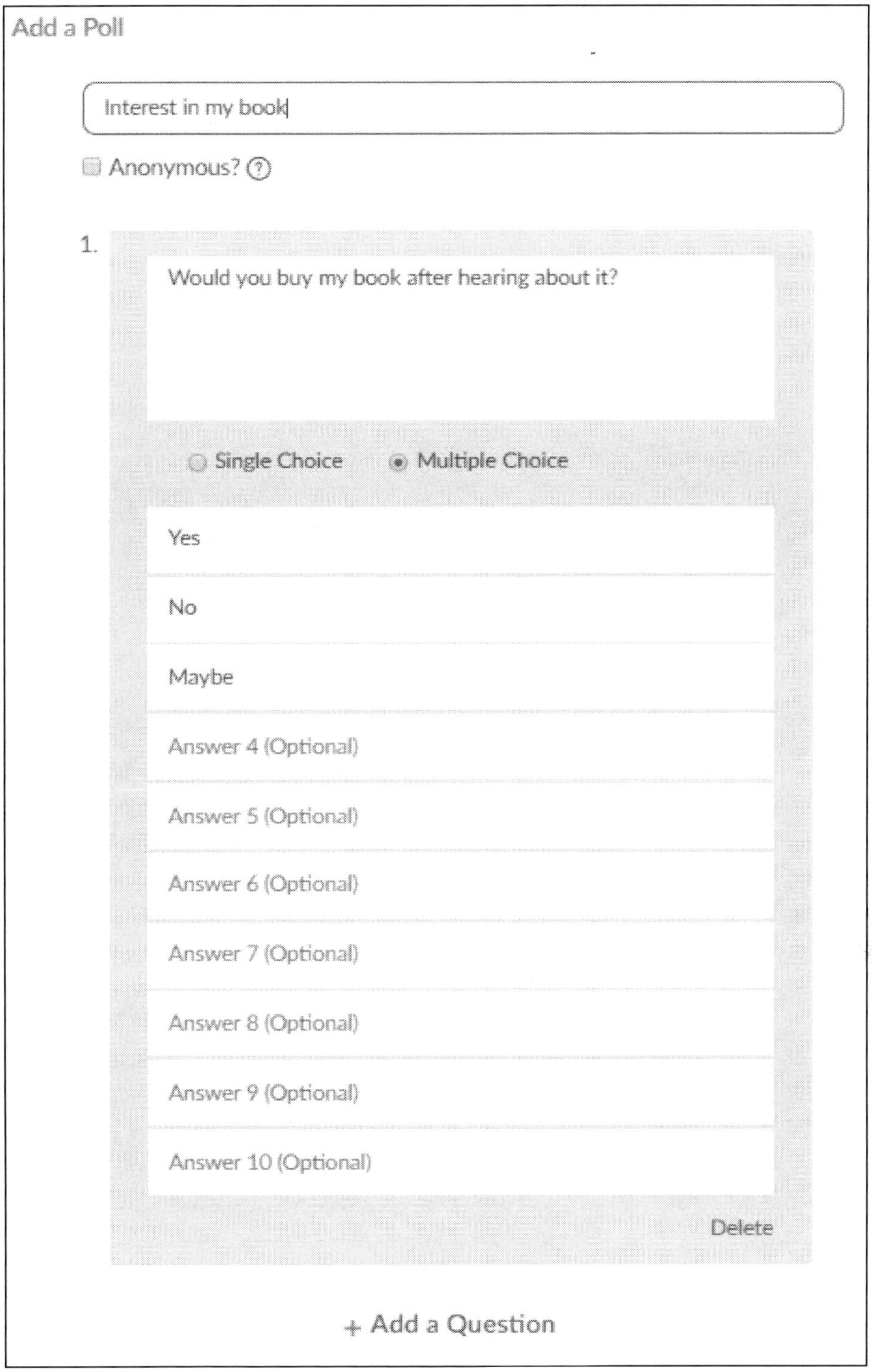

Add a Poll

Interest in my book|

☐ Anonymous? ⓘ

1.

Would you buy my book after hearing about it?

○ Single Choice   ⦿ Multiple Choice

Yes

No

Maybe

Answer 4 (Optional)

Answer 5 (Optional)

Answer 6 (Optional)

Answer 7 (Optional)

Answer 8 (Optional)

Answer 9 (Optional)

Answer 10 (Optional)

Delete

+ Add a Question

Figure 5.11

I will show you how the Poll feature works when I start the webinar.

Configuring Q&A (Question & Answer)

During your webinar, your attendees will be able to ask questions if you allow them to do so. If you go to the Q&A section under your webinar settings you can configure these options. I have changed some of the options from the default so I can show you how the Q&A feature works during the webinar.

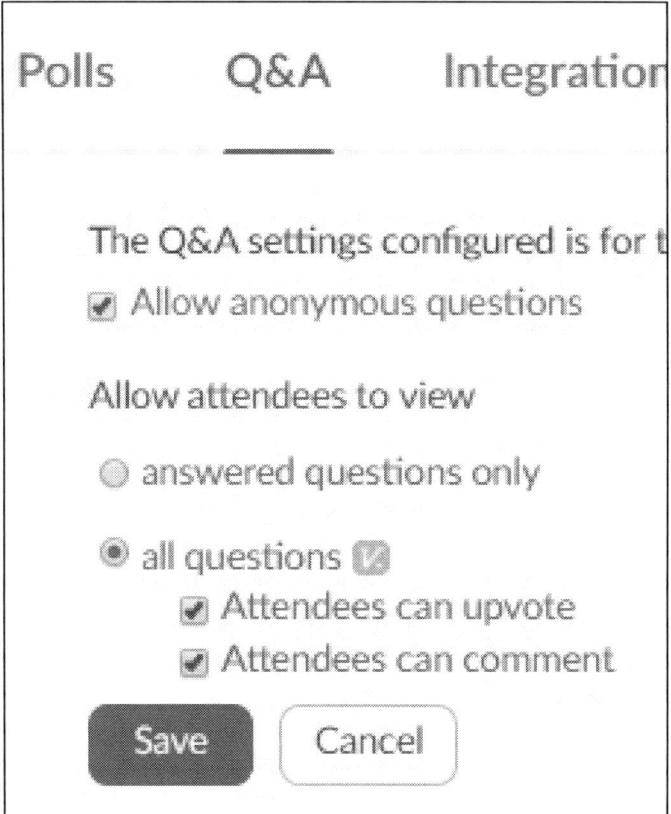

Figure 5.12

The *Allow anonymous questions* checkbox will let your attendees ask questions without providing their name to the host or any panelists.

Upvoting is when you agree with an answer given to a question so it's up to you if you want your attendees to be able to upvote or not.

Practice Mode

Before I start the real webinar I want to make sure things are working the way I want them to, so I set the webinar to use Practice Mode which lets me run it without technically starting it or letting in my attendees.

When I start the webinar it begins like it normally would where it asks you how you want to call in. I have the choice of using my phone and dialing in or using my computer audio. When you use one of the pay for plans then you will have this option for meetings as well. Zoom might eventually give you the phone call option for free accounts like they used to.

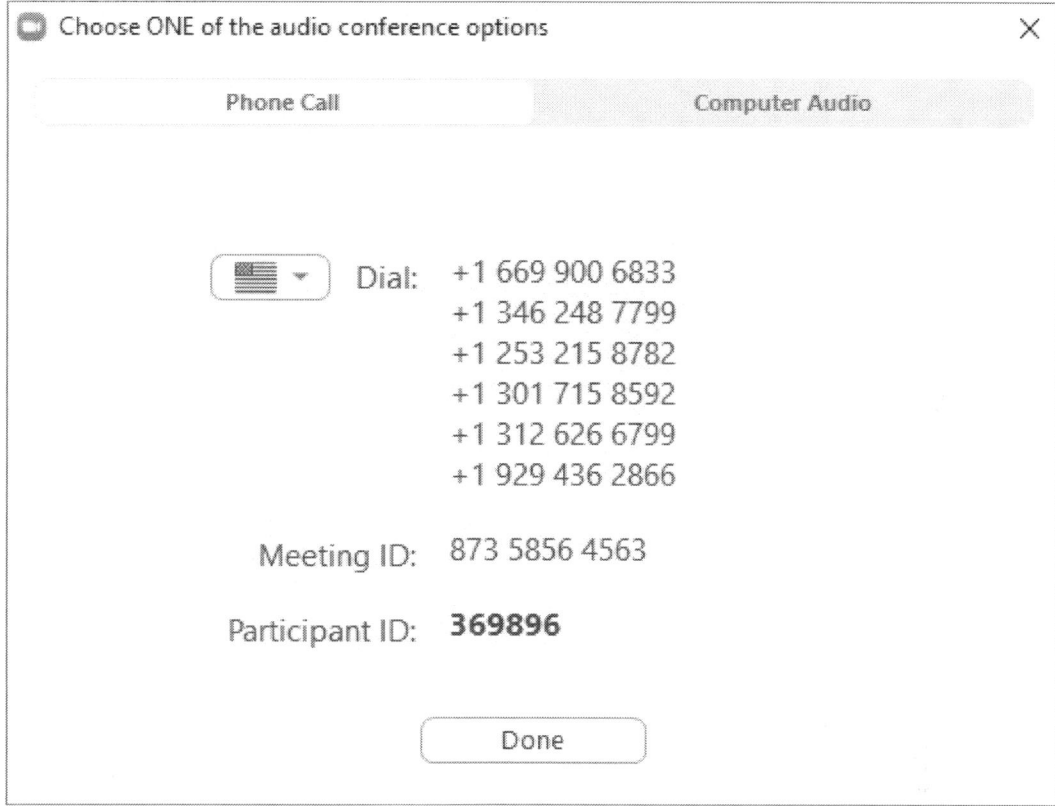

Figure 5.13

At the top of the Zoom client you will see a message saying that you are in Practice Mode and that your attendees can't join until you click on *Broadcast* which will start the webinar for everyone.

Figure 5.14

When you are ready to start the meeting for everyone, click the *Broadcast* button and you will get a message saying your attendees can now join.

User Registration

When my attendees get the invitation for my webinar they will be required to register since I chose the registration option in the webinar settings. Figure 5.15 shows the registration page they will be taken to when they click on the invitation link they receive.

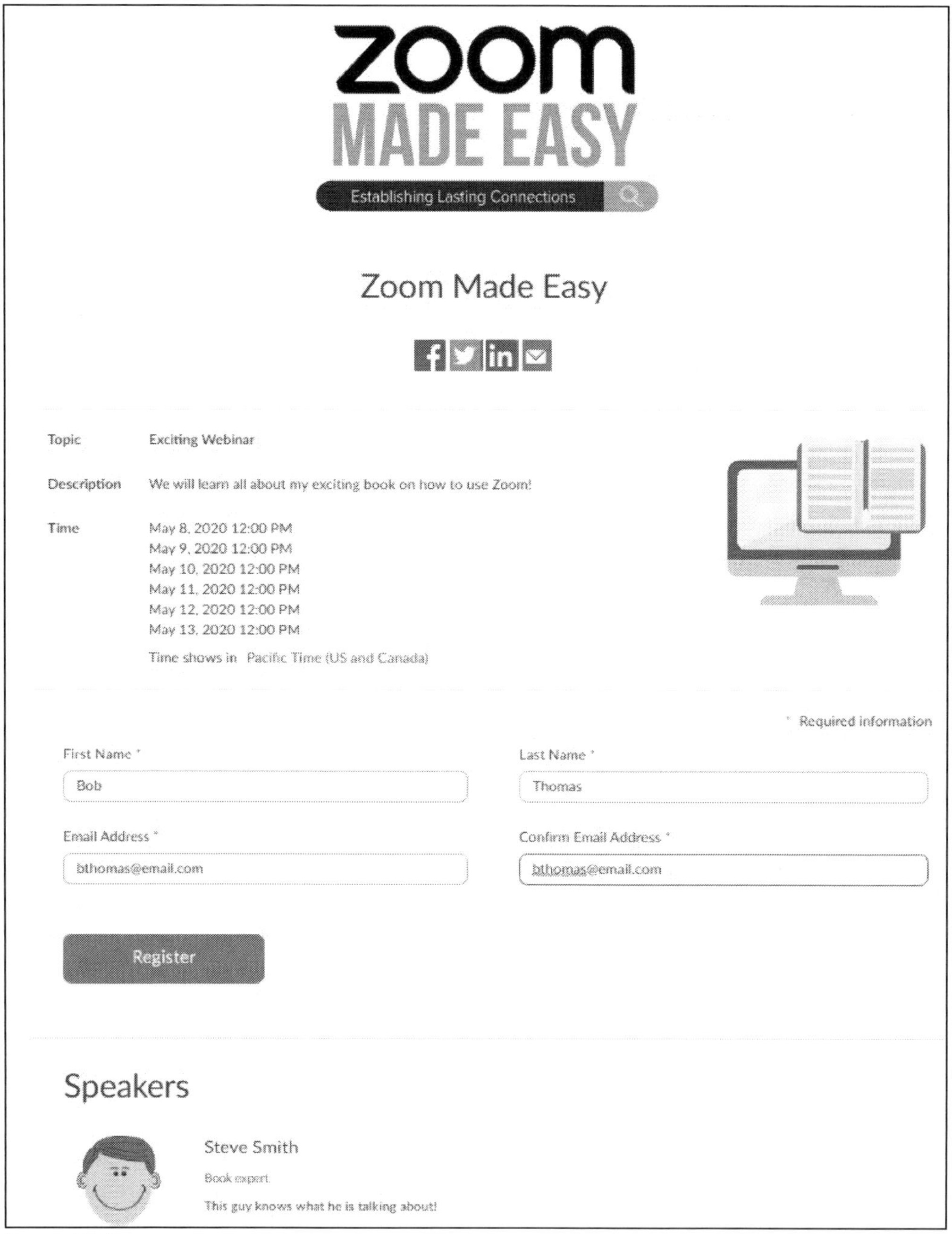

Figure 5.15

As you can see, the registration page has my banner graphic, logo and information about my featured speaker.

After the attendee fills out their name and email address they will click the *Register* button and will then be presented with a link that they can click on to join the webinar.

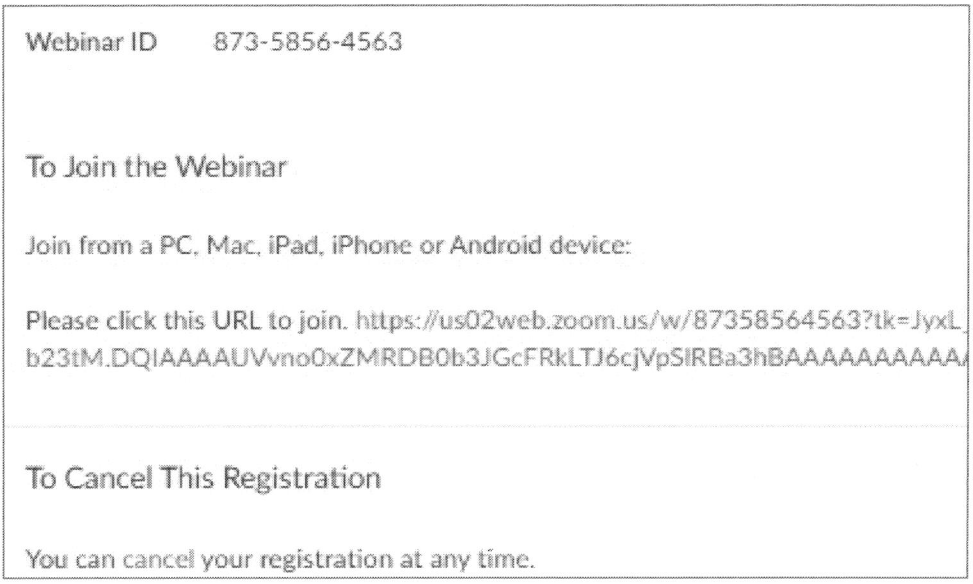

Webinar ID   873-5856-4563

To Join the Webinar

Join from a PC, Mac, iPad, iPhone or Android device:

Please click this URL to join. https://us02web.zoom.us/w/87358564563?tk=JyxL
b23tM.DQIAAAAUVvno0xZMRDB0b3JGcFRkLTJ6cjVpSIRBa3hBAAAAAAAAAA/

To Cancel This Registration

You can cancel your registration at any time.

Figure 5.16

After clicking the link, their Zoom client will open, and they will be taken to my webinar room. Since I don't have a video camera running they will see my profile picture as a placeholder (figure 5.17). I will go over how to configure a profile picture later in the book.

As you can see at the bottom of figure 5.17 that you have some options such as Chat, Raise Hand and Q&A that you can use to participate in the webinar. These options are showing up because I allowed them in the webinar configuration. Many people don't like to have interruptions during their webinars and won't use these features.

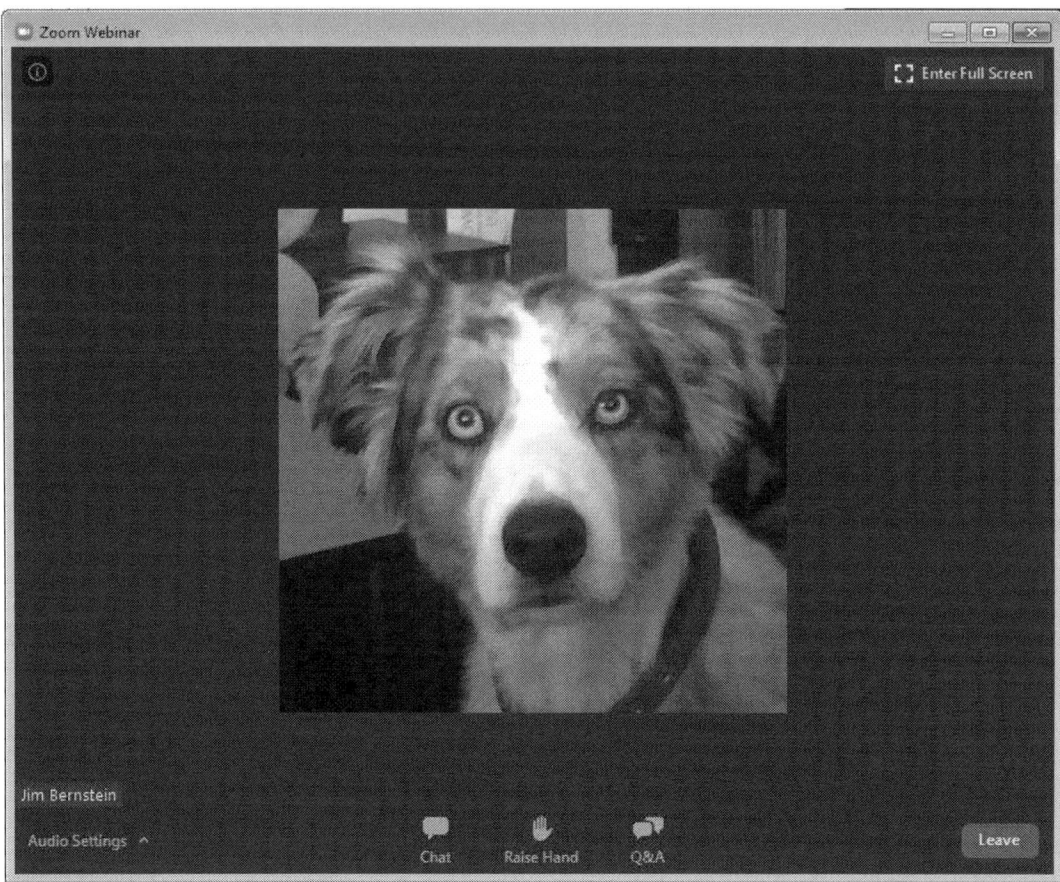

Figure 5.17

Once I start sharing my screen, the view that the attendees get will change and they will see what I am sharing. I will now share a picture of my book cover with my attendees and Figure 5.18 shows how they will see it in their Zoom client.

Now that everything has started and my attendees have joined I can start my presentation and let them hear all the great things I have to say!

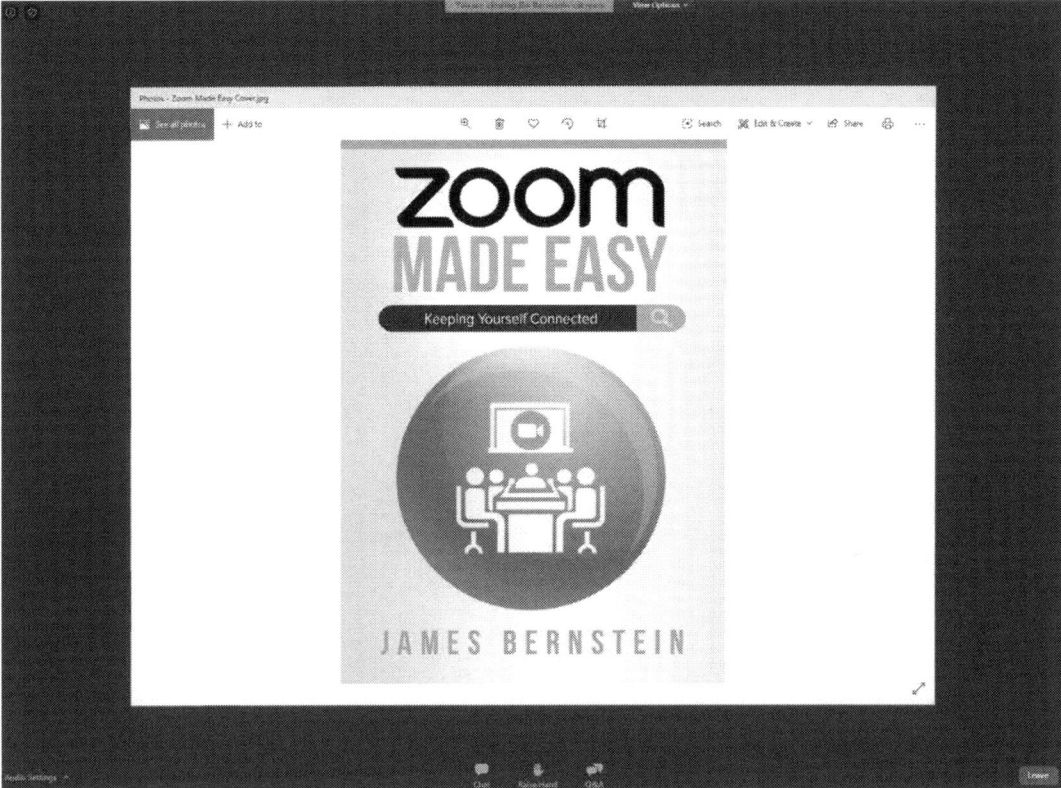

Figure 5.18

Make an Attendee a Participant

By default, the only people who can speak during a webinar are the host, co-host and any panelists you have invited. But there may come a time when you would like to hear from a particular attendee to hear what they have to say.

To enable the audio for an attendee you will need to go to the Participants button on the toolbar at the top of your screen and click on *Participants*.

Figure 5.19

Then you can choose a name from the list and then click on the *Allow to Talk* button as seen in figure 5.20. If you click on *More* you can see that you start a chat with an attendee or even promote them to a panelist. You also have the option to rename and remove them if the need arises.

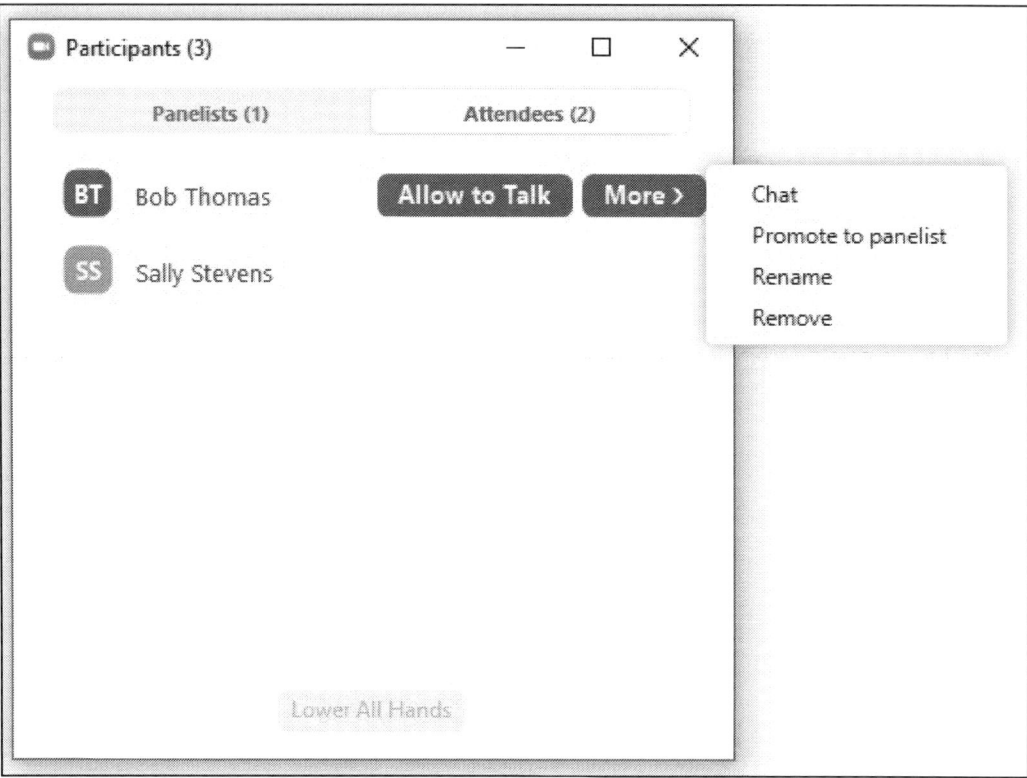

Figure 5.20

After you give an attendee the right to talk they will then have a microphone icon in their zoom client like they would if they were doing a meeting. Then they can click on the up arrow next to the icon to get some additional speaking options (figure 5.21).

Figure 5.21

Chat

The chat feature for webinars works the same way as it does for meetings and all you need to do as a host or panelist is click on the *Participants* icon in your toolbar, select a panelist or participant, click on *More* and start a chat session. You can either send a message to a particular person, just the panelists or everyone on the webinar as shown in figure 5.22.

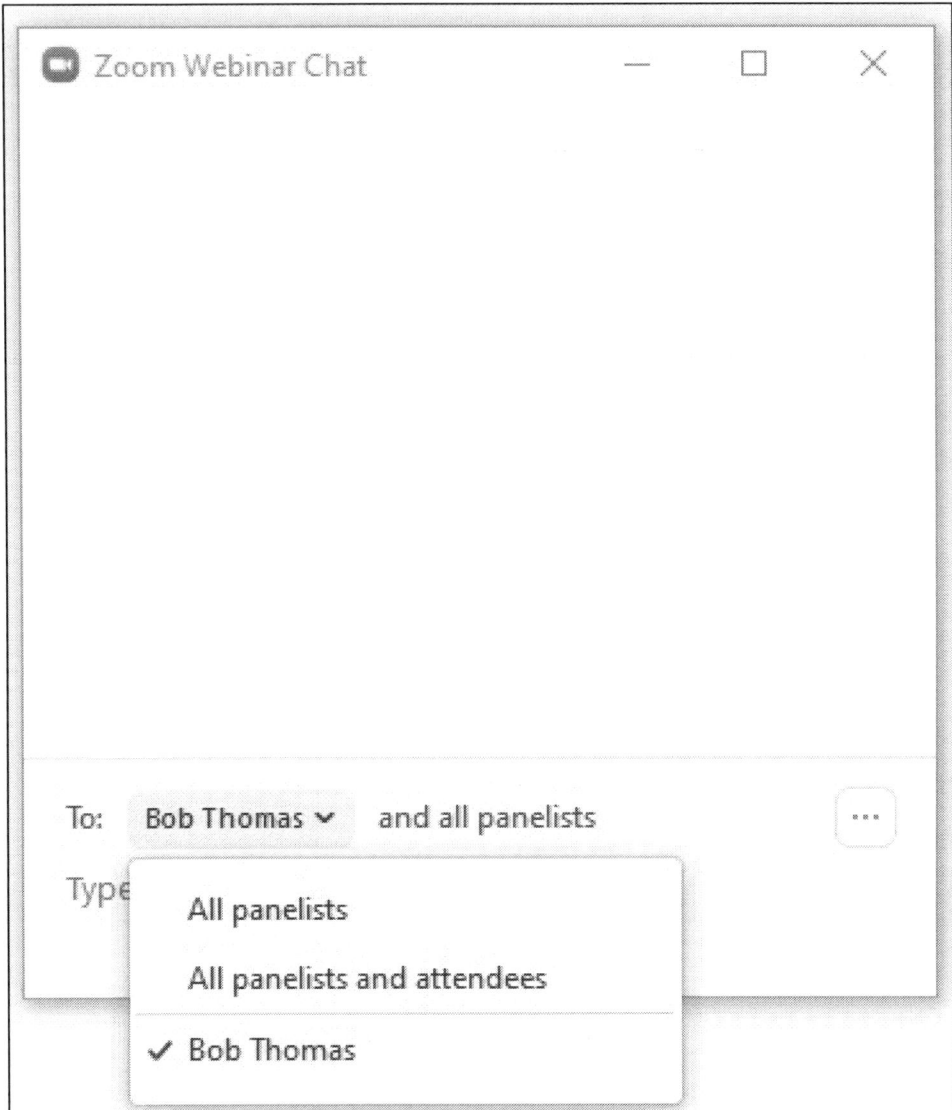

Figure 5.22

Figure 5.23 shows the options you get when you click on the ellipsis at the lower right hand side of the chat window when you select a certain person to chat with. You can choose one of these options to determine who your participants can chat with. The choices are chat with no one, all the panelists and all the panelists plus the attendees.

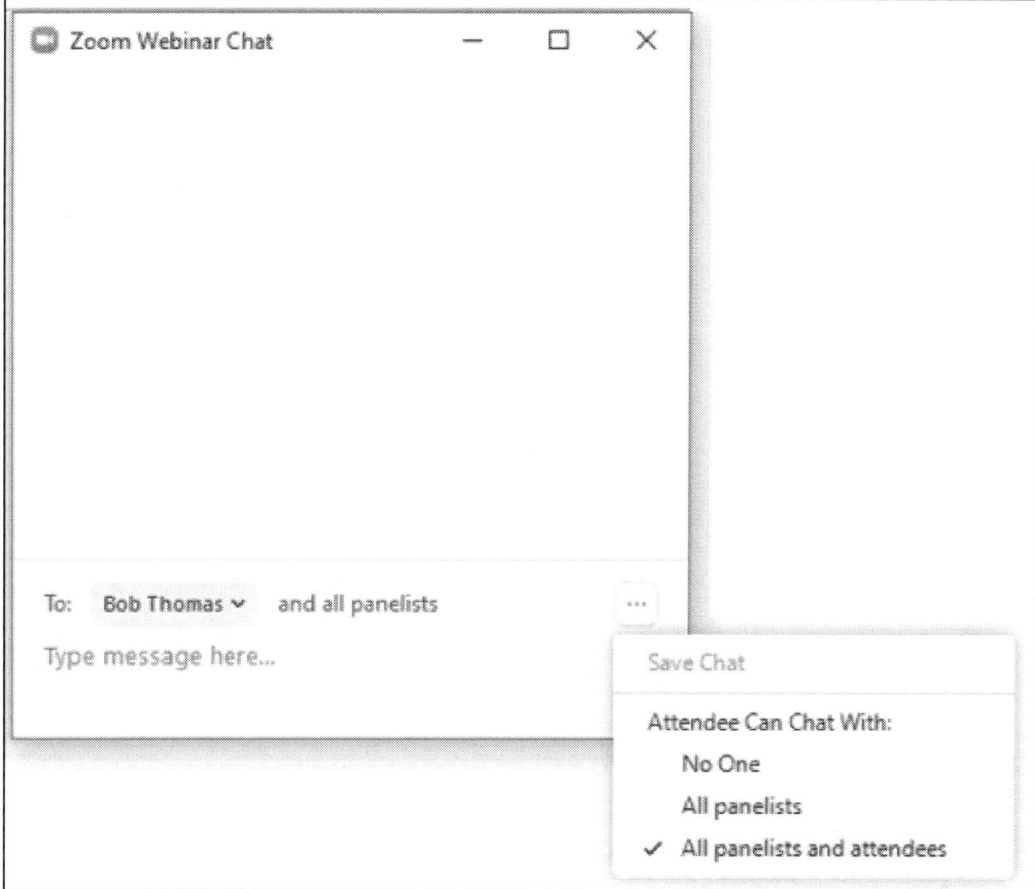

Figure 5.23

When you want to chat as an attendee you have two options to choose from. You can either chat with only the panelists or with the panelists as well as all of the attendees.

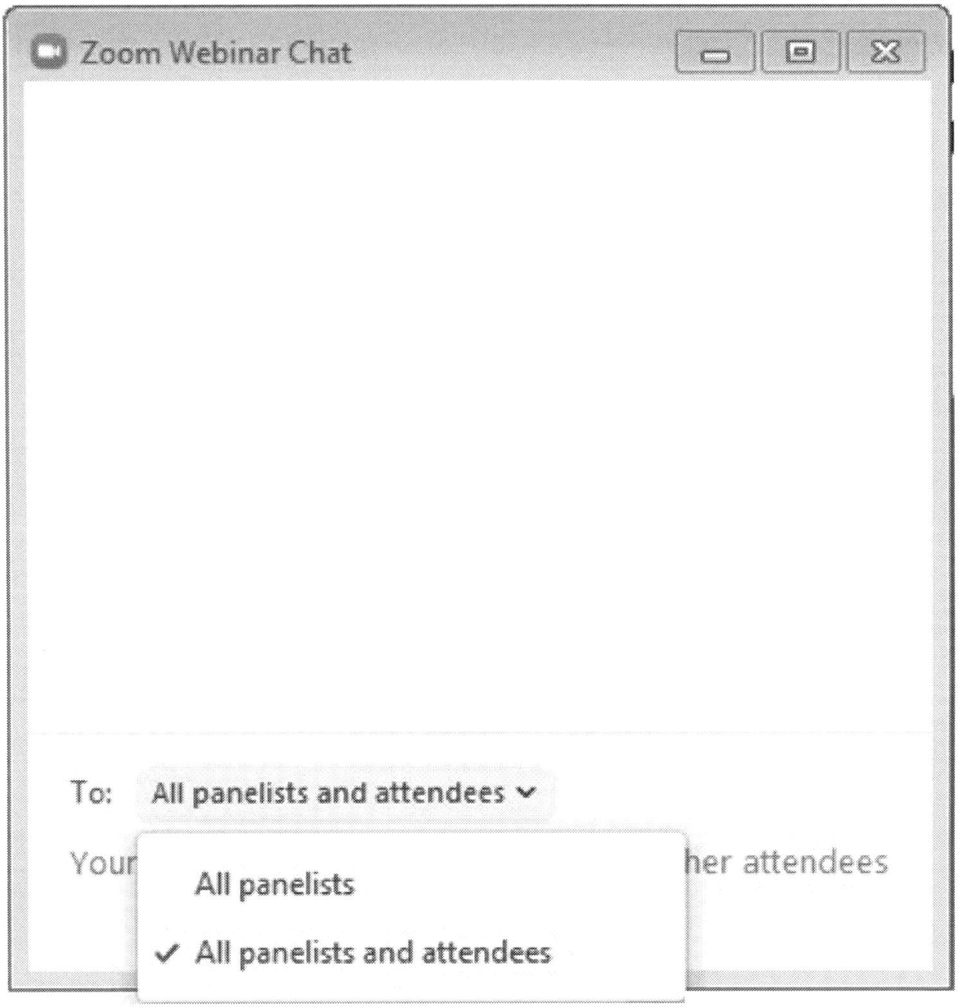

Zoom Webinar Chat

To: All panelists and attendees ⌄

Your   her attendees

        All panelists

      ✓ All panelists and attendees

Figure 5.24

Launching a Poll

You might recall during the initial setup of my webinar that I configured a poll asking my attendees if you would be interested in buying my book after hearing about it. Now it's time to launch the poll so I can have them vote and share their opinions.

To launch the poll all I need to do is click on the Polls icon in my Zoom toolbar.

Figure 5.25

Then my previously configured poll will appear, and I will be able to show it to my attendees by clicking on the *Launch Polling* button. If I want my other panelist to be able to vote as well I can check the box that says *Allow Panelists to vote*.

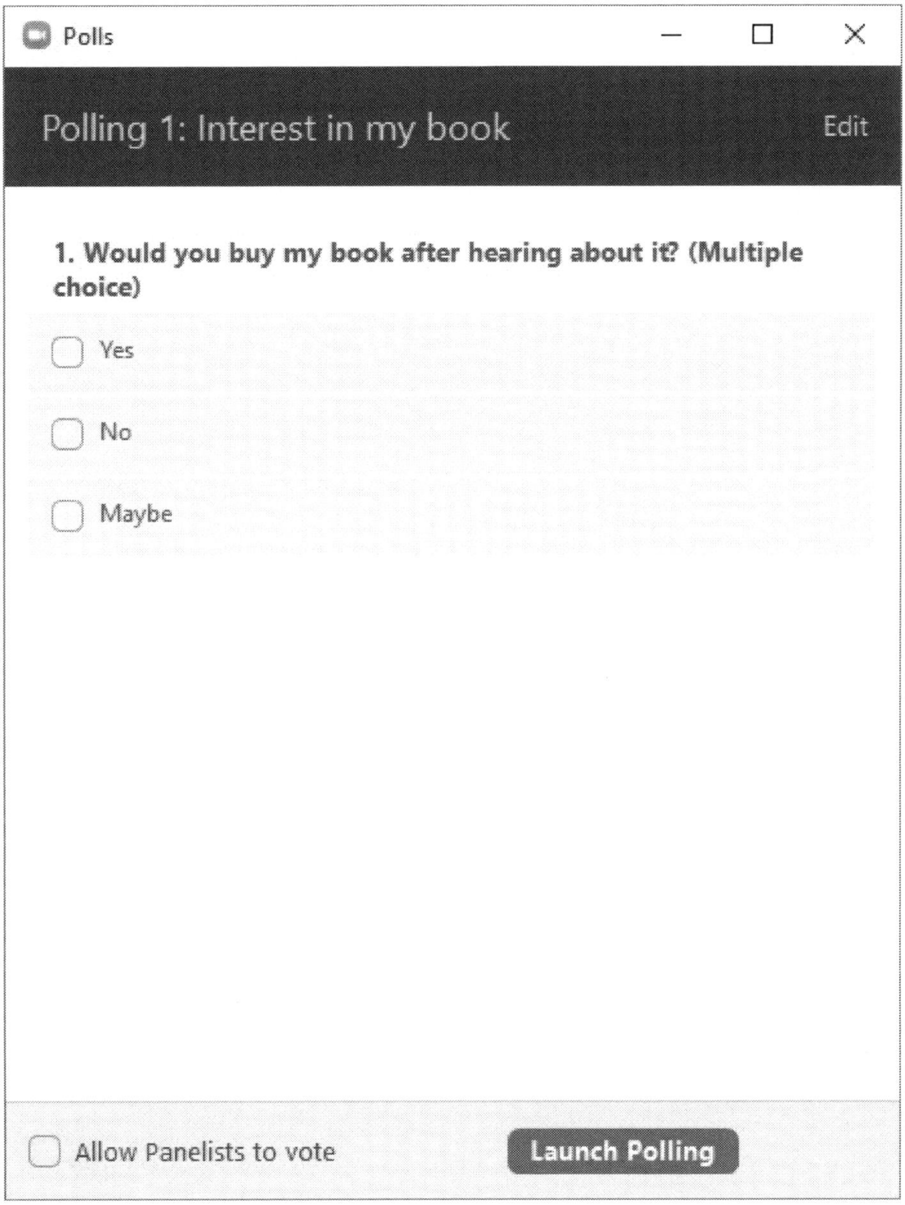

Figure 5.26

Now everyone who is attending my meeting will get a popup box similar to figure 5.27 where they can then vote by checking the box next to their selection. When they have made their choice they would then click the *Submit* button.

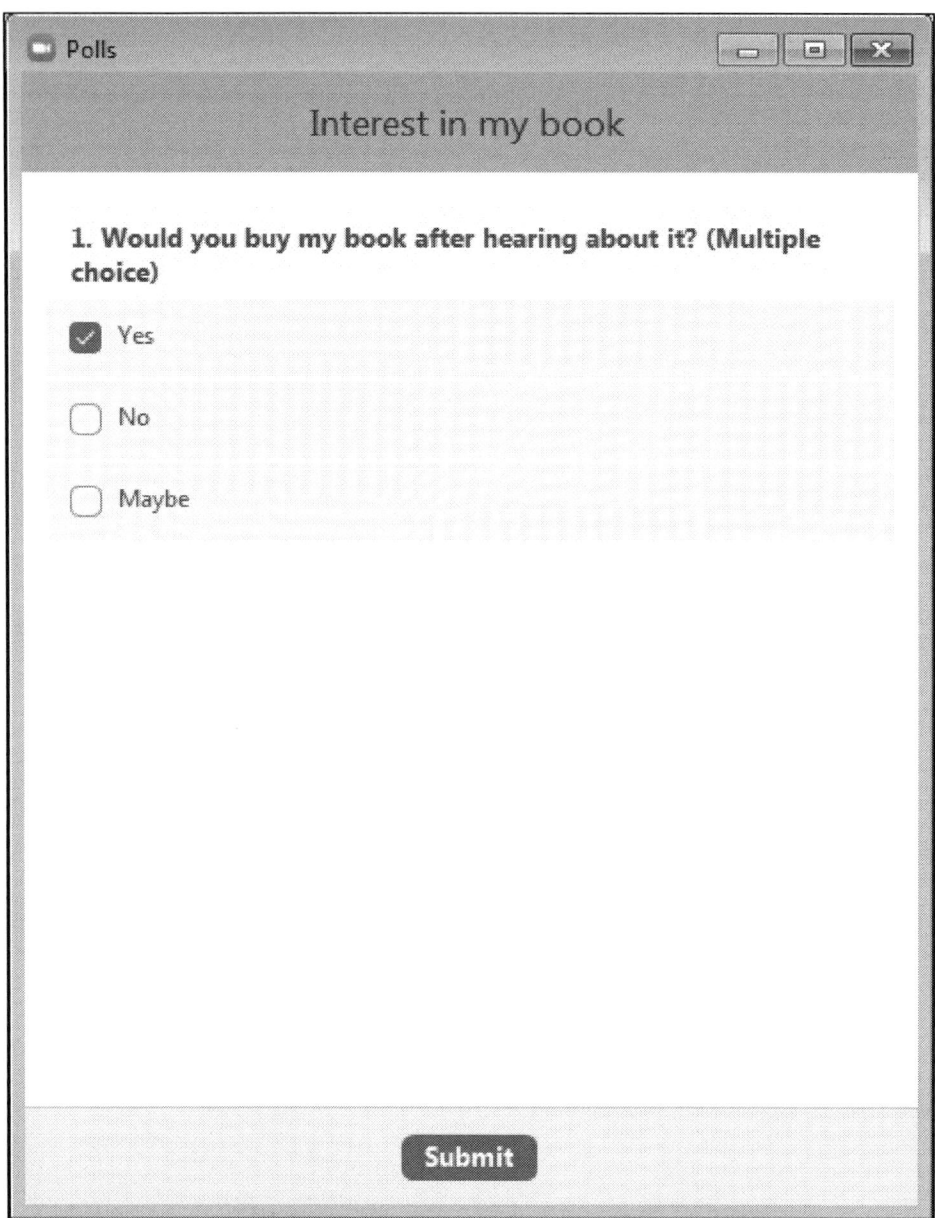

Figure 5.27

Figure 5.28 shows what the poll would look like on a mobile device, or in my case an Android smartphone.

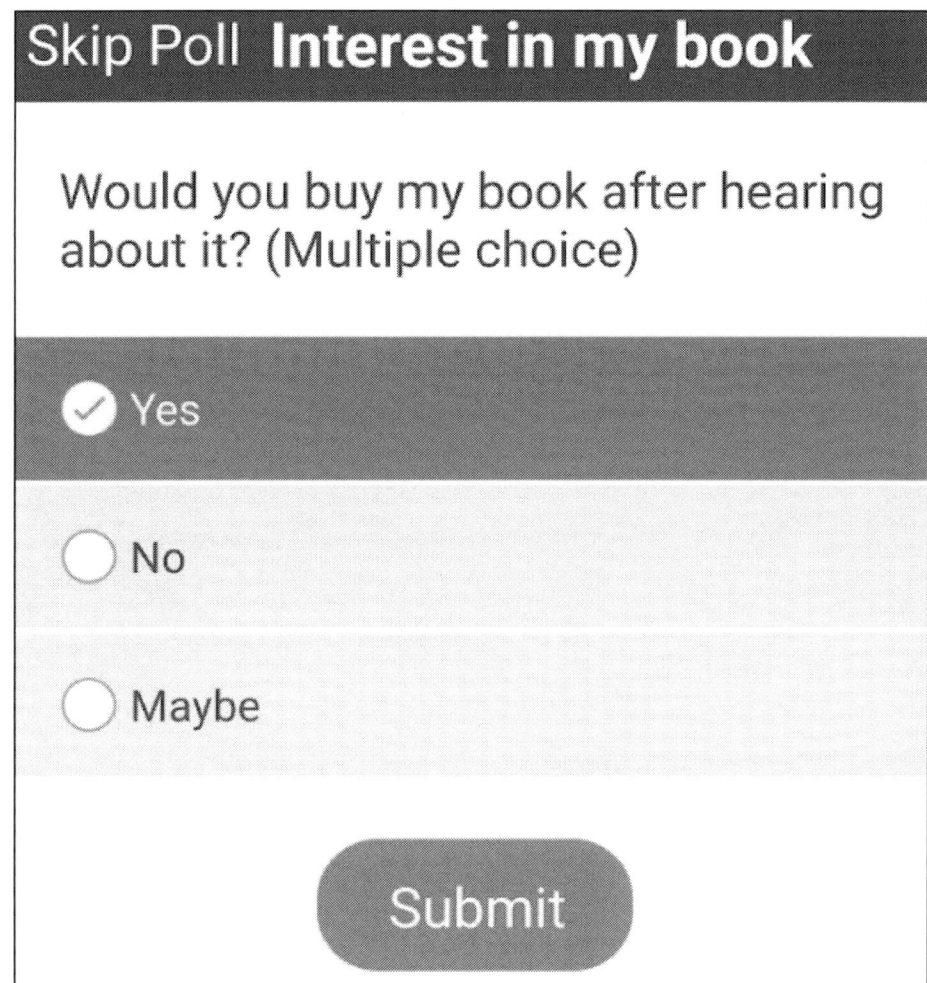

Figure 5.28

While the attendees are voting I can see the progress and see their answers. It will also show me how many of the attendees have voted. When everyone is finished voting I can click the *End Polling* button to finish the voting process. I can also click the End Polling button before everyone has finished if they are taking too long to vote.

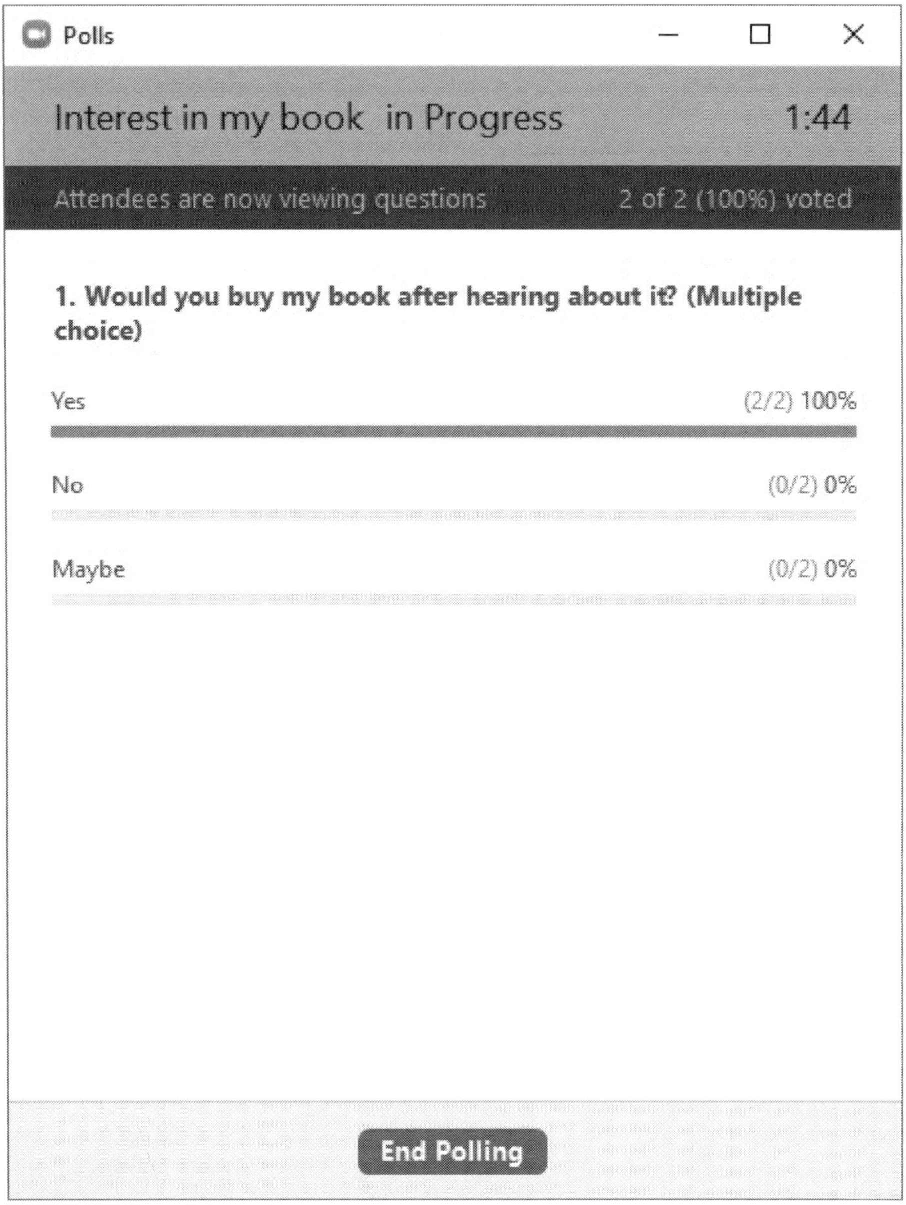

Figure 5.29

When the voting is complete I can share the results with my attendees, and they would see a popup box similar to figure 5.30.

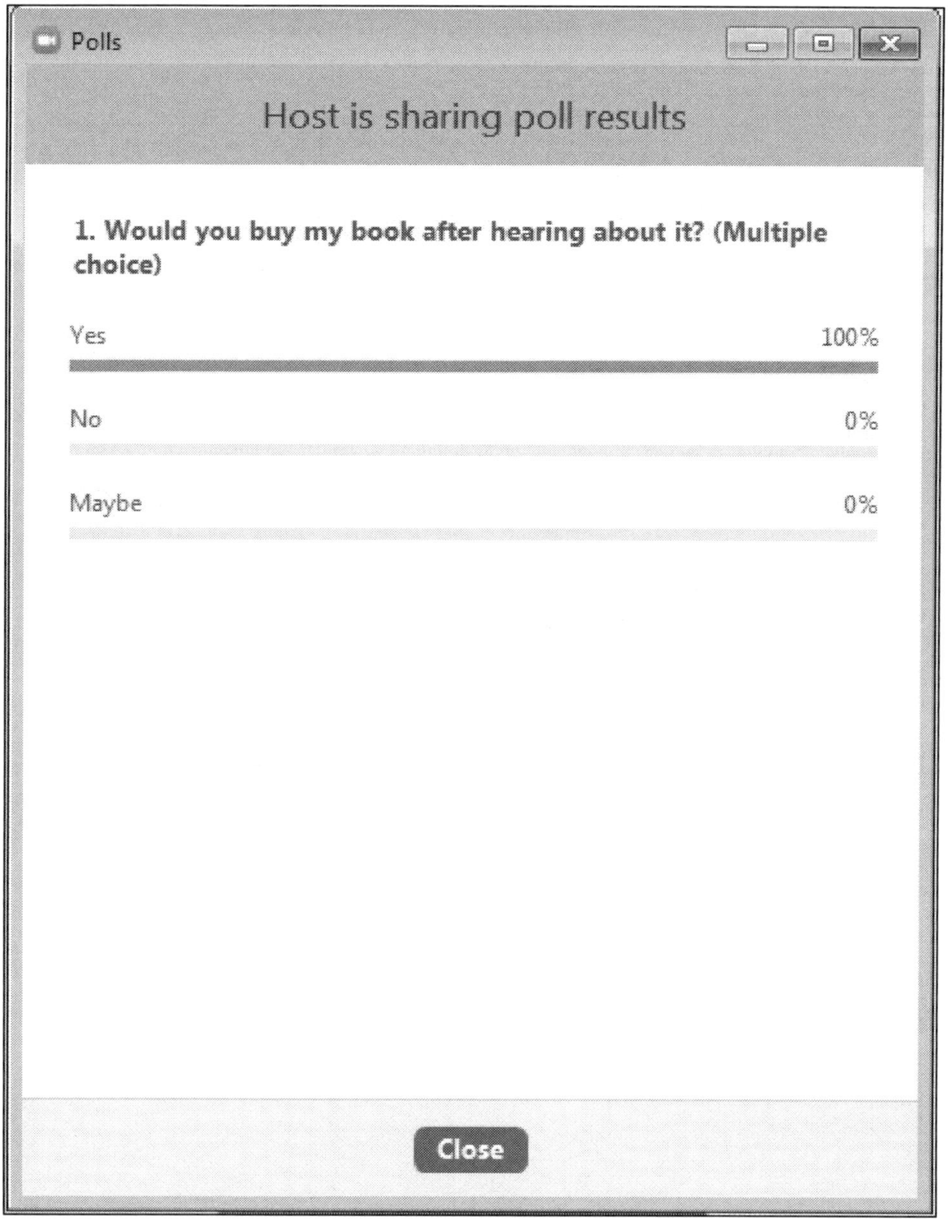

Figure 5.30

Live Streaming

Zoom gives you the ability to live stream your webinar on YouTube and Facebook in case you wanted to reach other people who were not invited to your actual Zoom webinar. By doing this you can make a post to your subscribers telling them that you will be live streaming your webinar at a particular time and then they can tune in to watch if they want to see your presentation.

If you click on the *More* button in the Zoom client toolbar you will have the option to go live on YouTube or Facebook.

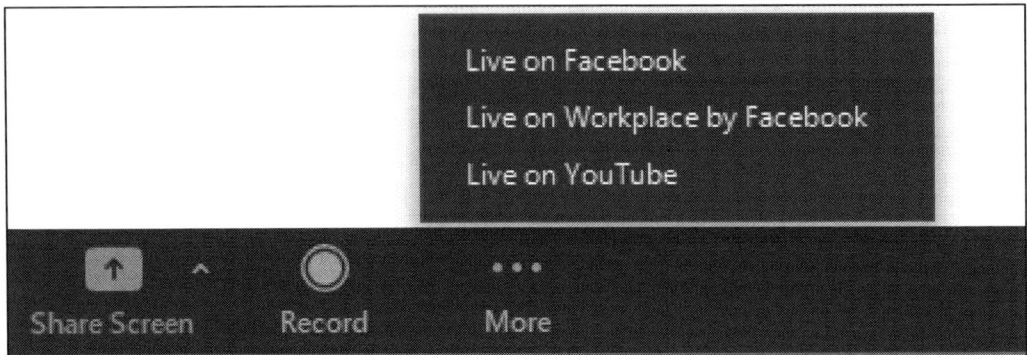

Figure 5.31

For my example, I will stream my webinar on Facebook, which is easier to do than YouTube, at least in my experience. To start with I will choose the *Live on Facebook* option.

Zoom will then take me to the Facebook website where I can login with my Facebook account. If you have any pages associated with your Facebook account you can stream your video on that pages rather than your own personal page. So if you happen to have a Facebook page that goes along with the content of your webinar you can stream it there.

For my live stream I will use my Online Computer Tips Facebook page and then click on *Next*.

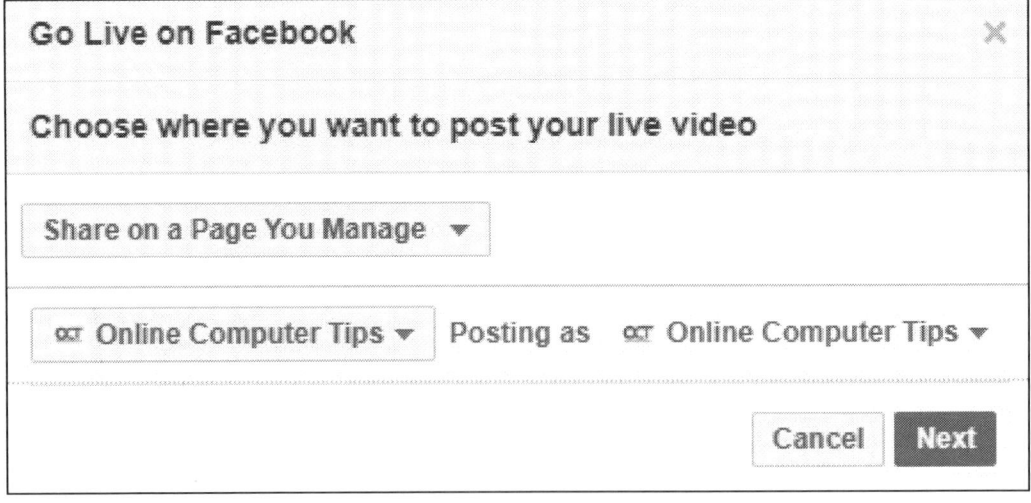

Figure 5.32

Zoom will then prepare the live stream to start on your Facebook page.

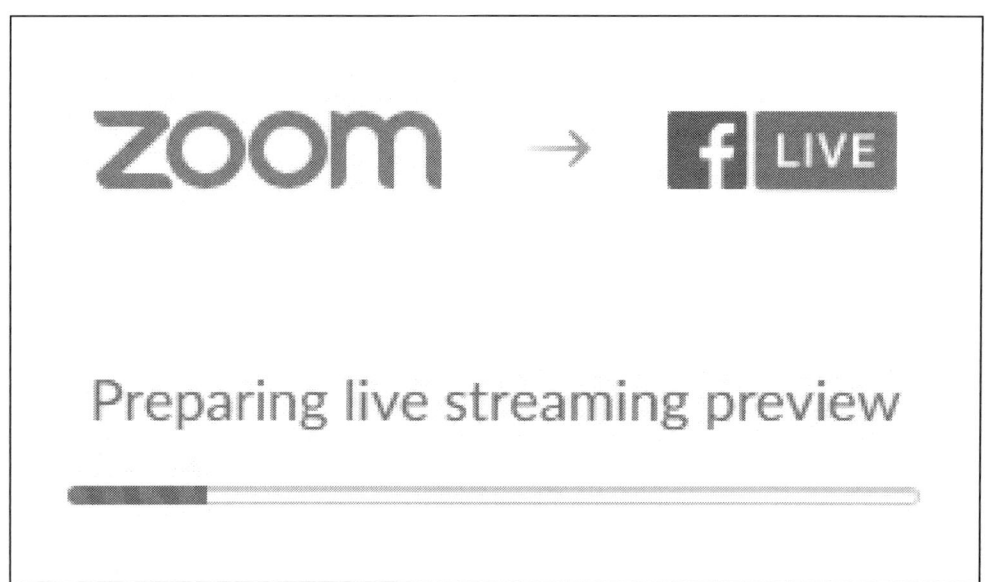

Figure 5.33

Next you will be presented with a preview page with some additional information and configuration options you can choose from. When you have things looking the way you want them to you can click on the *Go Live* button to start the live stream.

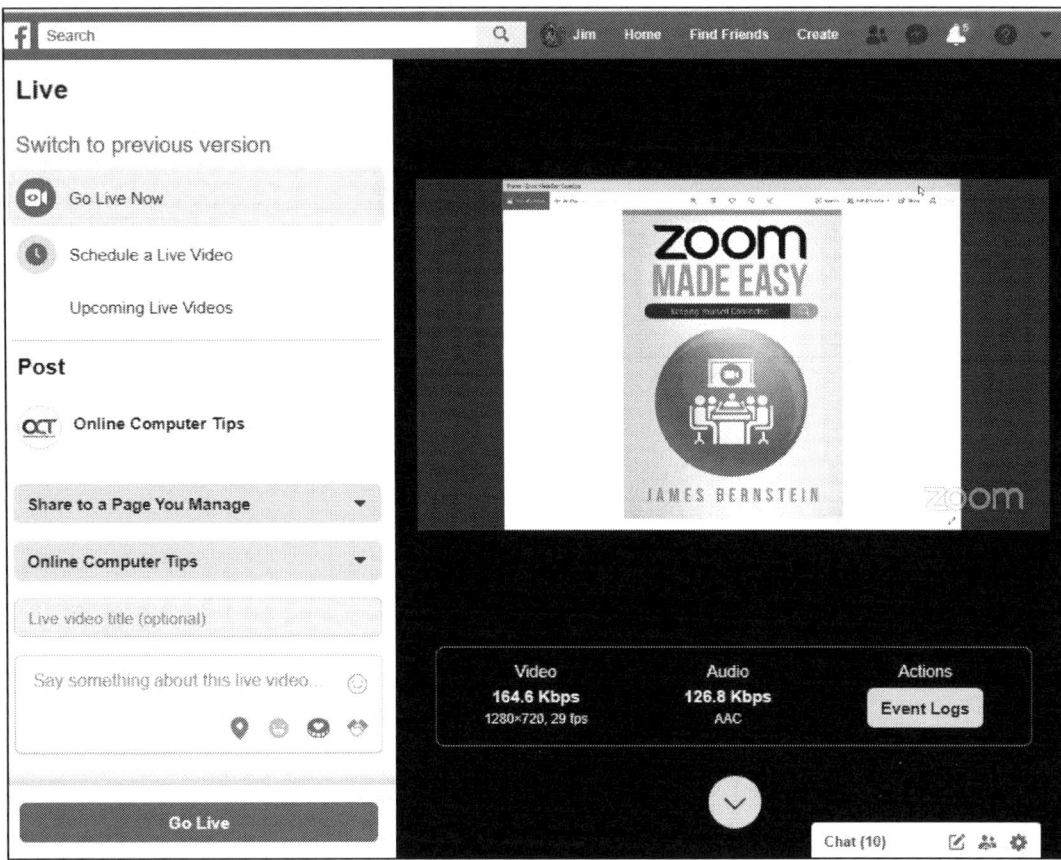

Figure 5.34

You will then notice that the Go Live button turns into a button that says *End Live Video* telling you that the streaming has begun.

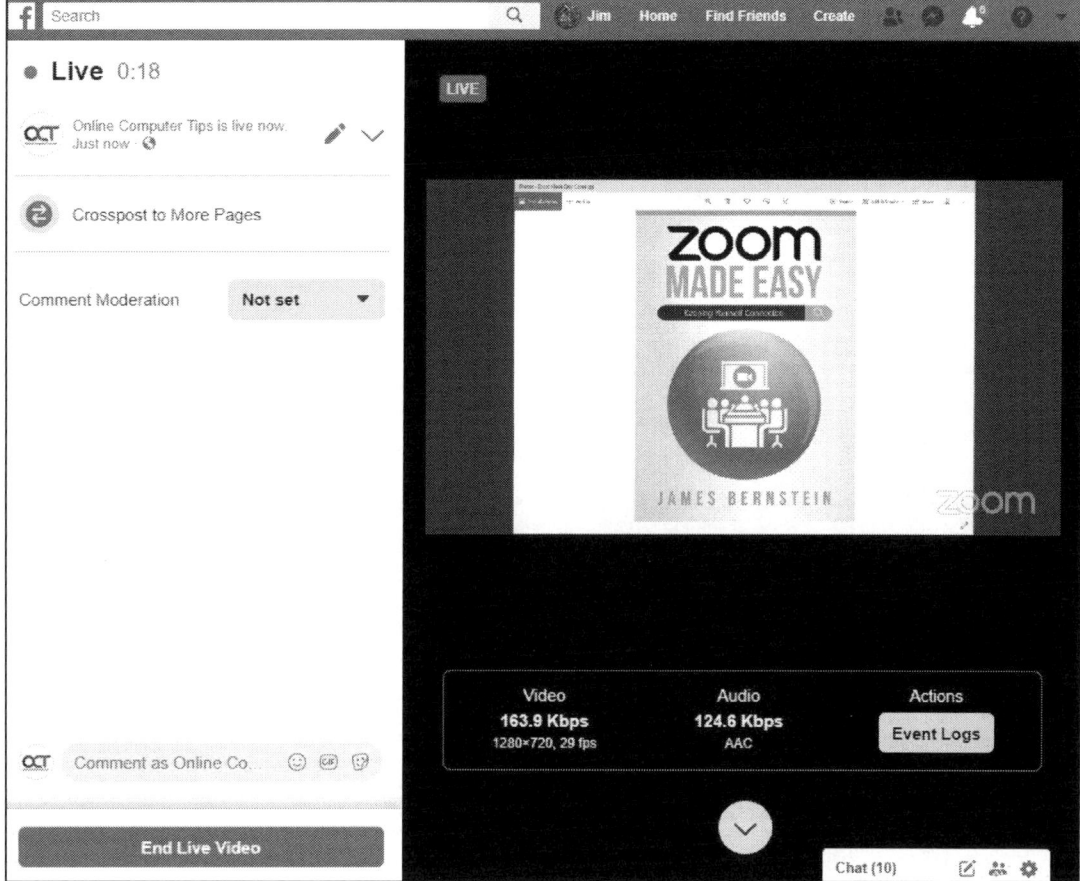

Figure 5.35

When someone goes to your Facebook page they will see that there is a live stream taking place and they will have the option to watch it by clicking on the *Watch Video* button.

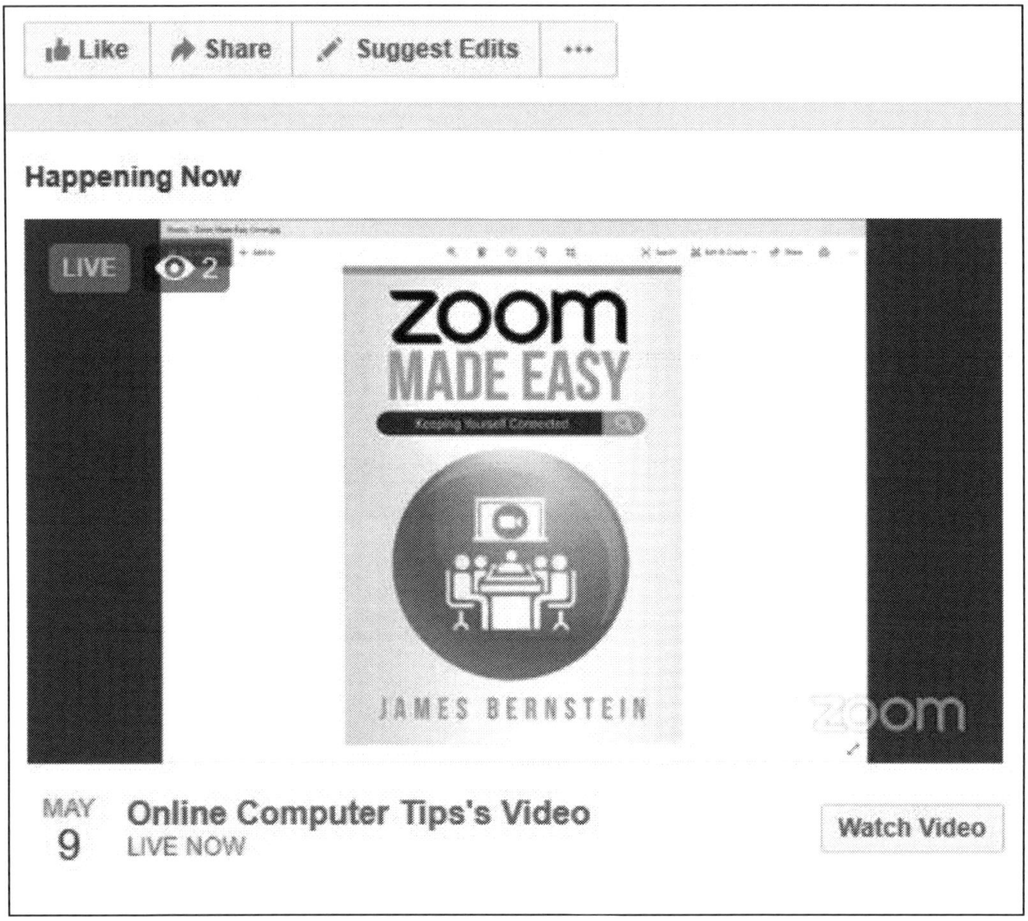

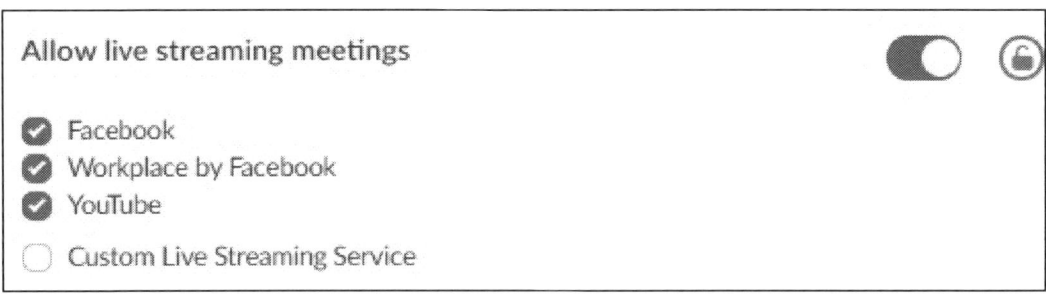

Figure 5.36

Zoom also allows you to live stream your meetings if you ever had the need to do so. To use this feature you first need to enable it by going to your meeting settings and finding the section labeled *In Meeting (Advanced)*, turning on the feature and selecting which Live Stream services you want to enable.

Allow live streaming meetings

✓ Facebook
✓ Workplace by Facebook
✓ YouTube
○ Custom Live Streaming Service

Figure 5.37

Chapter 6 – Settings

Just like with most other software, Zoom has a variety of settings available that allow you to adjust and customize the way the software works for you. For the most part you will probably be ok with the default settings or only need to change a couple of things but either way I will go over many (not all) of the settings that you can change within Zoom.

You can get to the settings from within the web interface and also from the Zoom client and I think using the client is easier to navigate and better organized so that is what I will be using for my demonstration. There are actually more settings I the web interface than in the client so you might want to poke around there as well. From the Home section within the Zoom client you need to click on the gear icon to get to the settings.

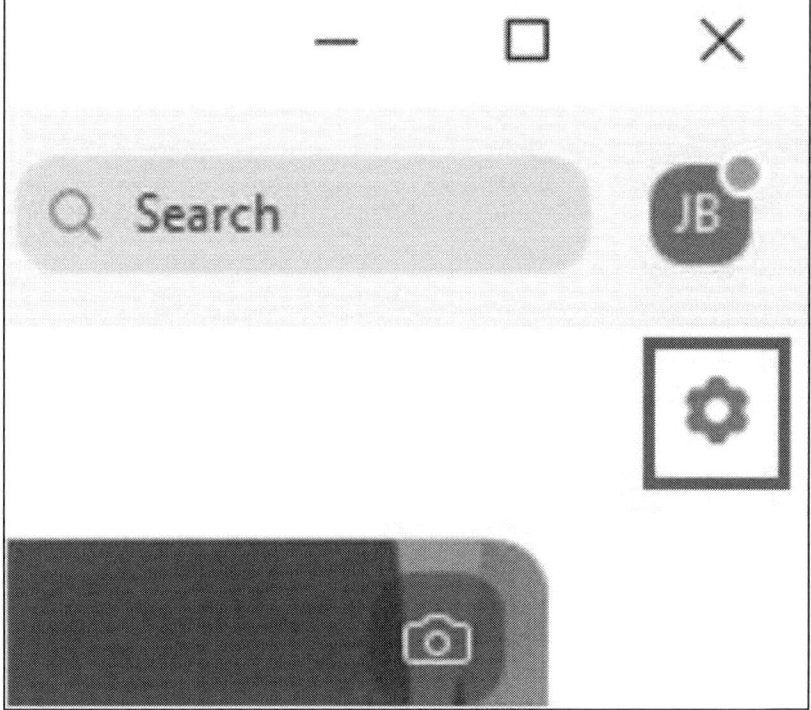

Figure 6.1

On the left hand side of the settings window you will see all the various categories of settings that you have to choose from.

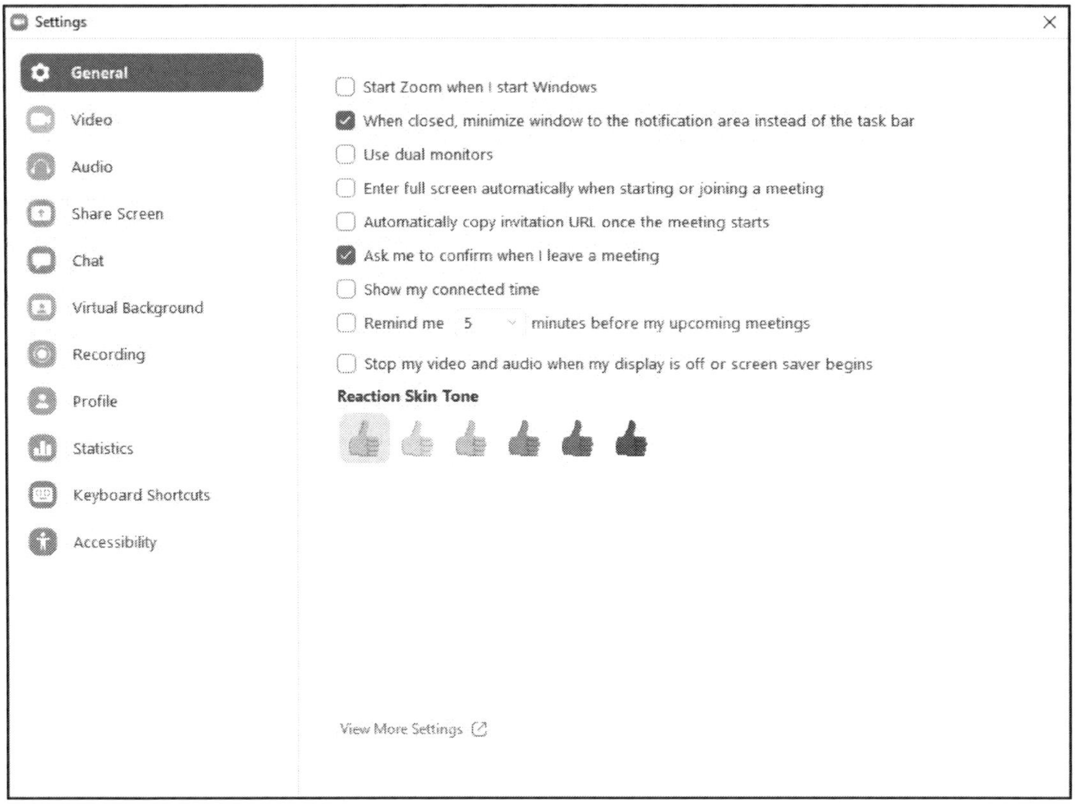

Figure 6.2

General

Here you can configure various things such as setting a reminder for your upcoming meetings and setting Zoom to load when your computer starts. The *Reaction Skin Tone* section is used for the color of the hand when you want to give a thumbs up or applause emoji\icon during a meeting.

You should be ok with the default settings here and I would definitely leave the checkbox for *Ask me to confirm when I leave a meeting checked* so you don't leave your meeting by accidentally clicking the End button.

Video

If you plan on using video in your meetings or webinars then you might want to check your video settings to make sure things are configured properly. When you first go in there you will see a variety of settings and if your camera is working you should see a live view of what it is pointed at.

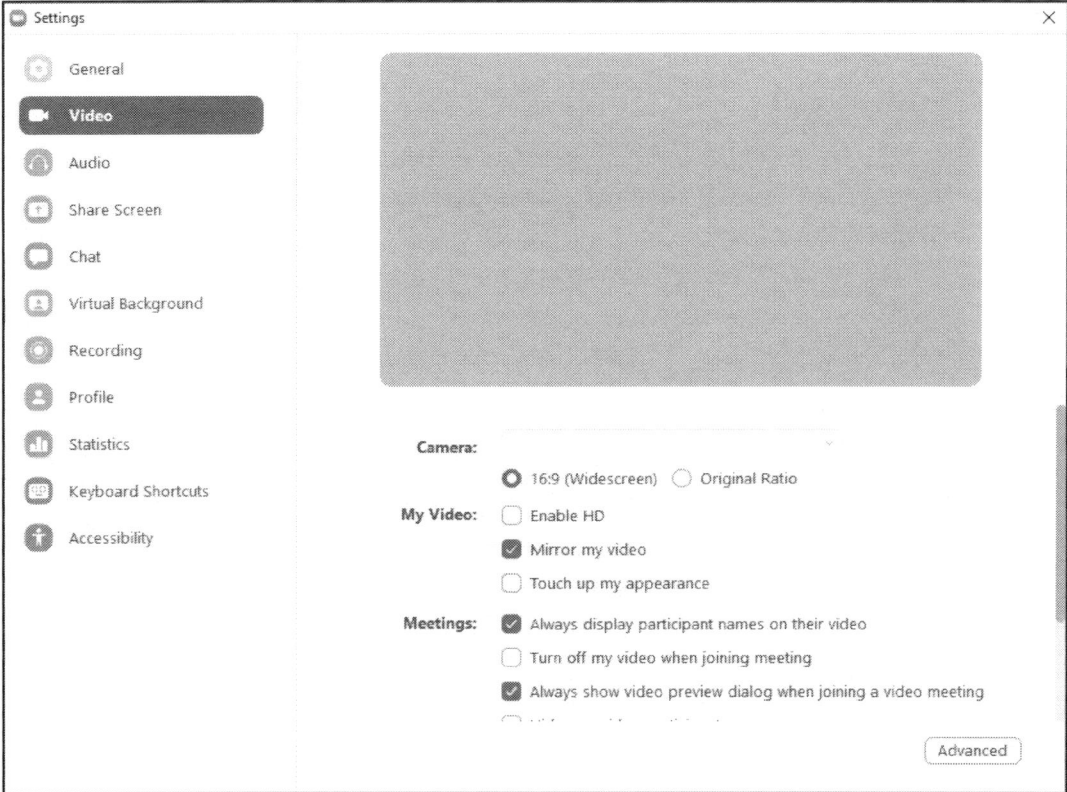

Figure 6.3

The options here are pretty self-explanatory. The *Mirror my video* setting will flip your video, so it mirrors your image rather than shows everything in reverse. The *Touch up my appearance* setting will apply a soft focus to your video to help "smooth things out".

If you click on the *Advanced* button you will see some additional options as seen in figure 6.4. I don't suggest messing with any of these because you might end up making things look worse rather than better or maybe not even work at all.

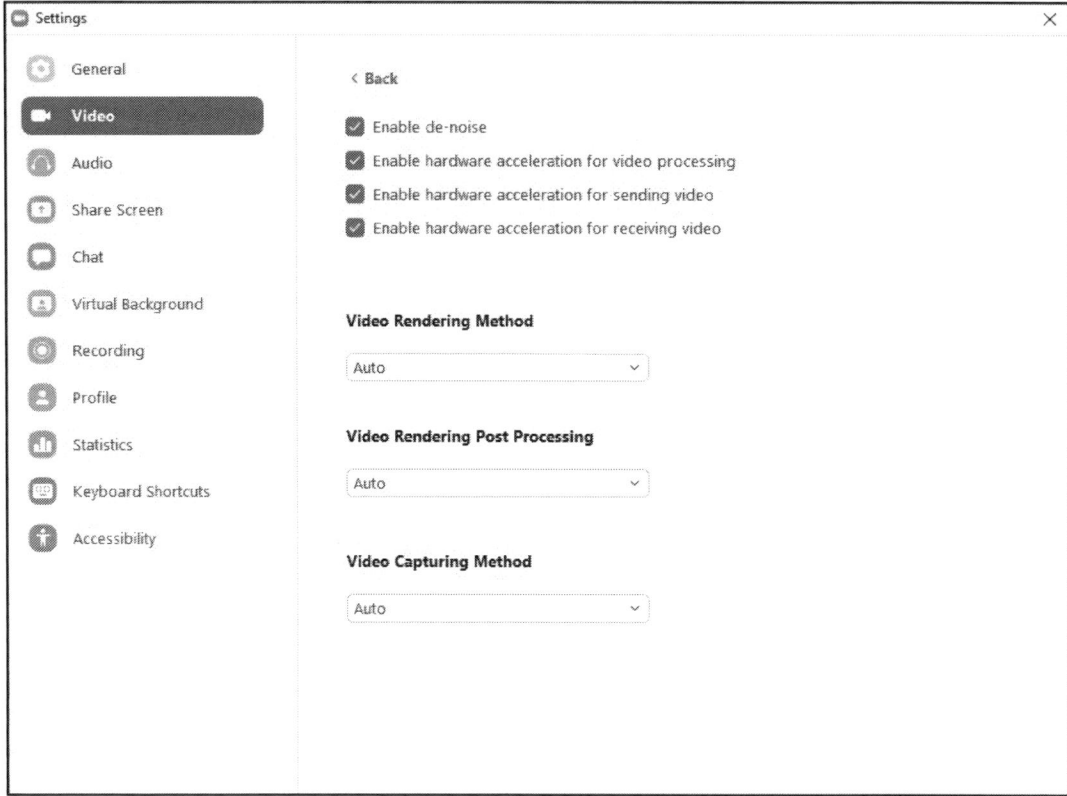

Figure 6.4

Audio

If you plan on using the microphone on your computer for your meeting audio then you can come to the Audio settings to make sure everything is configured the way you would like it to be.

Here you can do things such as test your speakers and microphone and also adjust the default speaker output and microphone input levels. If you have more than one microphone then you can choose it from the dropdown list from this section.

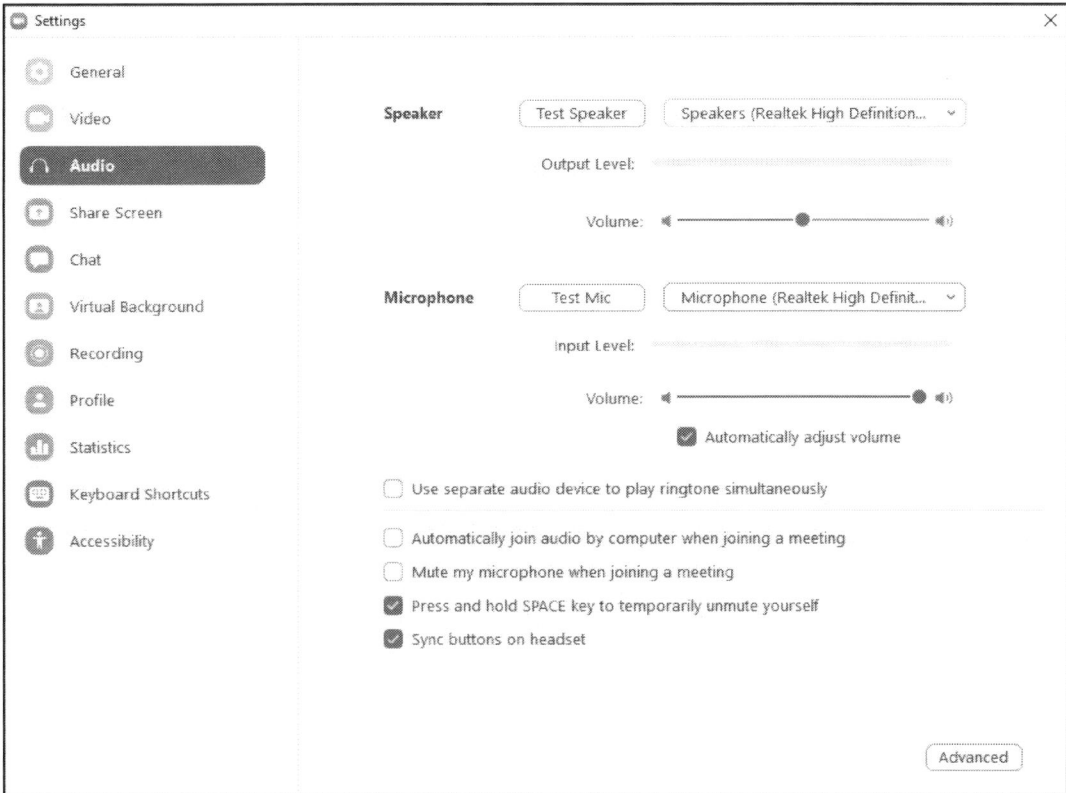

Figure 6.5

You most likely have noticed that you get prompted to join meetings with computer audio every time you start one. You can check the box that says *Automatically join audio by computer when joining a meeting* if you want this to happen automatically and not prompt you.

Share Screen

I spent quite a bit of time on how to share your screen with other participants in your meeting and if you would like to tweak how the process works then you have some options that you can change here.

You might have noticed that when someone shares their screen that your Zoom window becomes full screen and takes up your entire monitor. Some people don't like that because it covers the things they have open on their computer. Pressing the Esc key should take you out of full screen mode by the way. If you don't want the shared screen to work this way you can uncheck the box that says *Enter full screen when a participant shares screen*.

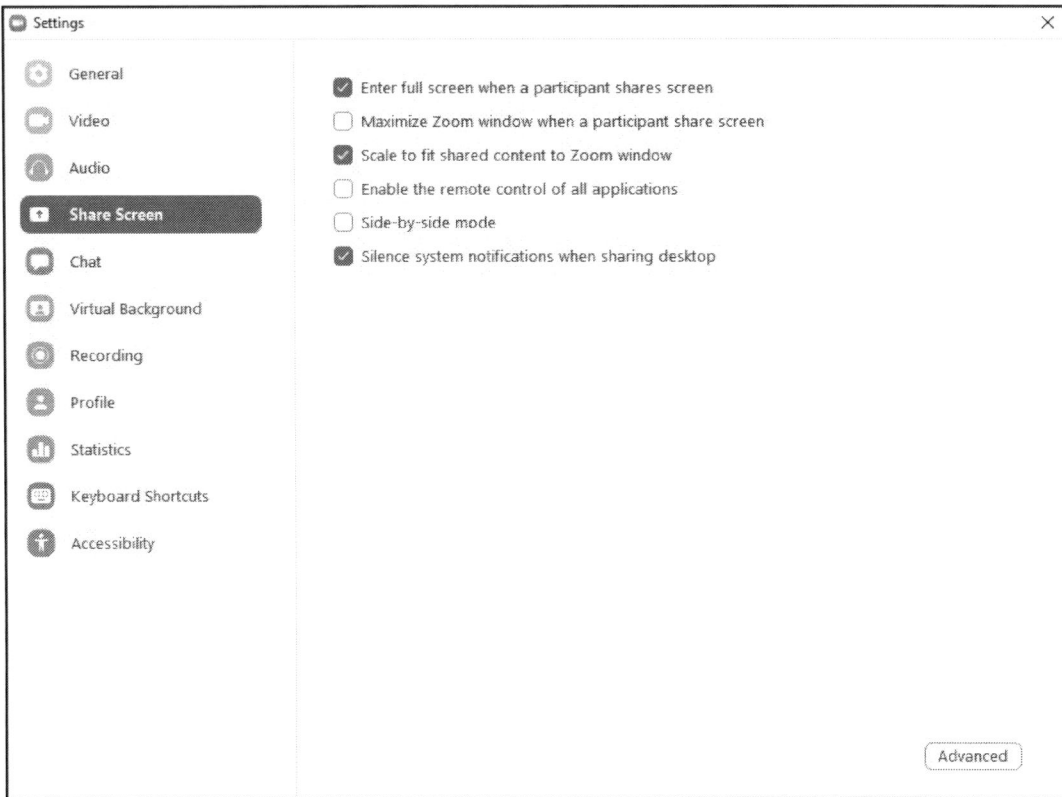

Figure 6.6

The other selections should be fairly obvious except for maybe *Enable the remote control of all applications* which will give remote uses the ability to control all aspects of the remote computer including any administrator prompts. This applied to Windows based computers. I will be discussing the Remote Control feature later in the book.

The *Side-by-side mode* option will allow you to see the shared screen alongside either the Speaker View or Gallery View, depending on which you are using.

Clicking on the *Advanced* button will give you a few additional options which you should probably leave set as is (figure 6.7). You might have noticed that when you share your screen there is a green box around the shared section. That only shows up on your computer and is there to let you know what your audience can see from your computer.

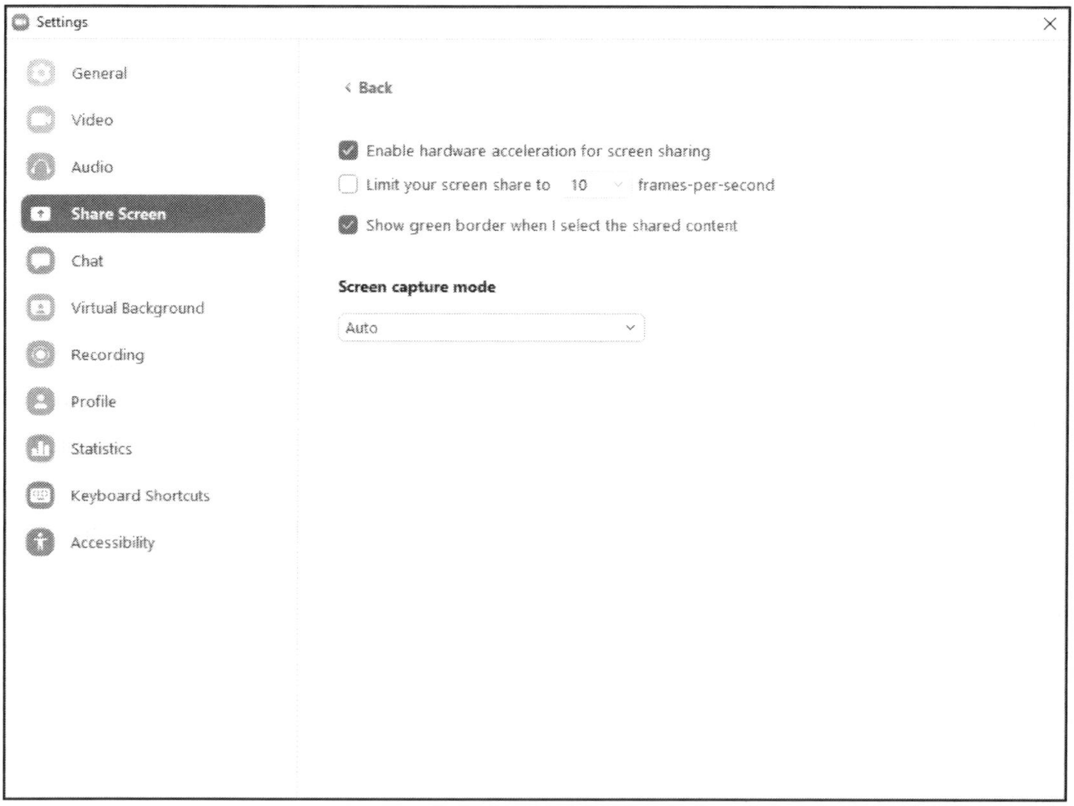

Figure 6.7

Chat

There are many things you can change from the Chat settings (figure 6.8) but once again the defaults should be fine for most people. Under the *Chat Settings* section there is an option to change your status to away when you are inactive for a set amount of time. This will tell others who send you messages that you are not at your computer, so they don't think you are ignoring them. The default is to kick in after 15 minutes of inactivity.

With the Zoom chat, you have the ability to block users from chatting with you if you don't want to be bothered by them or if they are getting rude for example. If you want to unblock any of them you can do so from the *Blocked users* section.

The *Unread Messages* section lets you decide what to do with any chat messages that you have not read yet so feel free to adjust those settings as needed.

The *Push Notifications* section allows you to configure how you are notified when you get a new message. The default is to notify you for all messages. The *Receive notifications for (Keywords)* option is interesting because you can add certain keywords and if someone types in one of those keywords you will get notified. So if you want to be notified when someone mentions "lunch" then you can add that by clicking on the Keywords button and adding it to the list.

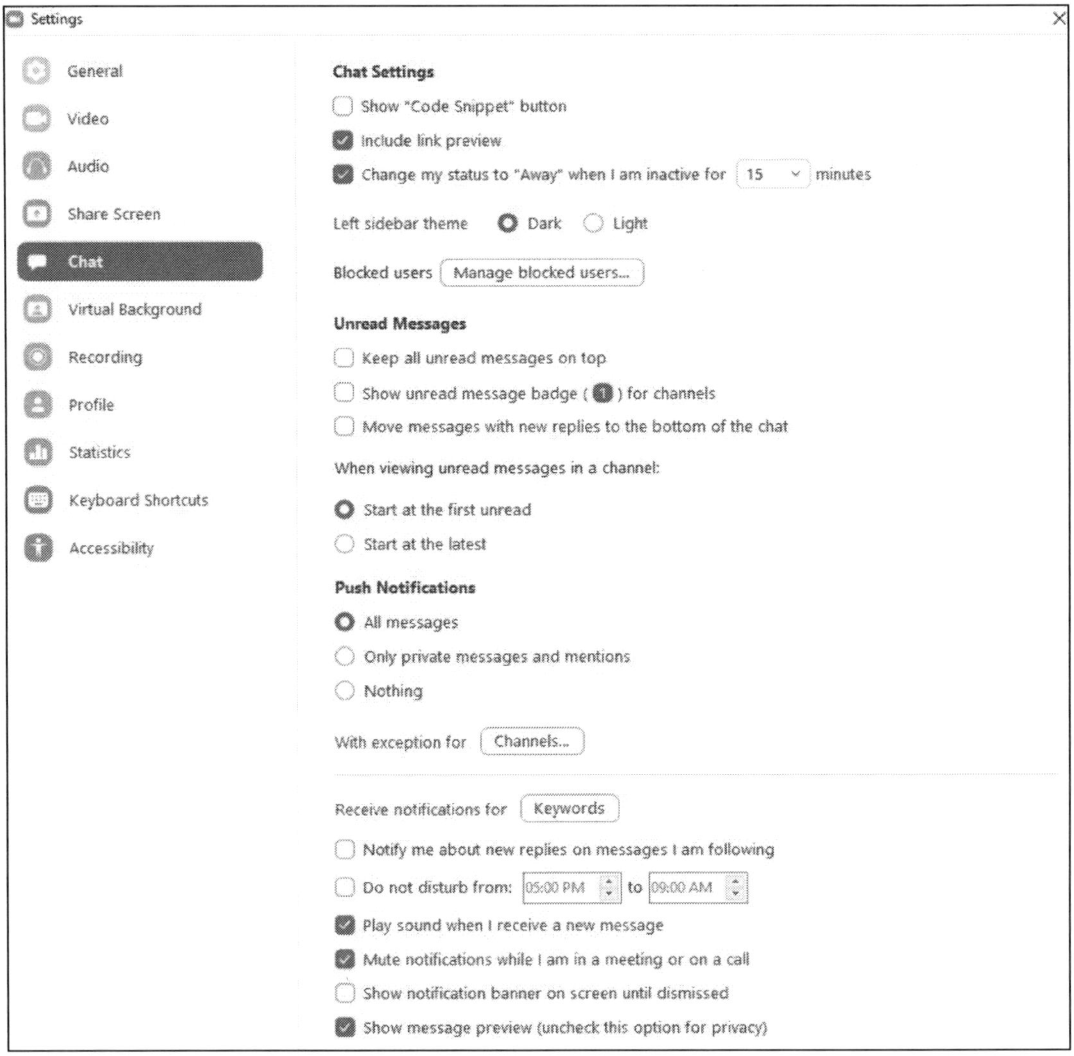

Figure 6.8

Virtual Background

I have already discussed how to add a background image or movie to your video when you are doing a meeting and you can come here to manage your current images or videos as well as add more if you would like some additional options. If you are super professional and have a green screen behind you then you can check the box that says *I have a green screen* to have Zoom improve the background image quality.

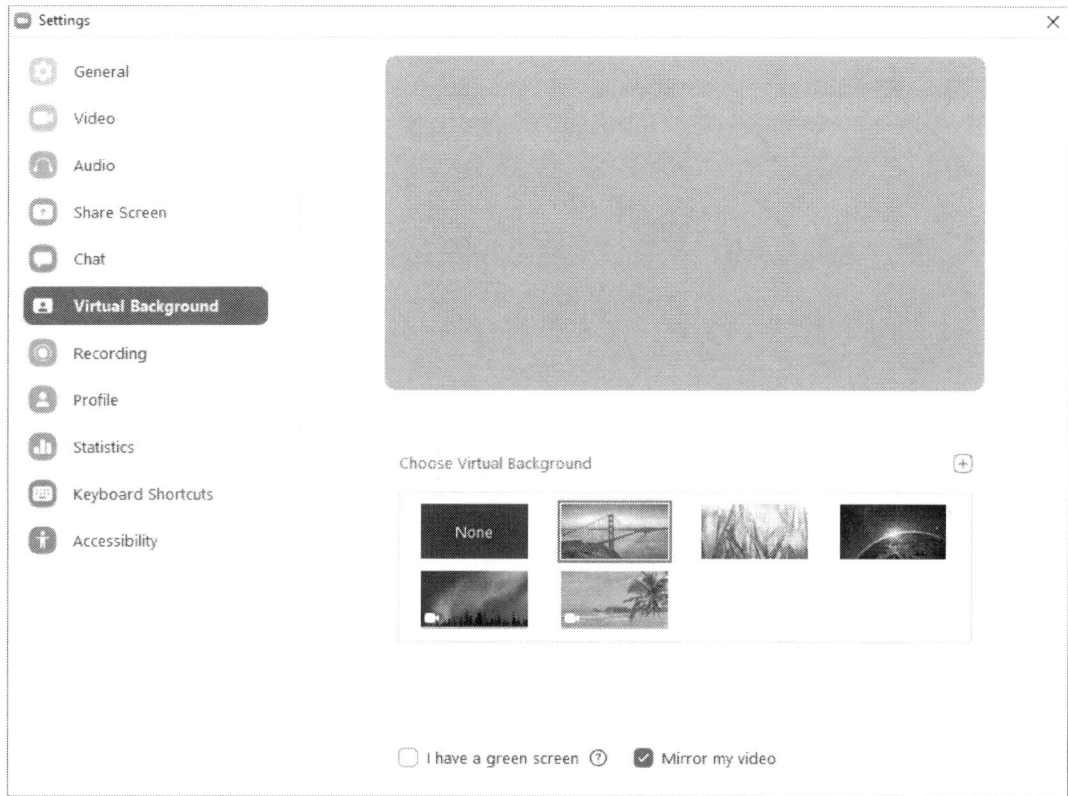

Figure 6.9

Recording

Here you can tell Zoom where to place the videos it records of your meetings if you don't want to use the default location which is shown in the *Location* box in figure 6.10. You can also check the box that says *Choose a location for recorded files* when the meeting ends if you want to get prompted each time when the meeting is over.

If you want to keep an audio record of each person who will be speaking during your meeting to review later then check the box that says *Record a separate audio file for each participant who speaks*.

The *Add a timestamp* option will add the date and time of your meeting to the video so when you review it later you will know exactly when it was recorded.

The *Record video during screen sharing* checkbox will make it so Zoom automatically records a video whenever screen sharing is being used.

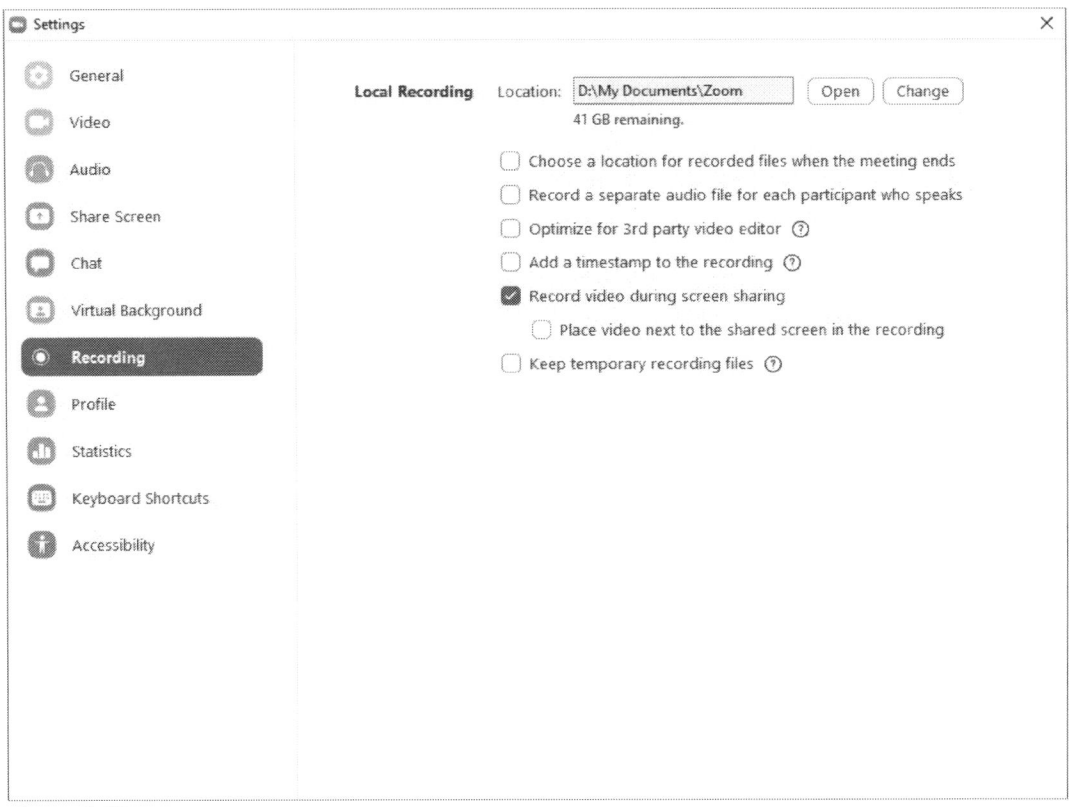

Figure 6.10

Profile
The Profile settings is basically just a shortcut to take you to your profile settings in the web interface in case you wish to make any changes. You can also upgrade your plan from this page which will take you to the Zoom website as well.

Statistics
This section is more informational than anything else. If you want to see what kind of toll Zoom is taking on your computer resources then you can check things out from here. If you come to this section without having a meeting running then you really won't see much since you need to have a meeting running to get any real information.

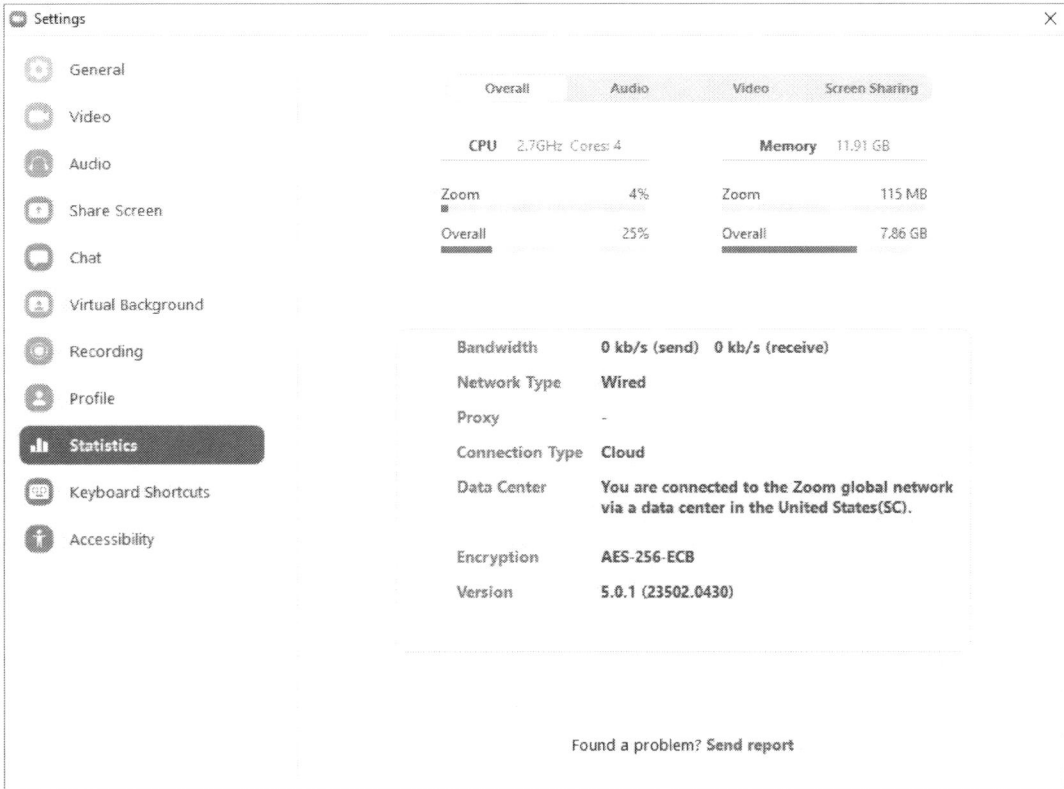

Figure 6.11

Keyboard Shortcuts

If you have been using a computer for some time then you are most likely aware of what keyboard shortcuts are used for. Some examples include *Ctrl-C* for copy, *Ctrl-V* for paste and *Alt-Tab* to switch between open programs.

Zoom allows you to enable or disable its default keyboard shortcuts from here. You will notice that most of them are disabled when you go into this section but you can enable whichever ones you would like to use by checking the box next to that particular shortcut.

Description	Shortcut	Enable Global Shortcut ⑦
Navigate Among Zoom Popup Windows	F6	☐
Change Focus to Zoom Meeting Controls (On Top when Sharing Screen)	Ctrl+Alt+Shift	☑
View the Previous Page of Video Participants in Gallery View	Page Up	☐
View the Next Page of Video Participants in Gallery View	Page Down	☐
Always Show Meeting Controls	Alt	☐
Switch to Speaker View	Alt+F1	☐
Switch to Gallery View	Alt+F2	☐
Close Current Window	Alt+F4	☐
Start/Stop Video	Alt+V	☐
Mute/Unmute My Audio	Alt+A	☐

Settings panel left menu: General, Video, Audio, Share Screen, Chat, Virtual Background, Recording, Profile, Statistics, **Keyboard Shortcuts**, Accessibility. Restore Defaults

Figure 6.12

Accessibility

If you have any conditions that require special assistance when it comes to using your computer then you might want to come to the Accessibility settings to see if you can make any changes that will make Zoom easier to use.

Here you can change things such as the font size for the closed caption text, have the meeting controls always be shown for easy access and also increase the size of the chat window.

Chapter 6 – Settings

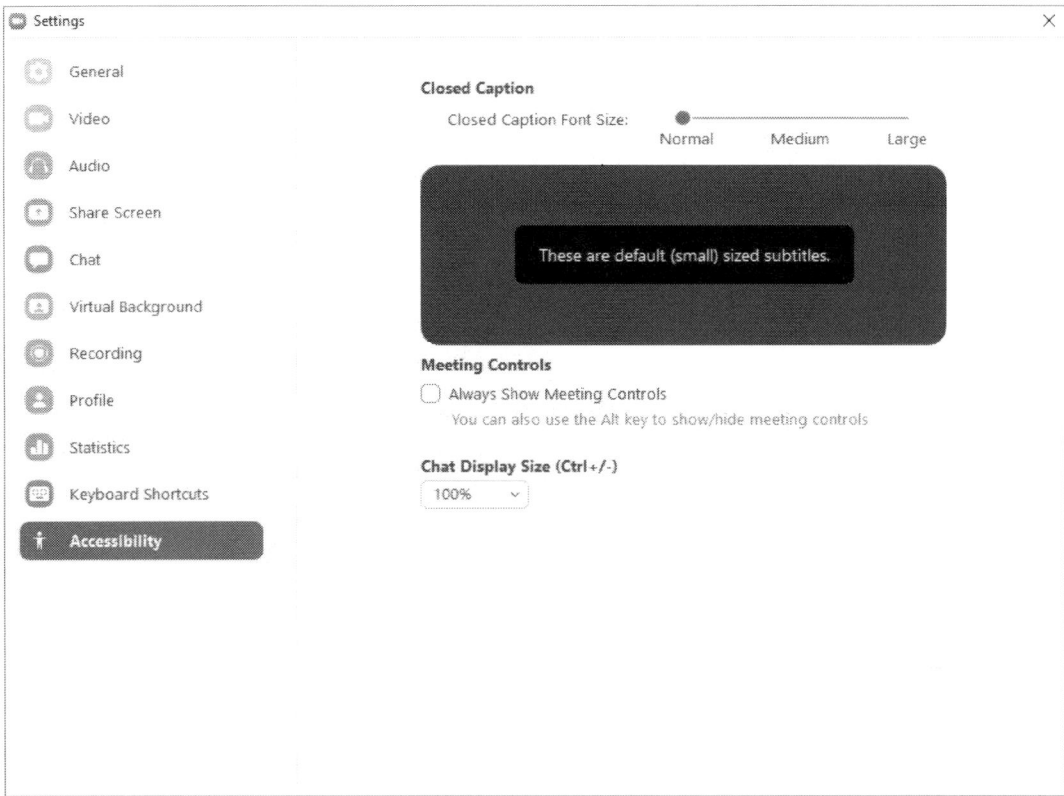

Figure 6.13

Chapter 7 – Using Zoom on Your Mobile Device

Since smartphones and tablets are as popular if not more popular than desktop computers, it makes sense that you should be able to have your meetings on your mobile devices since they are always with you and you never know when you might have something you need to discuss with others!

Using Zoom on a mobile device is similar to using Zoom on your computer but obviously there will be some differences as well as some limitations. Smartphones and tablets are great, but they still can't do everything that a desktop or laptop computer running Windows or Mac OS can do.

Downloading and Installing Zoom on Your Mobile Device
The first step in using Zoom on your smartphone or tablet is to download and install it. This process works the same way as any other app you have ever installed on your device. So assuming you have installed an app before, this process should be fairly simple.

To begin you will need to go to the Play Store (Android devices) or the App Store (Apple devices) and search for Zoom. Just be sure it's the real Zoom app and not another one with a similar name. The developer's name should be **zoom.us**.

Since I have an Android smartphone I will be demonstrating on that but if you have an iPhone the process should be pretty similar. Once you find the right app simply install it and wait for the process to complete.

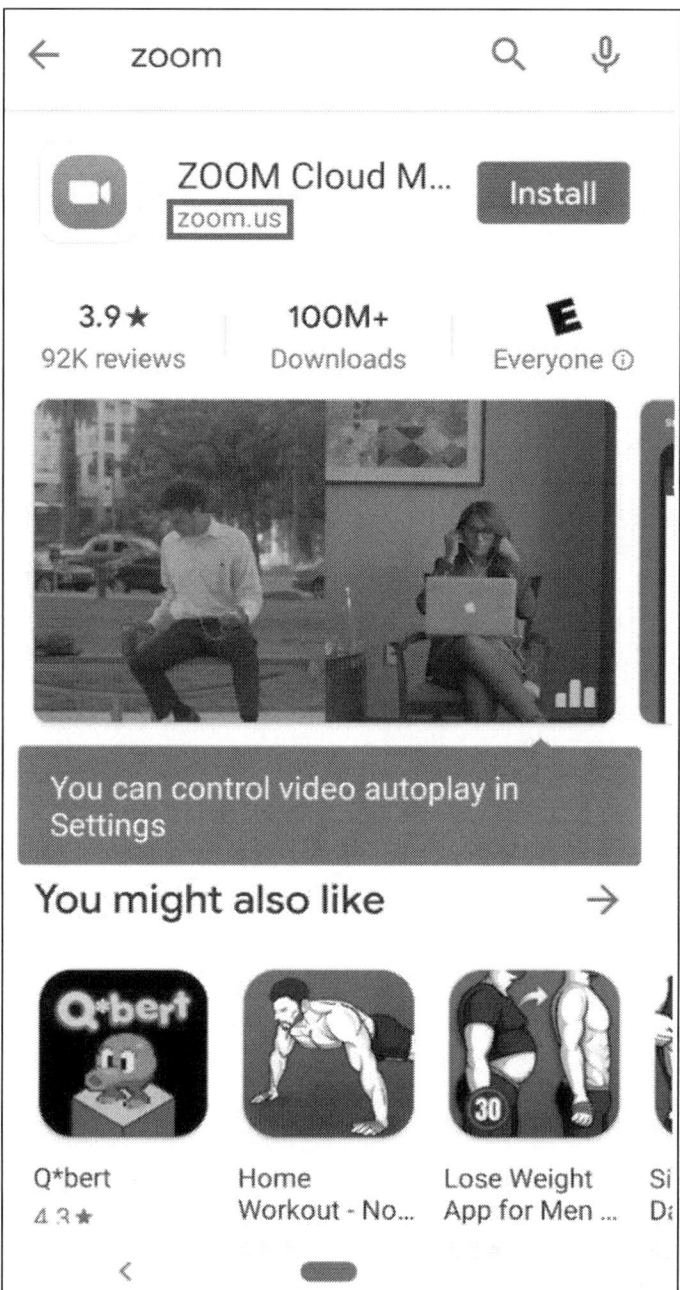

Figure 7.1

Next, you will open the app from your app list or main screen and sign in with your normal Zoom email address and password.

Figure 7.2

Using Your Zoom App For Meetings

Once you are logged in you will see the same choices that you have with the Zoom client such as starting a new meeting, joining a meeting, scheduling a meeting and sharing your screen. If you tap on your name you will be taken to what Zoom calls your *personal space* where you can add notes and files etc. to be used later.

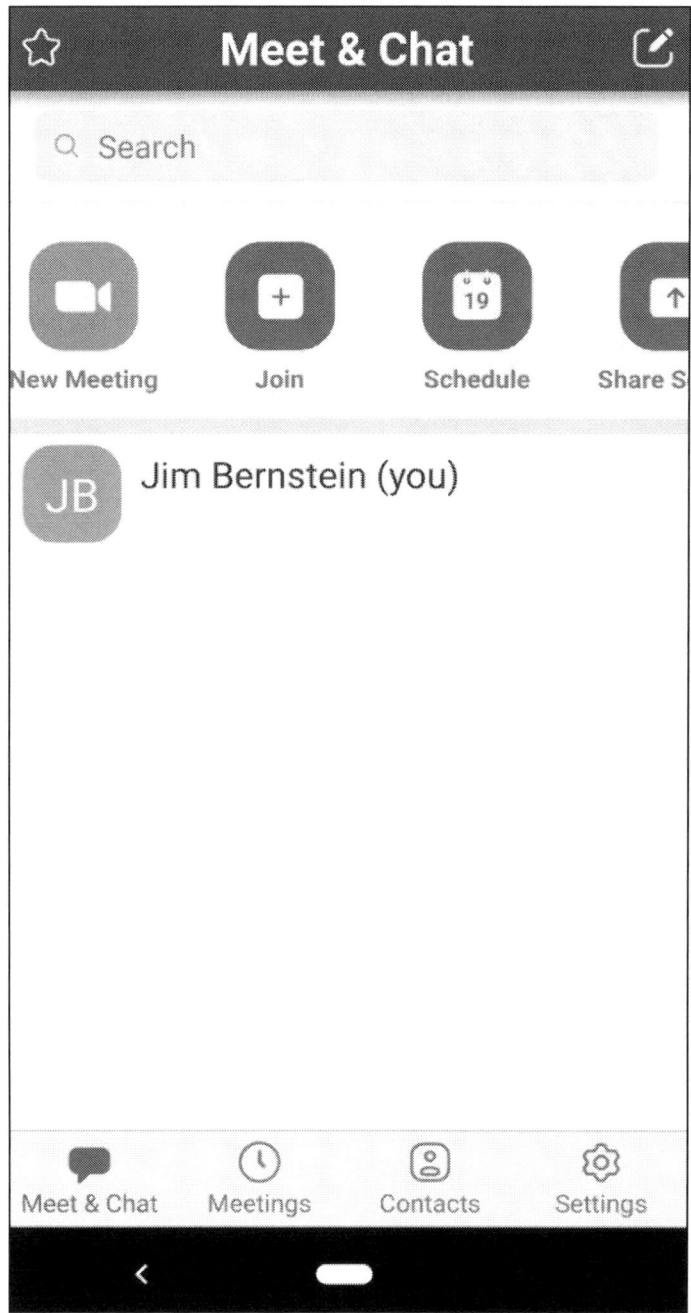

Figure 7.3

Now that the Zoom app is installed on my phone when I get an instant meeting invitation it will ring my phone and show me who is calling for the meeting as seen in figure 7.4. Then I can either accept or decline the call. If I accept the call I will be joined to the meeting.

Figure 7.4

Then I will be in the meeting and be able to see whoever is speaking on my phone and they will be able to see me as well. My video preview window is in the lower right corner of the screen. Since I don't have a video camera on the computer I started the meeting from I added my own video preview screen just for the visual effect!

Figure 7.5

You should have noticed that you have the same controls such as mute, share, participants etc. on the phone as you do with the Zoom client on the computer. Clicking on More (figure 7.6) with give you additional options such as starting a chat session or raising your had to get the host's attention.

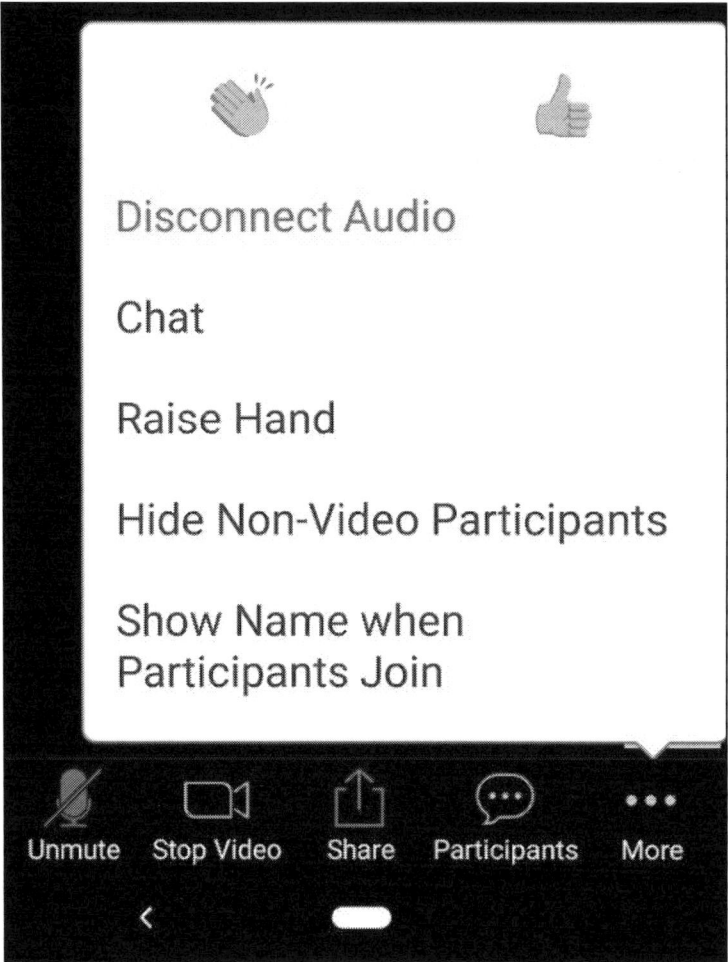

Figure 7.6

Not all meetings will be on the spot so if you have an email with an upcoming meeting invitation you can simply tap the *Join* button the main Zoom screen and type in the meeting ID and connect to the meeting at the time it is scheduled to begin (figure 7.7).

You can also disable your audio and video before joining the meeting if you don't want to be seen or heard.

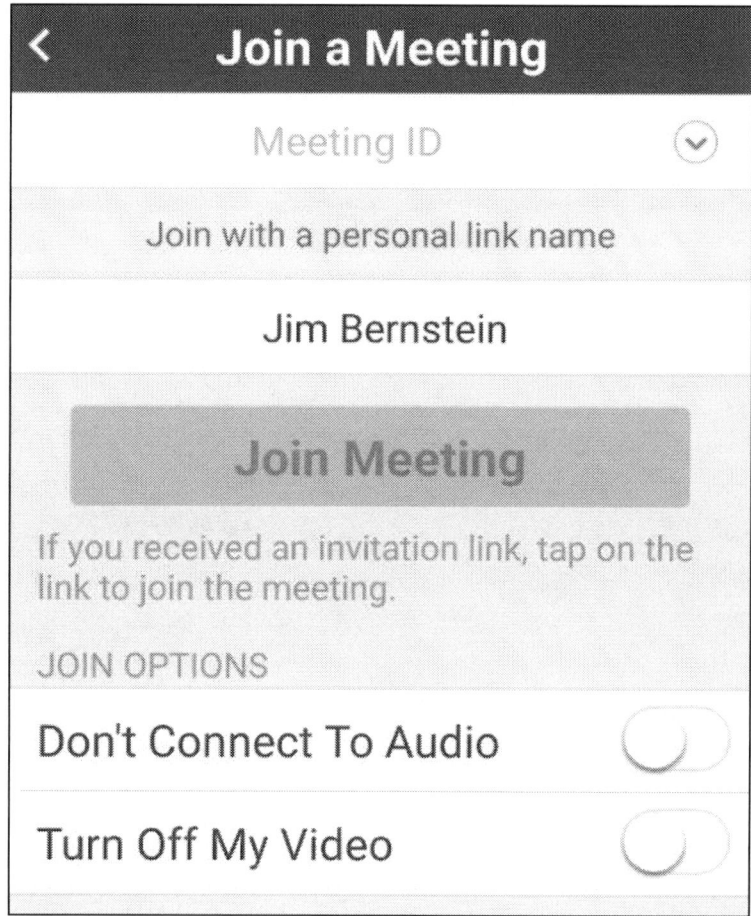

Figure 7.7

Sharing Your Mobile Device From Your Computer

If you are in the middle of a meeting on your computer yet you would like to share something from your smartphone or tablet then this is possible to do… assuming you have an Apple device such as an iPhone or iPad. I will get to us Android users in a moment.

Zoom gives you the ability to connect to your iPhone or iPad via the *Share Screen* interface that I have already discussed back in Chapter 4. By using this feature you can share your device with your audience giving them the ability to see exactly what you are seeing on your phone or tablet.

To enable this mobile device screen sharing you will want to choose iPhone/iPad from the list after you click on Share Screen as seen in figure 7.8.

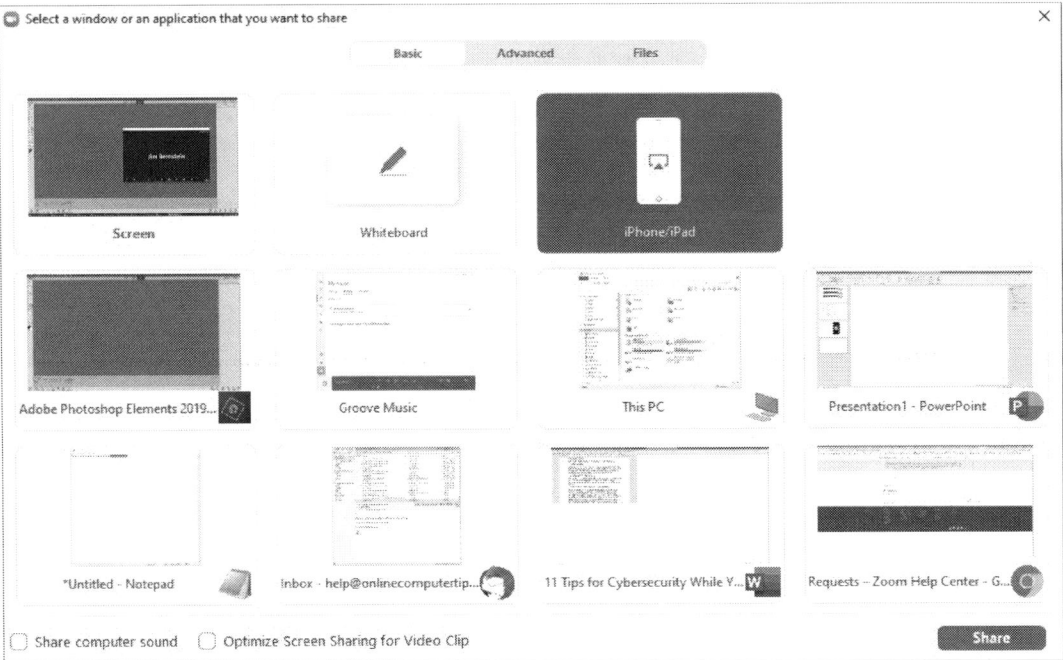

Figure 7.8

Next, you will be prompted to download and install a plugin for your Zoom software. This will only occur the first time you perform this type of sharing.

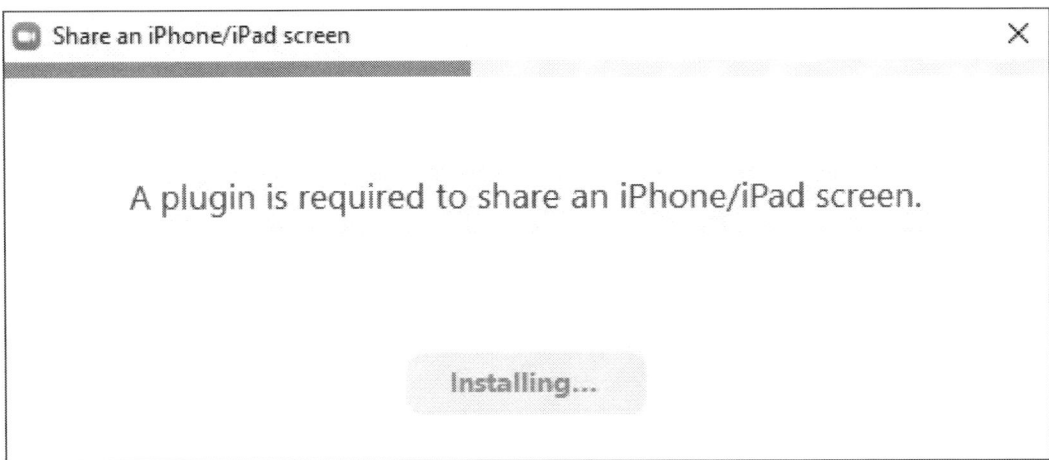

Figure 7.9

Then you will get a message telling you to look on the screen of your iPhone or iPad and connect to the network and then tap on *Screen Mirroring* and finally tap on the Zoom connection name (figure 7.10).

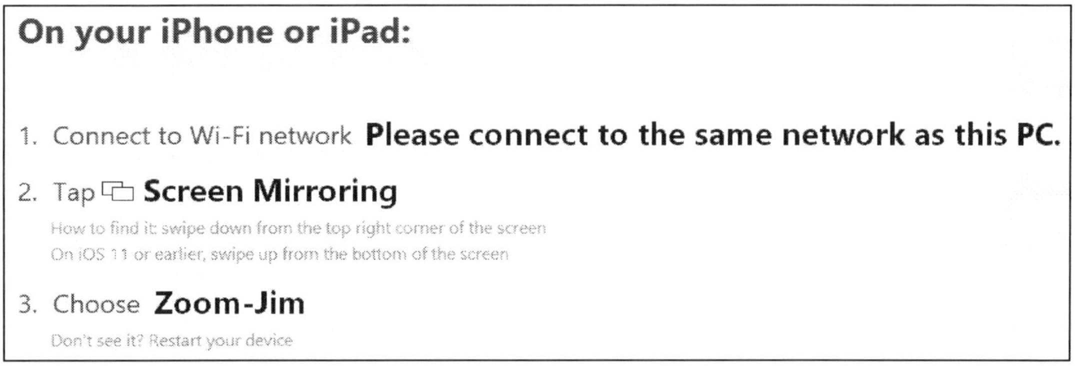

On your iPhone or iPad:

1. Connect to Wi-Fi network **Please connect to the same network as this PC.**
2. Tap ⬚ **Screen Mirroring**
   How to find it: swipe down from the top right corner of the screen
   On iOS 11 or earlier, swipe up from the bottom of the screen
3. Choose **Zoom-Jim**
   Don't see it? Restart your device

Figure 7.10

Finally, you should be connected and then you should be able to see your iPhone or iPad screen within the meeting.

For us Android users the only option we have to accomplish this is to join the meeting on our phone or tablet at the same time we are joined on the computer. You can join the meeting from more than one device with the same account.

Next, you will want to tap on Share and choose what you want to share on your device. You can share photos, documents, web URLs, bookmarks, your entire screen or start a whiteboard session.

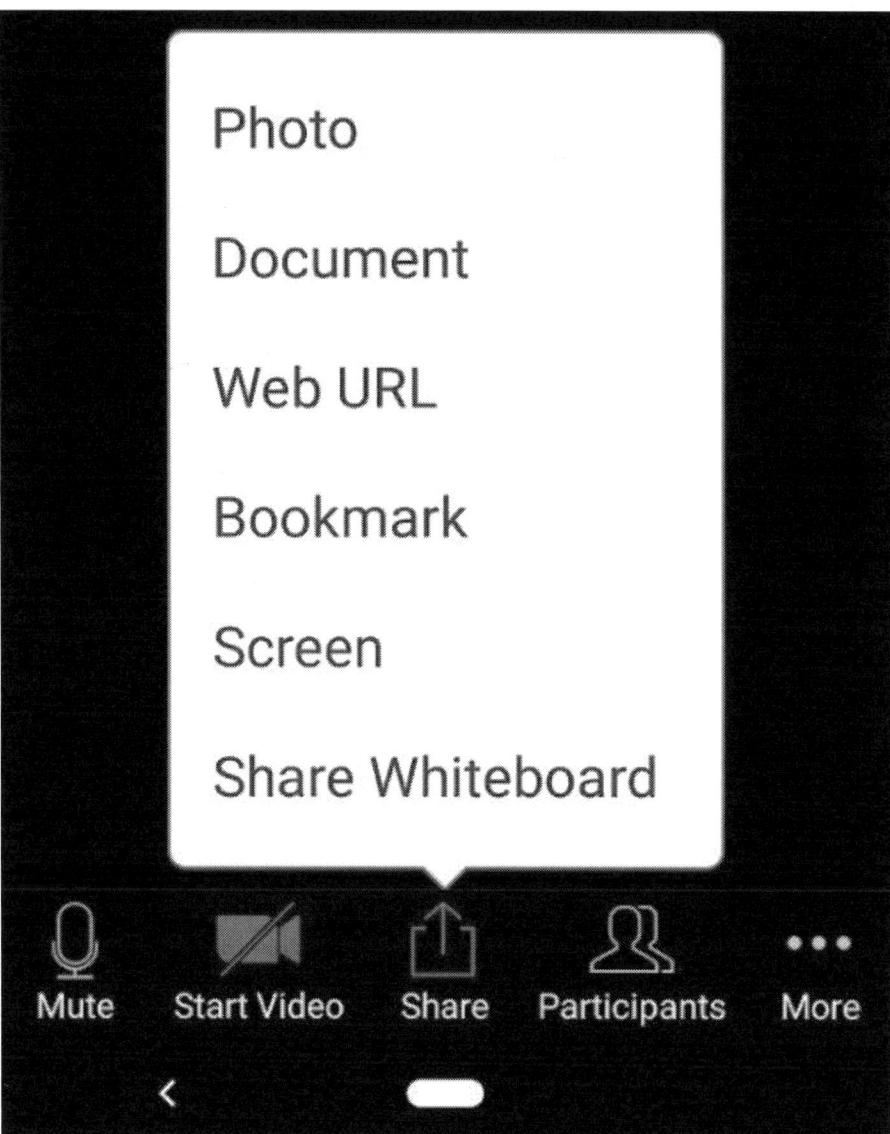

Figure 7.11

For my example, I will share a photo and now I can see on my phone that the photo is being shared and have the option to stop sharing it or make some markups with the Annotation button (figure 7.12).

Figure 7.12

Figure 7.13 shows how the shared photo from my phone looks on the Zoom desktop client.

Figure 7.13

Chapter 8 – Additional\Advanced Zoom Features

Now that you have all the Zoom basics down I wanted to take a little time to go over some of the extra, more advanced things you can do with the software\service. You might never have the need to do any of the things I will be discussing in this chapter, but it will be beneficial to at least know they are there.

Breakout Rooms

Breakout Rooms can be used to separate your participants into groups within their own room so they can collaborate on their own. This way you don't have a large group of people fighting for attention, but you can rather split up people into groups based on things such as common assignments or how well they get along.

To use Breakout Rooms you first need to enable the feature in your Zoom Settings from the web interface. Once you get to Settings simply click on *In Meeting (Advanced)* under the *Meeting* tab.

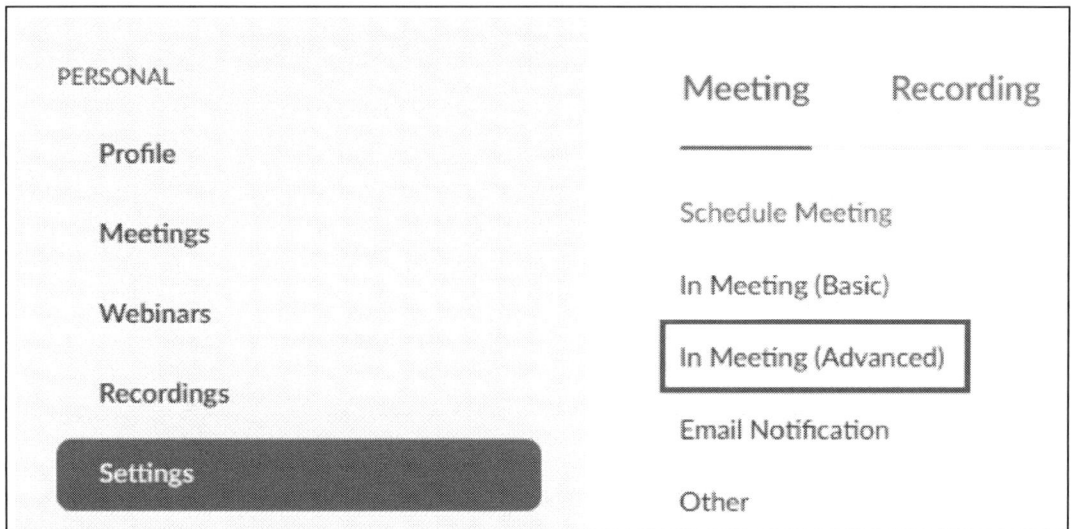

Figure 8.1

Next, you will enable the Breakout Room by moving the slider to the right, so it turns blue as seen in figure 8.2. If you check the box that says *Allow host to assign participants to breakout rooms when scheduling* you will be able to choose who will be put in a room with who before the meeting starts.

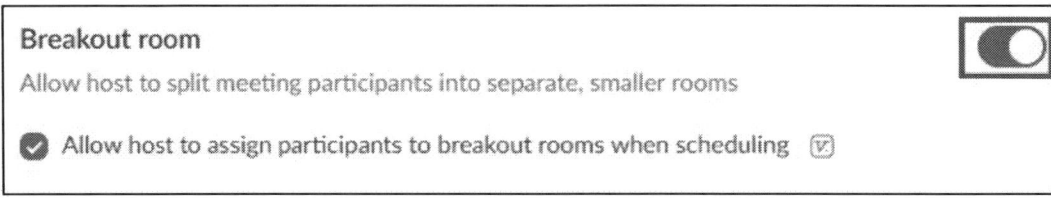

Figure 8.2

Then the next time you host a meeting you will have a Breakout Rooms button on your Zoom client toolbar.

Figure 8.3

When you create breakout rooms during the meeting you will need to select how many rooms you want to create which will determine how many people are put into each room. Since I have three participants in my meeting plus myself I can make two breakout rooms which will put two participants in one room and one in the other.

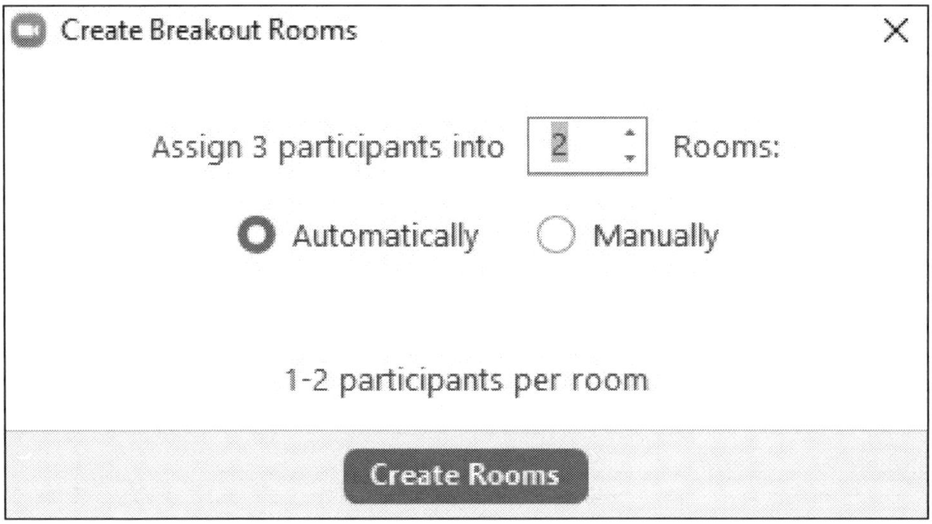

Figure 8.4

The *Automatically* option will choose who goes into what room on its own or you can choose the *Manually* option and decide for yourself. I will choose the Automatically option and see what Zoom does with the participants.

Figure 8.5 shows the results of the breakout room creation and as you can see the status says *Not Started*. You will need to click on *Open All Rooms* to have your participants placed into their respective rooms

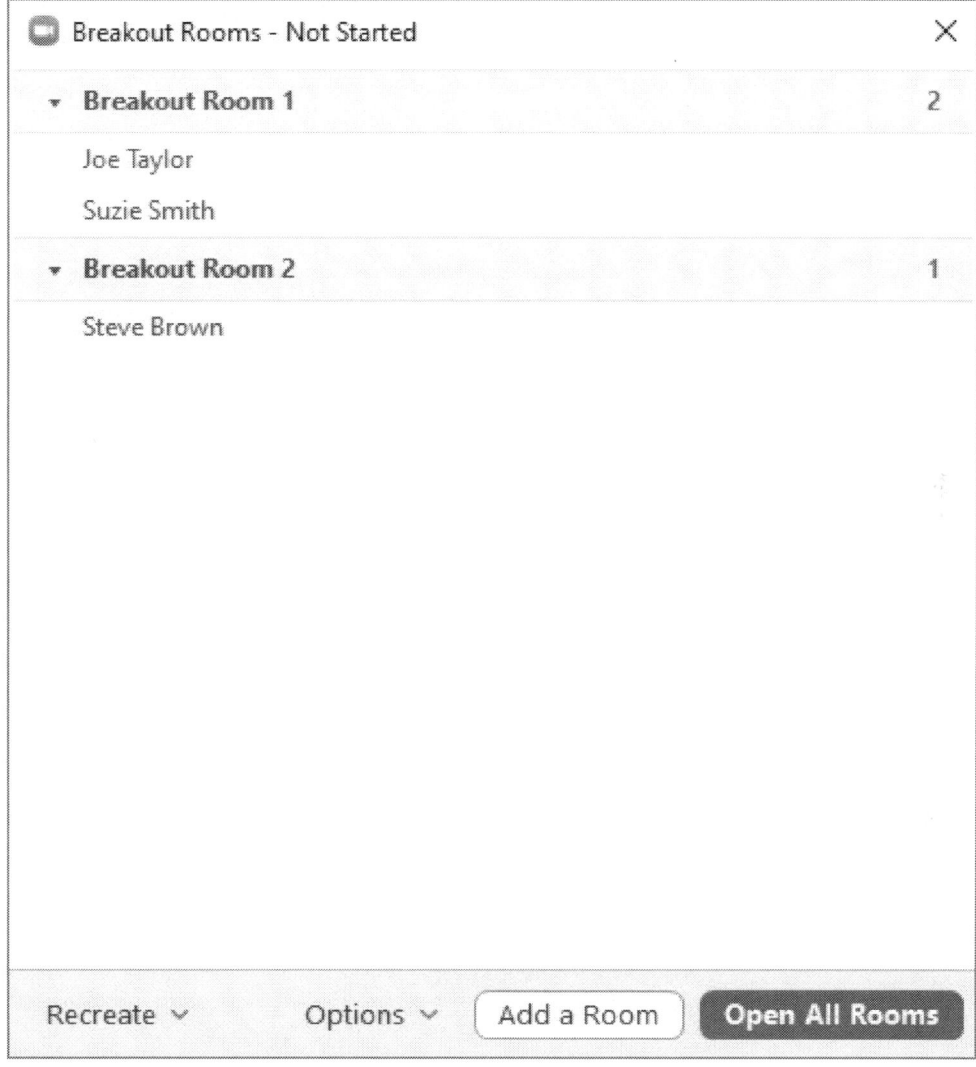

Figure 8.5

You can also click on *Add a Room* to create an additional room if needed or *Recreate* to have the rooms recreated from scratch.

Clicking on *Options* will bring up some settings that you can change as seen in figure 8.6. You can do things such as give the participants the ability to return to the main room whenever they like or put a time limit on how long the rooms will stay active.

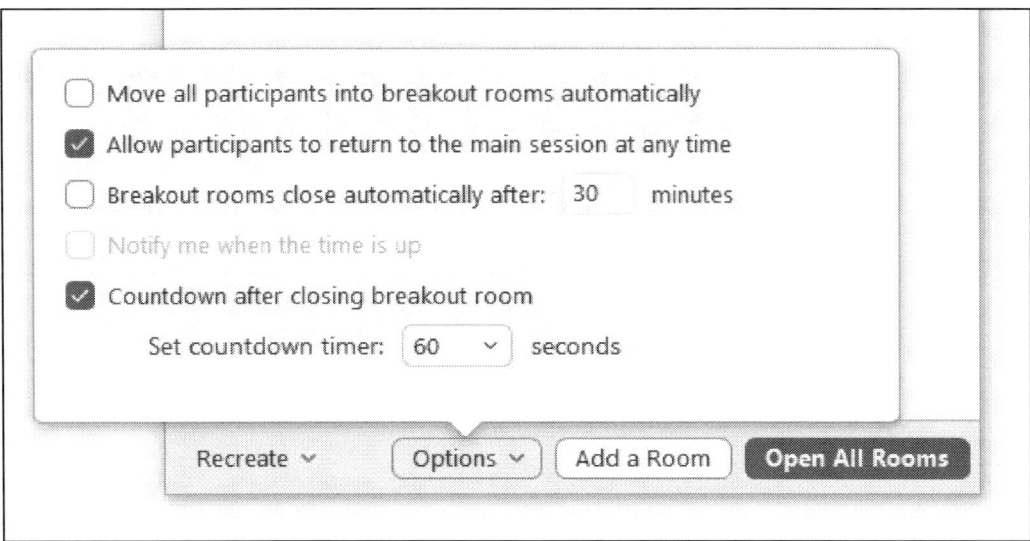

Figure 8.6

Once you open the rooms the participants will get a message on their screen telling them that they can now join their Breakout Room.

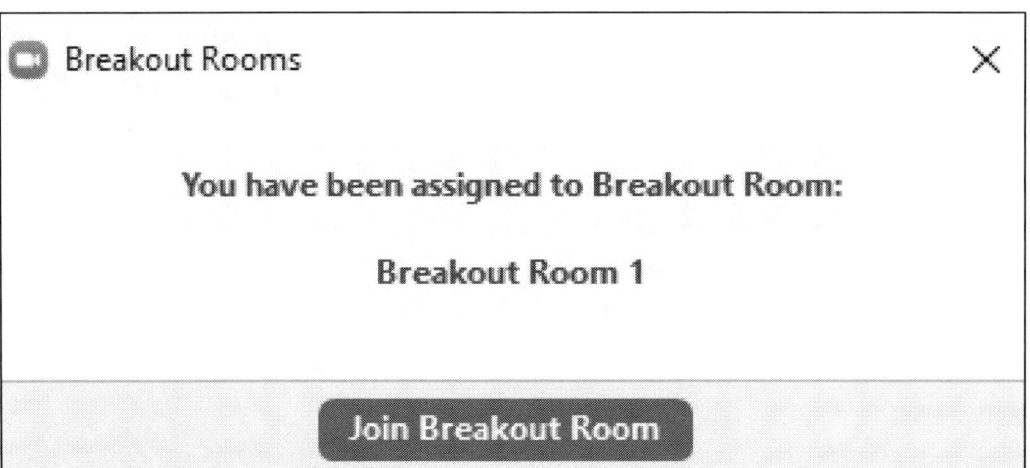

Figure 8.7

Once everyone has joined their rooms you will see their status and then have the ability to do things such as send a message to everyone in all the rooms or close all the rooms at once and bring everyone back to the main room.

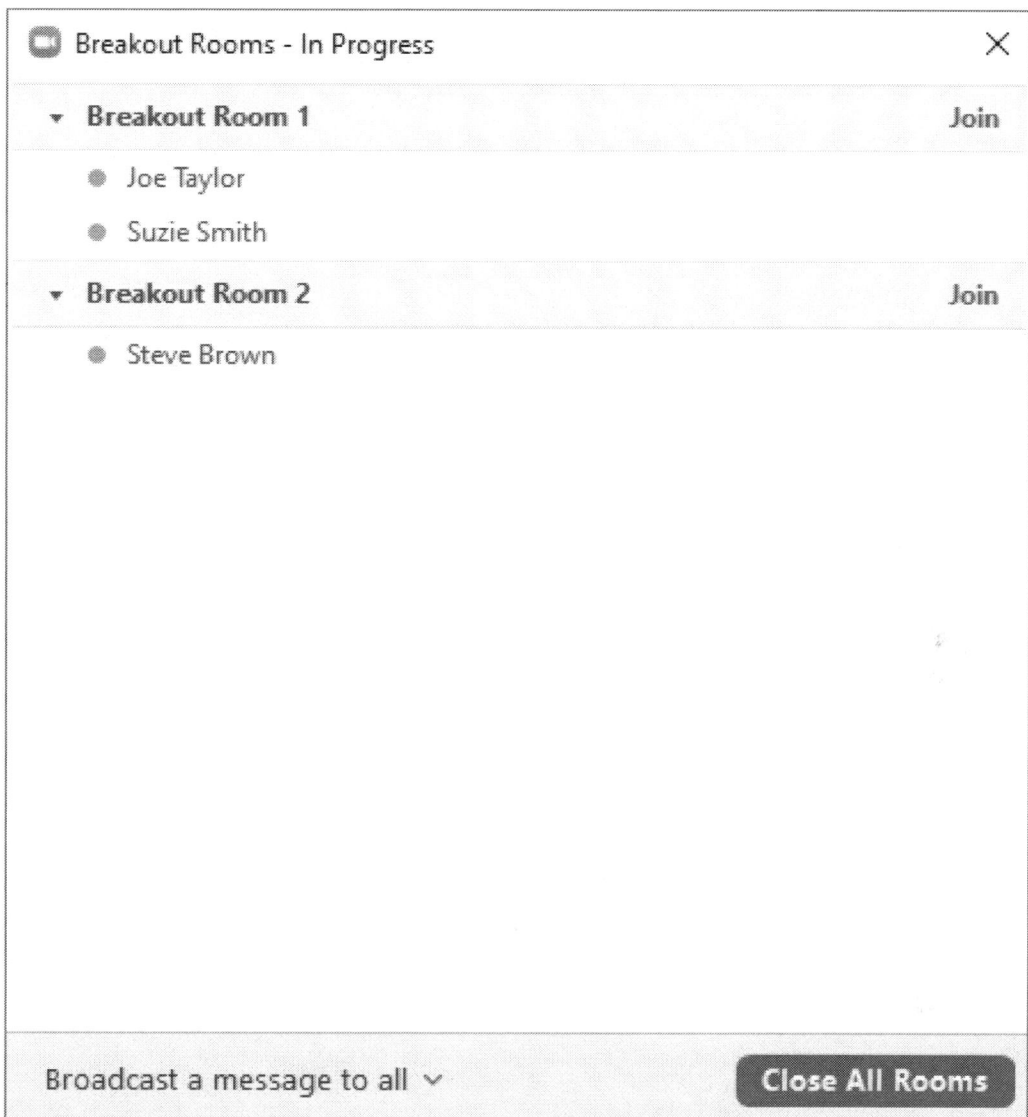

Figure 8.8

As the host, you have the ability to join any room you like or rearrange your participants into other rooms if needed.

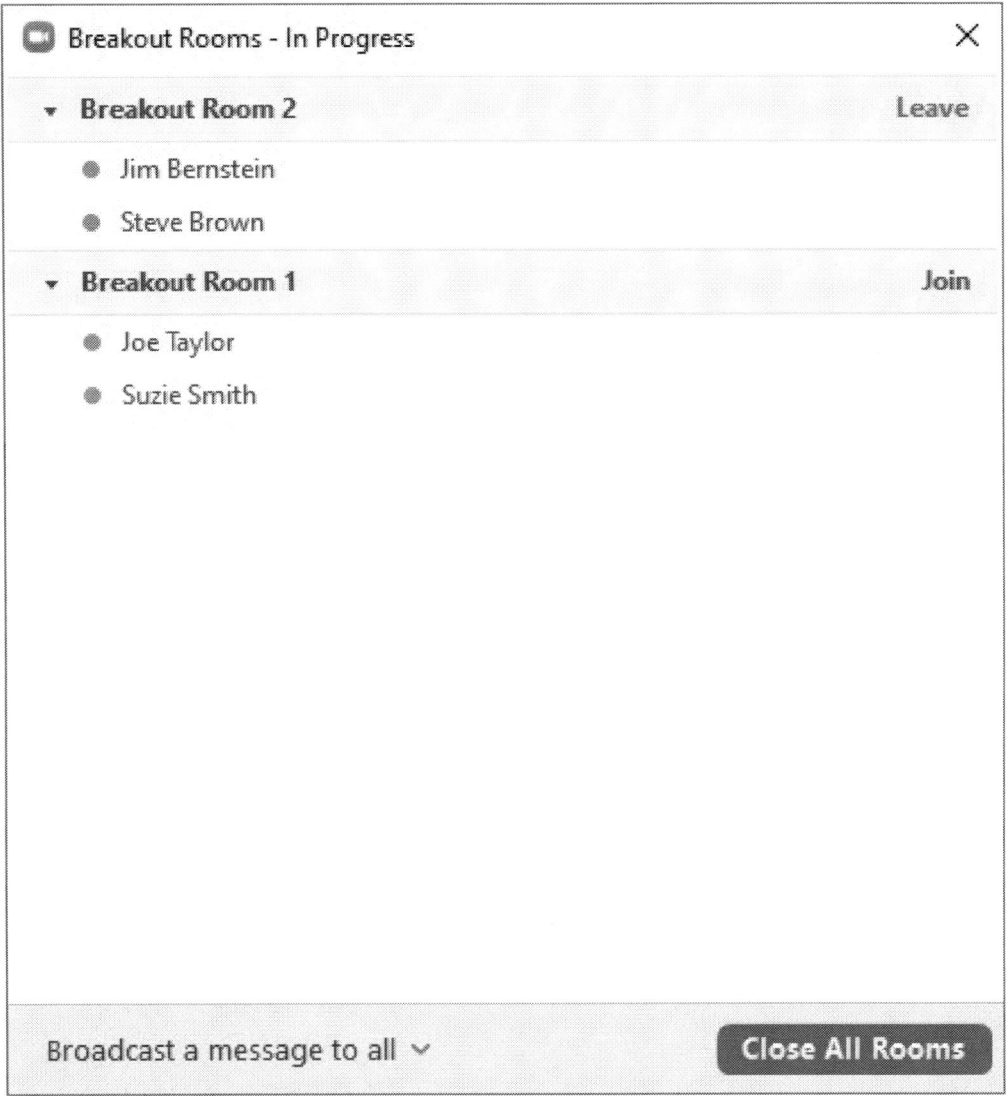

Figure 8.9

When you are ready to bring everyone back you can give them a 60 second warning, so they know it's time to wrap things up. You can adjust the time limit from the default 60 seconds if needed.

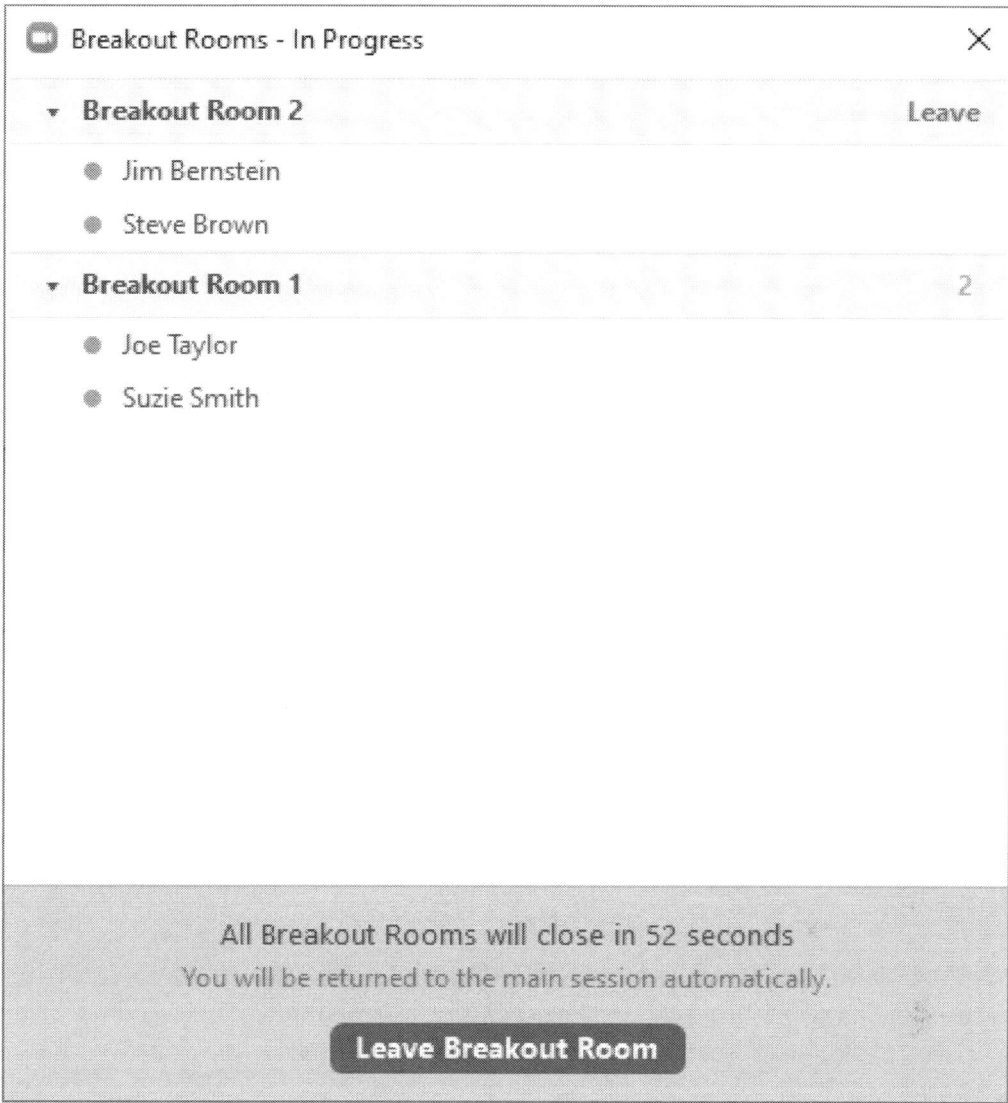

Figure 8.10

Nonverbal Feedback

You might have noticed how you can raise your hand or give applause during a meeting but Zoom offers some additional participation options that they call *Nonverbal Feedback*. This way you can do things such as agree with someone or tell someone to slow down without having to put it in a chat.

To use this feature you will need to enable it first from the Zoom web interface on your account. To do so go to the Settings section, Meeting and then *In Meeting (Basic)*.

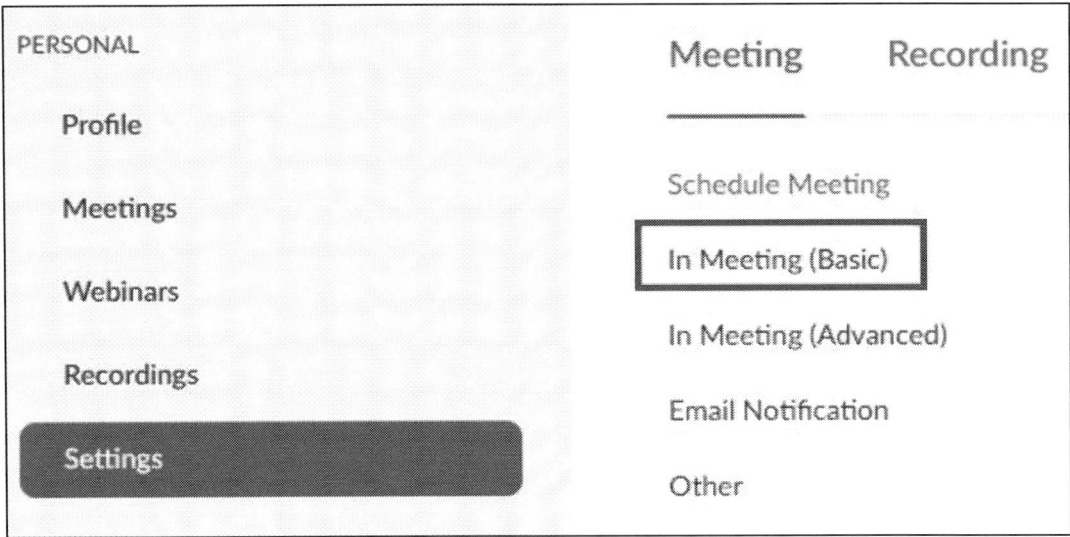

Figure 8.11

From there find the section that says Nonverbal feedback and move the slider to the right so it turns blue to enable this feature.

Nonverbal feedback

Participants in a meeting can provide nonverbal feedback and express opinions by clicking on icons in the Participants panel. ☑

Figure 8.12

Now when you go to the participants list you will see some choices on the bottom of the window as seen in figure 8.13. You can perform actions such as raise your hand, agree, disagree, say you want the presenter to go slower or say you want them to go faster.

Figure 8.13

Clicking on *more* will bring up some additional choices as shown in figure 8.14. You can also give a thumbs up, thumbs down, applause, say you need a break or say you will be away for a bit.

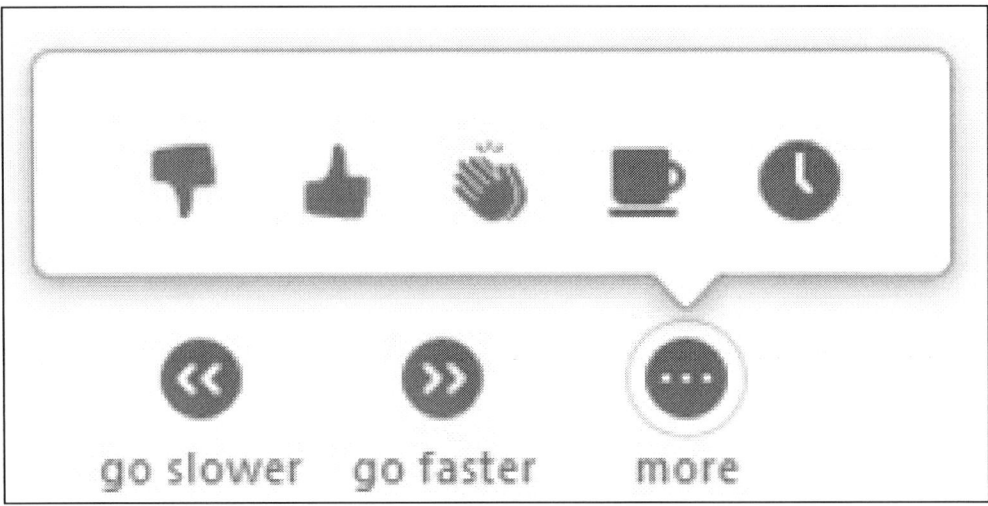

Figure 8.14

When you have your participants list open in the Zoom client you will be able to see the nonverbal feedback of the people in your meeting.

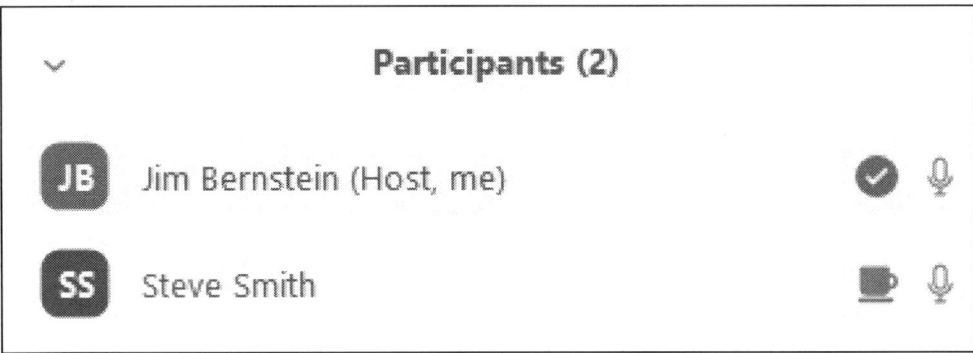

Figure 8.15

Remote Support and Control
Zoom has a handy feature that will allow you to help your fellow computer users with their issues by allowing you to remotely control their computer over the Internet or network. This way you can use their computer as if you were sitting at the local keyboard.

Before you can use this feature you will once again need to enable it in the Zoom web interface settings. It will be in the same *Meeting\In Meeting (Basic)* section and this time you will need to enable *Remote support* and *Remote control* (figures 8.16 – 8.18).

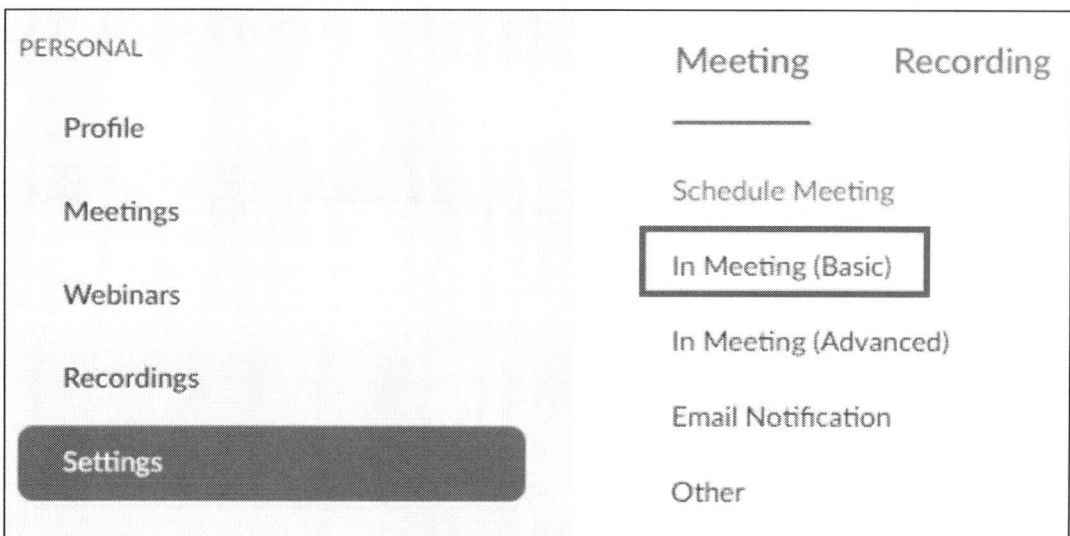

Figure 8.16

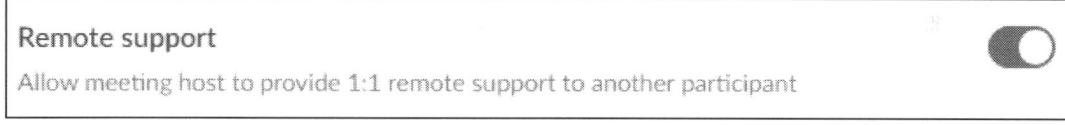

Figure 8.17

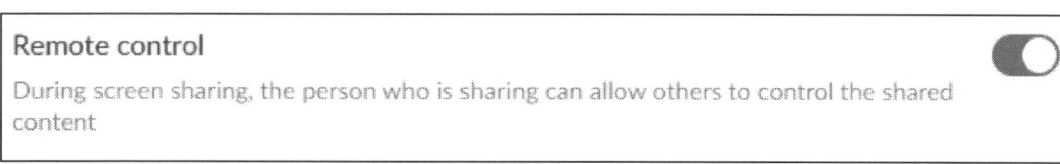

Figure 8.18

Once this is enabled you will then have a *Support* icon on the toolbar of your Zoom client. Clicking on this will bring up the option to request desktop control, application control or a restart of the computer.

Figure 8.19

You will most likely want to use the *Request Desktop Control* option so you can access all of the functionality of the remote computer.

The user on the other end will get a popup message on their computer asking to grant permission to the person who requested access to their computer. They will need to click on the *Grant Permission* button to allow the remote control to take place.

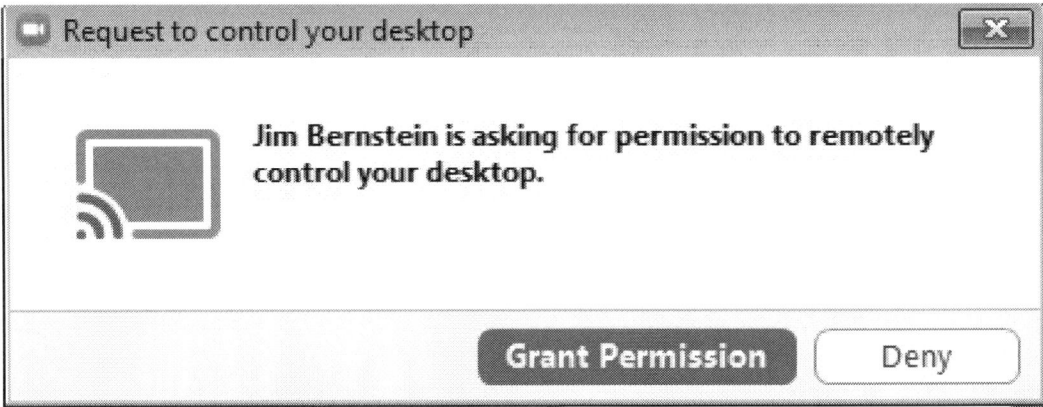

Figure 8.20

Then they will have a new dropdown bar on their screen showing them that it is being controlled remotely. They will have the capability to stop the remote control if they don't want the other person on their computer any longer.

Figure 8.21

If you are the one who is controlling the remote computer then you will have a window on your computer showing their computer screen and you will be able to use it as if you were sitting at their actual computer.

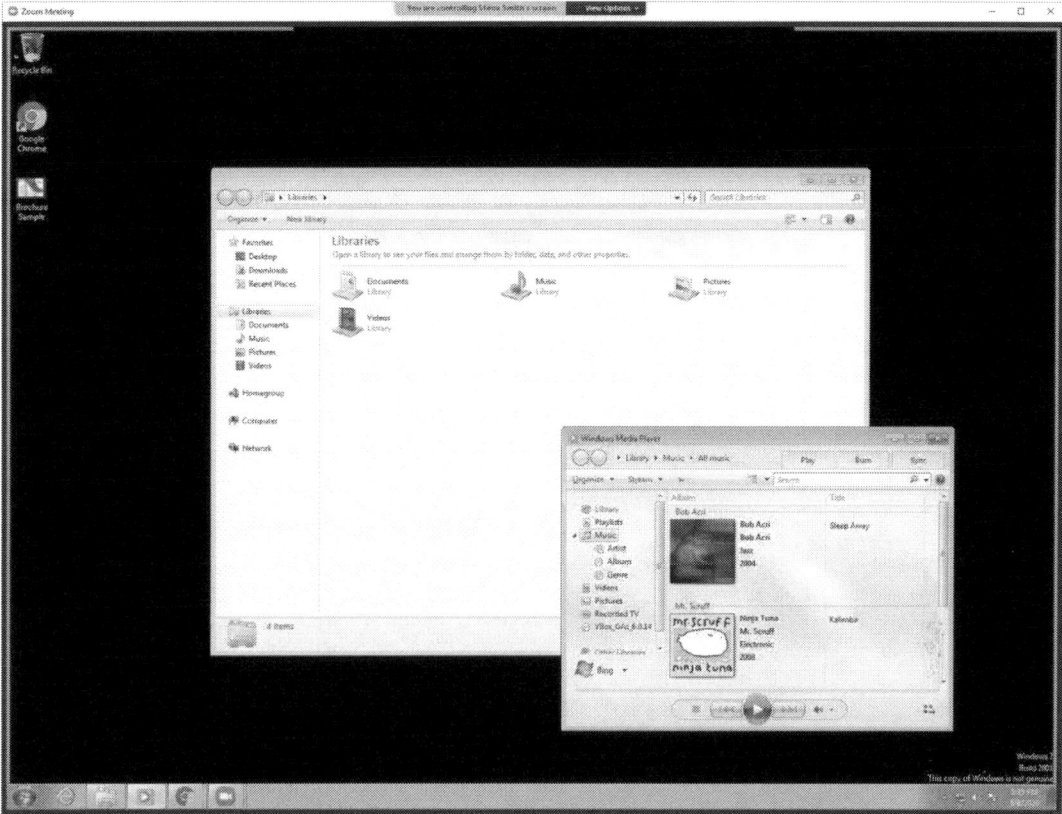

Figure 8.22

Changing Your Profile Picture

One last thing I wanted to discuss is how to change your profile picture because if you don't have one and are not using your video camera for your meetings then nobody will be able to put a face with the voice. Then again maybe you want to keep anonymous, but if not then adding a profile picture is something you might want to configure.

The first step in this process is to find a picture of yourself that you would like to use. Make sure its cropped so it mainly shows your head since the picture will be cropped into a circle by Zoom.

Next, you will want to log into the web interface and click the drop down arrow by your name and then select *Edit my profile.*

149

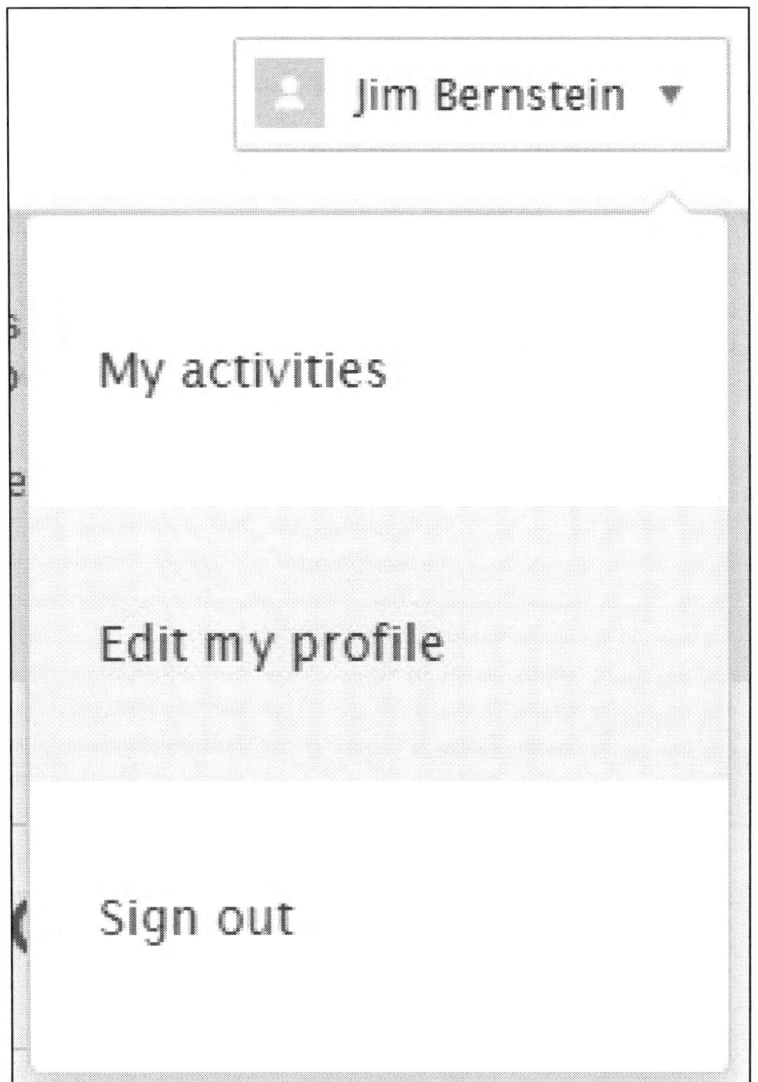

Figure 8.23

Next, you will want to click on the *Change photo* button, browse to the location of the photo you want to use and then select it. When you are finished you can click on the OK button and you will be ready to go!

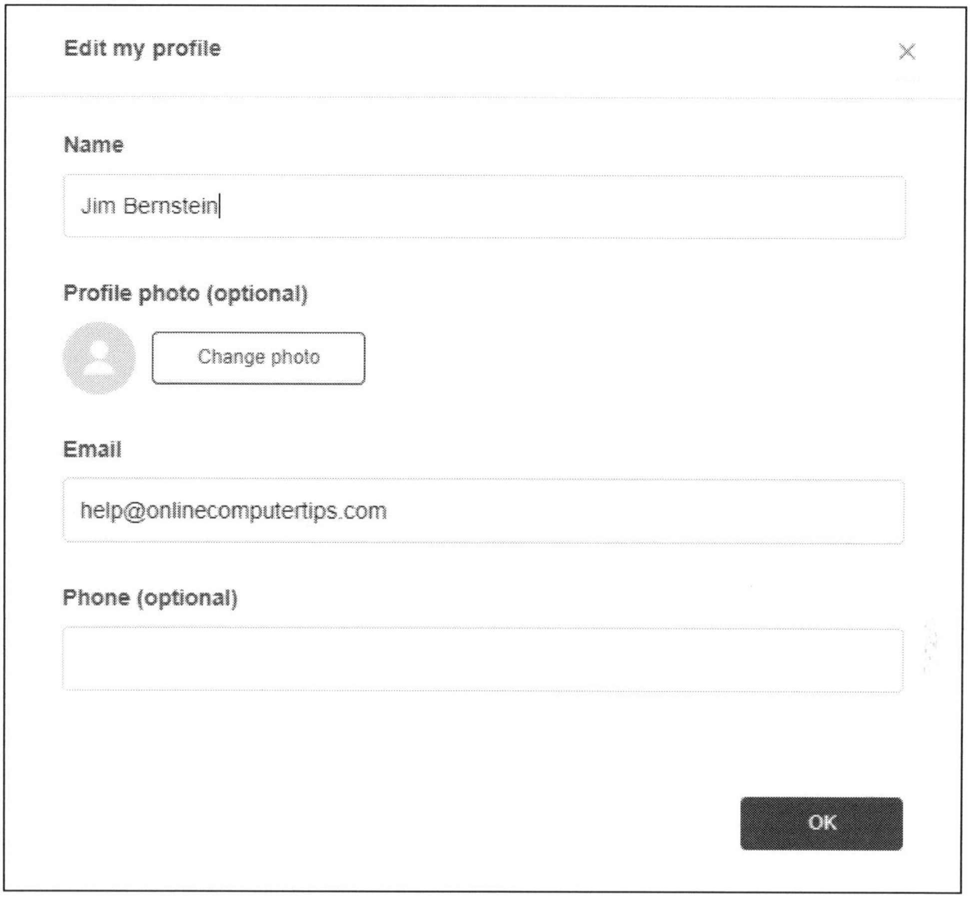

Edit my profile   ✕

Name

Jim Bernstein|

Profile photo (optional)

Change photo

Email

help@onlinecomputertips.com

Phone (optional)

OK

Figure 8.24

Another way to change your photo is from your Profile settings in the web interface. Simply click on the *Change* link under your current picture upload a picture from your computer using the *Upload* button.

PERSONAL

Profile

Meetings

Webinars

Change

Recordings

Figure 8.25

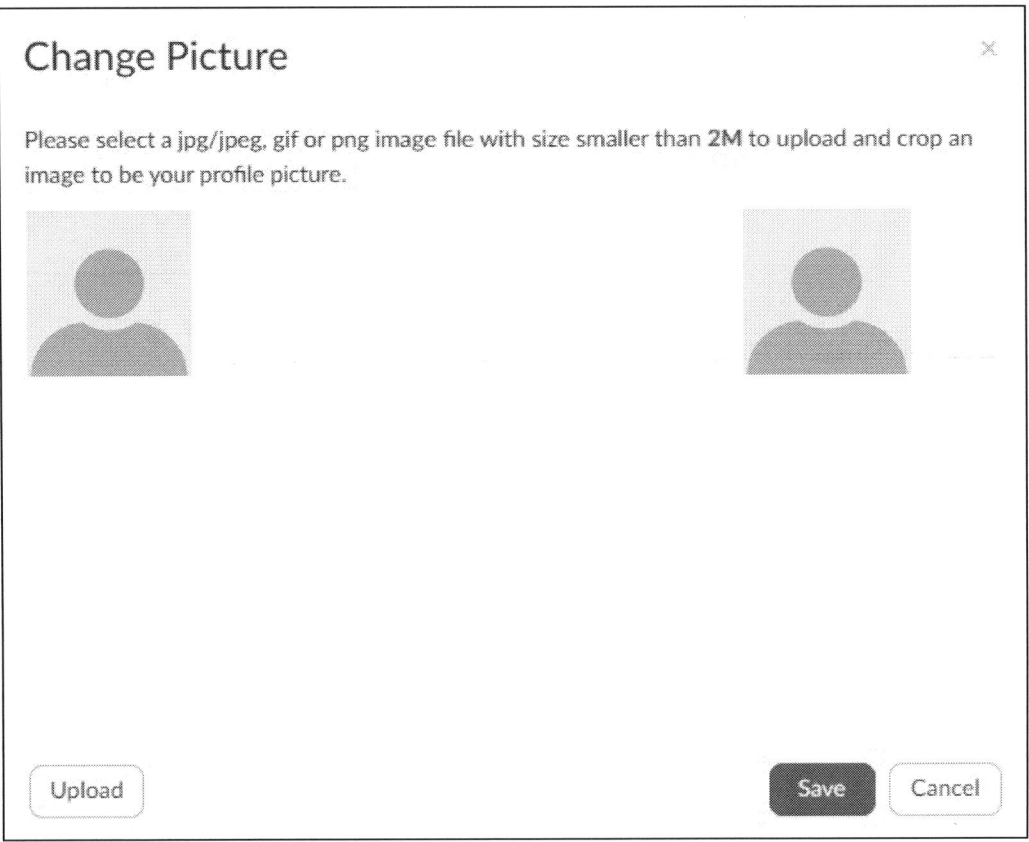

Figure 8.26

Once you have your picture selected you can then crop it to show just the part of the picture you want to use and then click on Save when you are finished.

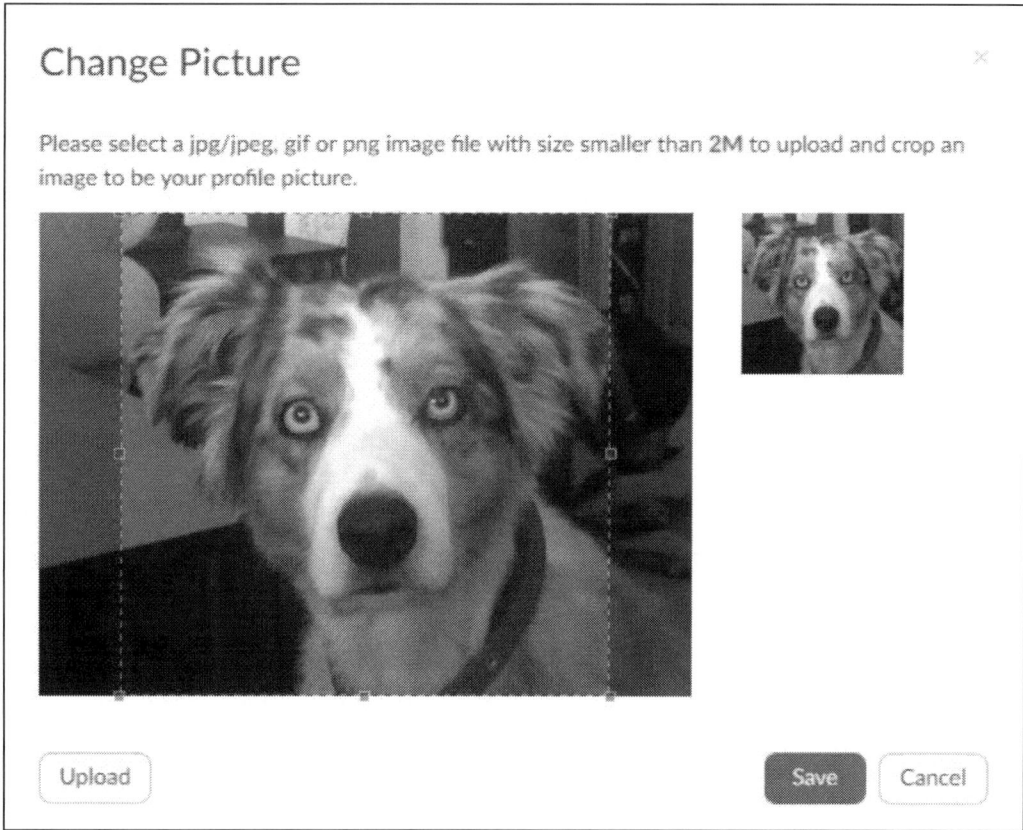

Figure 8.27

Figure 8.28

As you can see, there is a lot you can do with the Zoom software and service, even if you only use the Basic\free version, especially if you don't have the need to host webinars. Like I mentioned at the beginning of this book, the Basic plan will probably work just fine for most people so I would start with that and see if you need to upgrade later on.

Don't be afraid to play with all the features and tweak the settings so you can get the software working just the way you like it. Then once you are confident with your Zoom abilities, start hosting some meetings!

What's Next?

Now that you have read through this book and learned how Zoom works and what you can do with the software, you might be wondering what you should do next. Well, that depends on where you want to go. Are you happy with what you have learned, or do you want to further your knowledge of Zoom and online meetings or even take the next step and learn about other online meeting platforms such as GoToMeeting?

If you do want to expand your knowledge and computers in general, then you can look for some more advanced books on basic computers or focus on a specific technology such as Windows or Microsoft Office, if that's the path you choose to follow. Focus on mastering the basics, and then apply what you have learned when going to more advanced material.

There are many great video resources as well, such as Pluralsight or CBT Nuggets, which offer online subscriptions to training videos of every type imaginable. YouTube is also a great source for instructional videos if you know what to search for.

If you are content in being a proficient Zoom user that knows more than your friends, then just keep on practicing what you have learned. Don't be afraid to poke around with some of the settings and tools that you normally don't use and see if you can figure out what they do without having to research it since learning by doing is the most effective method to gain new skills.

Thanks for reading Zoom Made Easy. If you liked this title, please leave a review. Reviews help authors build exposure. Plus, I love hearing from my readers! You can also check out the other books in the Made Easy series for additional, computer-related information and training.

You should also check out my website at **www.onlinecomputertips.com**, as well as follow it on Facebook at **https://www.facebook.com/OnlineComputerTips/** to find more information on all kinds of computer topics.

About the Author

James Bernstein has been working with various companies in the IT field since 2000, managing technologies such as SAN and NAS storage, VMware, backups, Windows Servers, Active Directory, DNS, DHCP, Networking, Microsoft Office, Photoshop, Premiere, Exchange, and more.

He has obtained certifications from Microsoft, VMware, CompTIA, ShoreTel, and SNIA, and continues to strive to learn new technologies to further his knowledge on a variety of subjects.

He is also the founder of the website onlinecomputertips.com, which offers its readers valuable information on topics such as Windows, networking, hardware, software, and troubleshooting. James writes much of the content himself and adds new content on a regular basis. The site was started in 2005 and is still going strong today.

Made in the USA
Middletown, DE
20 October 2020